All That Matters

All That Matters

What Is It We Value in School and Beyond?

Edited by
Linda Rief
and Maureen Barbieri

HEINEMANN
Portsmouth, NH

Heinemann
A division of Reed Elsevier Inc.
361 Hanover Street
Portsmouth, NH 03801-3912
Offices and agents throughout the world

Every effort has been made to contact the copyright holders for permission to reprint borrowed material where necessary. We regret any oversights that may have occurred and would be pleased to rectify them in future printings of this work. The editors and publisher wish to thank those who have generously given permission to reprint borrowed material:

Excerpt from *Harris and Me: A Summer Remembered.* Copyright © 1993 by Gary Paulsen. Reprinted by permission of Harcourt Brace & Company.

Figure 2–1 from "The Authoring Cycle: A Theoretical and Practical Overview" reprinted by permission of Deborah W. Rowe, Jerome C. Harste, and Kathy G. Short. In *Creating Classrooms for Authors: The Reading-Writing Connection,* edited by Jerome C. Harste and Kathy G. Short (Heinemann, A division of Reed Elsevier, Inc., Portsmouth, NH, 1988).

Excerpt from *I'm in Charge of Celebrations* by Byrd Baylor. Copyright © 1986 by Byrd Baylor. Reprinted by permission of Atheneum Books for Young Readers, an imprint of Simon & Schuster Children's Publishing Division.

Library of Congress Cataloging-in-Publication Data
All that matters : what is it we value in school and beyond? / edited
   by Linda Rief and Maureen Barbieri.
     p.   cm.
   Includes bibliographical references.
   ISBN 0-435-08848-3
   1. Language arts.   2. Teaching—Philosophy.   3. Teacher-student
relationships.   I. Rief, Linda.   II. Barbieri, Maureen.
LB1576.H6126   1995
372.6—dc20
                                                       95-6643
                                                        CIP

Editor: Toby Gordon
Production: J. B. Tranchemontagne
Cover design: Judy Arisman

Printed in the United States of America on acid-free paper
99 98 97 96 95 EB 1 2 3 4 5

∾⊘ Contents

♪ *Acknowledgments*

All That Matters: What Is It We Value in School and Beyond? grew out of teachers' determination to find meaningful ways to celebrate their students' and their own achievements and growth. We appreciate all teachers who work towards this end in their classrooms and in their communities. Whether they are represented in these pages or not, they are the heart of this book.

Originally titled *Workshop 7: What Do We Value?* this collection was to be the seventh in a series begun by Nancie Atwell at the suggestion of Donald Murray in 1989 to give classroom teachers a voice in the professional literature. We appreciate Don, Nancie, editor of *Workshop 1, 2,* and *3* and Tom Newkirk, editor of *Workshop 4* and *5,* for their advocacy and their leadership. The high calibre of the early editions of *Workshop* has inspired us in our classrooms and, more recently, in our roles as editors. They encourage teacher-researchers everywhere to reflect on practice and to share discoveries with others.

Workshop 7 evolved into *All That Matters,* thanks to the sheer volume of heartfelt response we received to our call for manuscripts. We thank Toby Gordon for her steadfast commitment to teachers as writers and for her vision in urging us to expand our book. Toby trusts teachers and is determined to give us continued access to publication in future edited collections of classroom research.

Many thanks to Karen Ernst for listening to our new concept for the book with such insight and care. The title, *All That Matters,* is her gift to us, and we will always be grateful.

"Like water," my father echoed, "be gentle and strong." I gazed amazed at the ocean waves that sounded like thunder and swelled like tears. "Be gentle enough to follow simple paths in the earth, but strong enough to rise up and reshape the world—like that first flood."

——Brenda Peterson, *Living by Water*

Introduction

It's a personal thing. Whenever I come back to the ocean in Maine it happens. All the anxiety, pressure, and tension in my life seem to dissipate. As I stand at the sea and stare out to the horizon, everything seems to fall into perspective; what I've worried about seems suddenly smaller and somehow less consequential than I had thought. I can feel my shoulders let go of the weight they've been carrying. My breathing changes. I am quieter.

Sometimes the sea is serene, other times ferocious, and some days it catches the light in ways that turn it a dozen different shades of blue. At night I fall asleep listening to the sound of the waves crashing against the rocks or lapping gently in steady rhythm. The sea is in a state of constant change. But the rocks are not. These rocks have been here for centuries, thousands and thousands of years, here by the sea withstanding the ocean's terror, the ocean's steady crashing, lapping, caressing. Together, the notions of change and of constancy calm me. They remind me of what it is that matters in my life.

In the busy world of teaching, it's often easy to lose track of what matters to us as we wrestle with the day-to-day issues confronting us as professionals. Are we offering our students the best possible instruction? Are our methods based on the latest learning theory? Do we even know the latest learning theory? Do we keep up with our professional reading, writing, and attending of conferences? Are we addressing the needs of each student as well as the needs of the whole class and the community that extends beyond the classroom walls? Essentially, are we meeting expectations—both our own and our districts'? As teacher-researchers and teacher-writers we often feel as if we are juggling a myriad of challenges, and we keep juggling—indeed become more adept at juggling—because we love our work. Caring as we do for our students, our work becomes in a very real sense who we are. When we ponder what it is we value, we are quick to realize that we value our students, their learning, their literacy, and their welfare. We value the relationships that we forge with them every day we are together.

When Linda and I began to think about this new collection, we anticipated lots of great articles on evaluation. Teachers, we knew, were designing innovative ways to honor their students' strengths and growth as learners. We were excited at the prospect of learning more about portfolios and other meaningful forms of assessment in schools. We posed the question, "What is it we value?" as broadly as we could in hopes of eliciting stories of teachers' professional development as well as accounts of students' achievement. As submissions poured in, we were amazed at the range and the diversity of topics teachers chose to share with us. We discovered that, for these teachers, evaluation is not something that happens at the end of learning; rather, it is ongoing, a part of classroom life from *day one*. These teachers have built in ways to celebrate the signs of growth and insight that traditional methods often miss: They help kids produce videos, ask questions about personal obsessions with nature or computers, and give class time over to real conversation; in short, they notice more. The concept of focusing on children's strengths, of listening closely, and of paying a new kind of attention strikes us as characteristic of all the teachers here, teachers who cherish those moments, often serendipitous, when the act of making knowledge is palpable in the room.

Mark Goodman writes of "opening our hearts again to a new group of kids" and reminds us that the whole idea of relationship is and always will be the key to a productive classroom, as it is to a productive life. Teachers who speak here of other important relationships in their lives are teachers who bring compassion, curiosity, and respect to every encounter with a child. Mary Catherine Bateson writes:

> The gift of personhood is potentially present in every human interaction, every time we touch or speak or call one another by name, yet denial can be very subtle too, inflicted in the failure to listen, to empathize, to attend.... Western culture associates independence and autonomy with strength, but there is a sense in which an awareness of being part of a larger whole, of being defined by context, a self in adaptation, can offer a different strength, leading to flexibility and constant learning. Caring and commitment are what make persons, and persons in turn reach out for community. Personhood arises from a long process of welcoming closeness and continues to grow and require nourishment over a lifetime of participation. (1994, p. 62)

These teachers who value "personhood" seek to bestow it on their students and their colleagues day in and day out. Understanding the importance of "participation," they are also teachers who are dedicated learners themselves. They learn not only from their students but also from one another. They develop more significant ways to evaluate their professional growth in their own buildings; they seek and heed the advice of the parents in the community; they reach out beyond school walls to become more than they are.

Real learning implies humility, risk, and vulnerability. I may not succeed at learning to play the piano or read Vietnamese or grow asparagus, and in the attempt to learn I may reveal frailties previously carefully camouflaged. But the teachers who write here are willing to chance failure because they understand that learning is as essential to our survival as breathing; learning is what keeps us alive. These are teachers who value living in the world. They often embrace art, music, poetry, gardening, or other family traditions for their own aesthetic and emotional fulfillment. In addition to developing literate habits of mind, these teachers seek to build in themselves attitudes of acceptance, respect, and compassion for humanity at large. What might it mean to a class full of children to have a teacher who writes a poem because she is moved by a whole town's courage?

We do not leave our passions outside the door when we come into our classrooms. If we care deeply about social justice, our concern will become part of the curriculum. Karen Smith writes of her passion for reading, but shows that it is something larger that drives her. She loves to read because literature gives her "multiple world views" and enables her to understand that no one perspective is superior to others. Karen's students' perceptions of the world are shaped by their literature and their teacher's belief in its real world significance. What we care about inside and outside of school coalesce.

In his book *On Being A Teacher* (1993), Jonathan Kozol argues that teachers' passions have a place in classrooms: "The hidden curriculum, as we have seen before, is the teacher's own integrity and lived conviction. The most important lesson is not what is written by the student on a sheet of yellow lined paper in the lesson pad; nor is it the clumsy sentence published (and "illustrated") in the standard and official text. It is the message which is written in a teacher's eyes throughout the course of his or her career" (1993, p. 20).

For this reason, *All That Matters* has become more than a collection of compelling classroom narratives. We have interspersed other kinds of writing here—poetry, memoir, personal essay—to honor all the ways these teachers recognize what matters to them in their lives. Teachers who take the time to remember quiet family moments and to record these in writing are not only modeling literacy; by bringing what they cherish into the room, they are honoring children by being themselves.

At times our teaching consumes us. When we are not with our students, we are thinking about them, reflecting on what has happened so far, and planning what we will do next. We are our work, of course, but we are other things as well.

"My life has forced me to adopt multiple levels of focus, shifting back and forth and embedding one activity within the other, parent and observer, teacher and student," writes Bateson. "I have been fortunate in living several lives simultaneously, the effect of layers of commitment. There is even room for awareness of the process of learning" (1994, p. 96).

We cannot separate our teaching lives from our personal lives—it is all personal to us when we "open our hearts"—but it is also vital that our lives be more than teaching. We need nourishment—the essays, novels, and poems we read for our own joy—our family relationships, friends, flowers, long walks in the woods, respect for the environment—growing vegetables, raising pigs, sewing, playing the flute, traveling, cooking and eating great food, appreciating good wine, or collecting antiques. Things that may never be an actual part of our teaching are parts of us and thus affect all the lives we touch. Who we are is woven into how we behave, how we approach colleagues and kids, how we envision our work, our world, and our future together.

All That Matters seemed to us at first a cavalier title, one that might be construed as presumptuous. But now we realize that "all that matters" is the heart of true evaluation. All that matters to us will always be a part of teaching; we cannot escape it. We need to take the time, no matter how hectic our days become, to stare out at the sea or to sit quietly in the yard or up on the rooftop and ask ourselves what it is we care about and how honestly we share our concerns, hopes, and passions with one another and with our students. New methods of instruction and evaluation will continue to evolve in direct proportion to who we are, and how much of that we are willing to bring into our teaching. This may be, in the end, all that matters.

Maureen Barbieri
with Linda Rief

References

Bateson, Mary Catherine. 1994. *Peripheral Visions: Learning Along the Way*. New York: HarperCollins.

Kozol, Jonathan. 1993. *On Being A Teacher*. Chatham, NY: Oneworld Publications.

Minnie Mae Cooks A Poem

Donald M. Murray

She decides to make lentil soup
but there are no lentils,
remembers soup begins with what you have at hand,
what is left over, ripe or not yet quite
rotten, what demands to be saved.

She examines the bones saved against
need: a turkey carcass, one pork chop
with no pork, shin bone that was intended
for the neighbor's dog but kept, steak bones,
pig's knuckles, chicken wings, lamb leg,
selects the ones that have not cooked
together before, imagines their soup.

When they fill the pot, she adds water,
turns up the flame.

In the evening she skims off the fat,
smells in the steam what she does not
expect: meals and friends, the house after
they leave, family worries, celebrations and, yes,
sees hunt, capture, the butcher cleaver
coming down.

Still she must make soup, there is a need
for what is not wasted.

The next day, she reaches under the counter,
chooses six red potatoes, ten yellow onions,
cuts them in quarters, scrapes one bunch
of carrots, slices, hacks a turnip
into squares, then beets.

Root crops were her ancestors' winter food.

She skims off more fat, adds what is cut and cleaned,
puts the cover back on.

From the refrigerator she takes a half head of cabbage,
the celery not yet eaten, last night's limas,
Sunday's peas, some of the fresh broccoli
bought for tomorrow's dinner, and yes,
the cauliflower that was not dipped
when those people who knew her
in another life dropped by
unannounced.

Stir and taste.
It is not what she expects.
She smiles and fits the cover tight.

Friday's summer squash smells all right,
dump it in. Slice last week's sausage, Italian hot,
three picnic hot dogs, one with mustard, trim the tomatoes
that need saving, and the peppers red and green and yellow
turning brown. Cut away what is too far gone,
preserve what is left.

She adds, stirs, notes how this steaming spoonful
tastes so different from the last. It is at last
making itself soup. She turns down the light,
lets it simmer until she goes to bed.

In the morning she wakes to the dream
of grandma's soup, thick as stew.

From the freezer, she selects last summer's
shish kebab, a cup of venison stew, one and one half
hamburg patties. Surprise. There is lentil soup.
She puts in the pot with shells and angel hair, marinara
and white clam sauce, these frozen salad greens will fit
right in. And oh, yes, where is that bag of spinach? Good, I
can save half the leaves. Stir them in.

She shakes in salt, grinds in pepper, dribbles in a touch of soy,
stirs and sips, adds some more and a dash of Worcestershire,
another shake, a third. It will make a company meal.

She forgets the garlic, hurries to peel one toe,
two, three.
She adds the rice left over from the Chinese chicken and cashews
ordered in, finds the chicken and cashews, plops
them in as well, and stirs,
then tastes.

It is not what she has ever cooked before.

Minnie Mae serves it steaming in their bowls,
watches as they taste, find the flavors
they need to make her soup their own.

Staying Off-Balance and Alive: Learning from my Students

Linda Rief

Each morning they meet and practice for a half hour before school starts. Sixth, seventh, and eighth graders. Jazz band. And each spring at their performance I'm in awe of how skilled these young men and women are: Greg on the saxaphone, Ayshe on drums, and Rachel at keyboard. I'm so impressed I want to do what they do. I ask Rachel if she'll teach me how to play the piano. "What do you know?" she asks. "Nothing," I say. "Nothing?" she questions. "Well, I know some keys are black and some are white—but I don't know why."

On my desk the next morning I find my first lesson: How to sit at the piano. Each day for the next seven days I find a new "lesson plan," and during our daily quiet study Rachel coaches me through each lesson (see Figures 1–1 and 1–2).

I practice at a table, my fingers tapping the edge. The only other sounds are my continual questions to Rachel: "Why *are* some notes black and some notes white? What does that fraction three over four mean, or four over four? What does that big 'S' mean? How do you know something is sharp or flat?" and her patient responses. Out of frustration Rachel sighs, "You know, Mrs. Rief, without a keyboard or piano, this is like you trying to teach me writing without paper and pen."

How to sit at the Piano

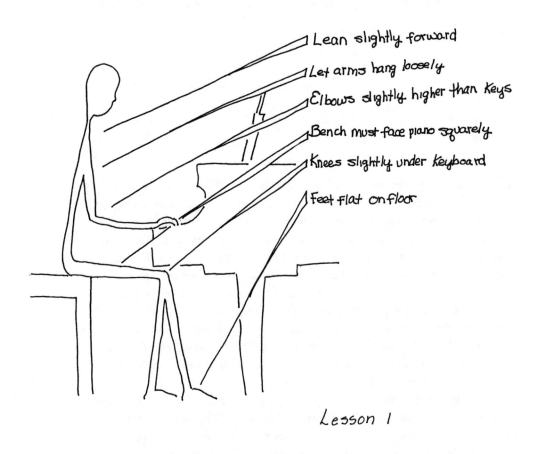

Lean slightly forward

Let arms hang loosely

Elbows slightly higher than keys

Bench must face piano squarely

Knees slightly under keyboard

Feet flat on floor

Lesson 1

Figure 1–1. *How to sit at the piano.*

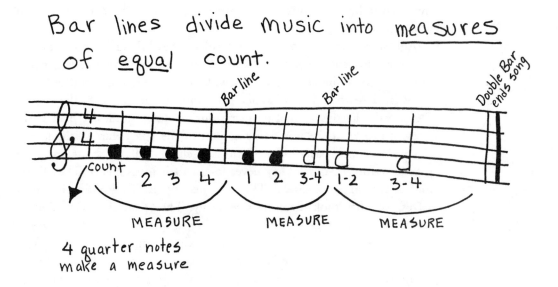

Figure 1–2. *Quarter note, half note.*

What possessed me to ask Rachel to teach me how to play the piano? I wanted to be like her. I admired her passion. I liked the way her music made me smile, or well up with tears from evoked memories; made me clap my hands, tap my feet. Made me relax. I took pleasure in the sounds she and the entire jazz band created. I admired Rachel the same way I admire Katie as a swimmer, Joe as a soccer player, Kristen as a reader, Molly as a hockey player, Patrick as a mathematician, Taylor as a chess player, and my mother as a seamstress. I admired Rachel's skill, her expertise, the ease with which she did something that looked so daunting, so complex, so foreign to me. I respected her patience with practices. She made time to play, and learned to play well, because it mattered to her. She took so much pleasure in what she did, I wanted to find that same pleasure.

And somewhere, deep in the back of my head, I was a little bit envious of a fourteen-year-old who knew so much more about music than I did. I wanted some of what she knew. Could it be that difficult to learn?

What I learned from Rachel had nothing to do with the piano. Despite the lessons Rachel gave me during quiet studies, I paid more attention to what she was doing as part of the jazz band. Without fail, Rachel and her peers showed up at school half an hour early to practice—for 180 days. They never forgot their instruments. They never fooled around at practices. They laughed often. They enjoyed themselves. Yet they took themselves seriously. They paid close attention to what their teacher Dave Ervin was doing: directing, playing, coaching, teaching, challenging. They shared a relationship with Dave. They respected him for what he knew and could do *for* them and *with* them. They were good, actually *excellent*, at what they did, because it mattered to them and it mattered to him.

Playing the piano and keyboard mattered to Rachel. She did everything she had to do to be the best she could be at it. And she had a teacher she admired and respected because he was what he taught—a player in the band.

When I first asked Rachel to teach me how to play the piano, I had the grand idea that one day I would be able to saunter over to a piano and let my fingers dance passionately across those black and white keys. The audience would applaud, and gasp and sigh in admiration, the same way I did and continue to do, when the jazz band plays in the spring.

I promised Rachel that I would find a keyboard we could keep in the room. But I never did. She never asked me when I would get it. The lessons stopped appearing on my desk. And I still don't know the difference between those black and white keys.

Why didn't I rent or borrow or buy a keyboard?

What if I *had* brought a piano or keyboard into the room?

What if Rachel had played music around me more often?

Would I have stuck with the lessons? Would I have learned to play more than "Chopsticks" with two fingers?

I might have. But I didn't. I don't think I really cared enough to learn how to play. I realized I was more interested in what made Rachel work so hard. Along the way Rachel taught me more important lessons. She taught me that I can't do it all. She taught me that I have my own priorities. She taught me to be the best that I can be at what matters to me. Writing matters to me. Teaching matters to me. Teaching kids to create, interpret, and appreciate language and literature matters to me. Helping kids become literate young men and women who contribute creatively and productively in our society by communicating with others, understanding the world in which they live, and finding their place in our complex, diverse society matters to me. Teaching kids to be the best that they can be at what matters to them is what matters to me.

As a writing teacher, my goal is *not* to make all kids great writers. It is to make them the best writers they can be in the time that I have with them. It's my job to surround them with the best models: authors to whom they can apprentice themselves, books they can lose themselves in, characters who tell them they're not alone, words that make them think and feel and learn. It's my job to provide the structure and time for them to practice writing. It's my job to guide, coach, challenge, and teach them. I want to be the best reader and writer I can be so that my students will want to read and write in the same way that Rachel and her peers want to play in that jazz band, because *they want to*. Because it matters to them.

The craft of teaching is inextricably tied to the craft of listening to our kids and acting on what they tell us. That's what Rachel did. She asked me what I knew, structured a plan to teach me based on my questions, and sat beside me as coach. She was there to teach me if I wanted to learn from her. That's the way I try to teach.

I learn from everyone around me. I learn from those people who are passionate about their learning, teachers like Tom Romano, Jane Kearns, Don Murray, and Maureen Barbieri. From the research of Nancie Atwell, Don Graves, and Mary Ellen Giacobbe, I know that my students learn the most when they are given choices into what they read and write, when they are given time to develop their ideas, and when they receive positive, constructive response to what they've done well and what they might try differently. I learn *the most from my students* every day. Kiki, an eighth grader last year, was one student who challenged me. In her log in May she wrote, "You're always saying you learn so much from me. *Exactly what is it* you've learned from me?"

In fourteen years of listening hard to seventh and eighth graders, exactly what is it I *have* learned from them?

I've learned that they trust me as a teacher, as a writer, as a reader, and as a human being when I'm reading, writing, and speaking about those things that matter to me.

I write about my mother's death, my father's drinking, the love of my grandparents, my confusion about Vietnam and war, growing up in the '60s, raising teenagers, world issues that baffle me, educational issues, family relationships, and the things my students say and do. I write about all those things that make me think, and feel, and question myself.

I've learned that students learn the most when they are reading, writing, and speaking about those things that matter to them.

Patrick has big questions. Often those questions arise in his reader's-writer's journal as he reads. From Patrick and those other students like him, I've learned to admit that I don't have all the answers, so I push them to find someone who does. I recommended he write to Carl Sagan (see Figure 1–3).

Despite the sincerity and honesty of Patrick's letter, I put little faith in a reply. Even I was surprised, and genuinely touched, by Sagan's return letter (see Figure 1–4).

Mark loves to read. He always has a Weis and Hickman or Piers Anthony book curled in his fingers. But he hates to write. From him I've learned to build on his strengths as a reader (by letting him read, feeding his appetite by handing him books that challenge his thinking, and

Carl Sagan
Director, Laboratory for Planetary Studies
Cornell University
Ithaca, NY 14850

Dear Mr. Sagan,

    I am an eighth grade student at Oyster River Middle School in Durham, New Hampshire. I just finished reading *Cosmos*, which I started after finishing *Contact*. I found *Contact* on a shelf in my attic, and thought I would give it a try. After the first few pages I was totally engrossed in the story, and could not stop reading until I finished some fifteen days later. When I had finished, I wanted to know if there was any possibility that the predictions made in *Contact* would ever come true. On the cover of *Contact* it said that you explain the universe in *Cosmos*, so I started to read that.

    I couldn't stop reading this book either. The information contained was enough to keep me more than occupied for the month it took me to read the book. The universe is so interesting! All of these laws and properties which are the same everywhere in the cosmos are truly fascinating. Kepler's second law, for example: that planets everywhere in the cosmos sweep out equal areas in their elliptical orbits for any set time. That this is true everywhere is what I think is the most exceptional part. I think Newton summed up this awe at the majesty and precision of the universe when he wrote: "I do not know what I may appear to the world; but to myself I seem to have been only like a boy, playing on the seashore, and diverting myself, in now and then finding a smoother pebble or a prettier shell than ordinary, while the great ocean of truth lay all undiscovered before me."

    While reading *Cosmos*, I found that facts about the universe also interest people who are not as scientifically inclined as me. Different facts appeal to different people. For example, one girl who sits at my table in language arts, was amazed that everything is in the cosmos. She kept pointing to objects in the classroom and asking if they were in the cosmos. Eventually I convinced her that everything she had ever seen and would ever see is in the cosmos, the same cosmos which she herself inhabits.

    Another person in my class thought it is interesting that people are made of starstuff. The molecules that make us all were ejected into the universe after the

Figure 1–3. *Patrick's letter.*

explosion of a star, perhaps on the other side of the galaxy. I learned about short-range nuclear force and the beginning of life on Earth with him.

I think that many of the facts in *Cosmos* should interest everyone. However, I do not think that many people in my class could read *Cosmos* cover to cover. Many people are intimidated by its size, and others by the fact that it is obviously not designed for eighth graders. As I was reading through the part about ancient Greek philosophers, a thought occurred to me: why not print another *Cosmos*, with less detailed information but still a broad and interesting range of facts? It could be designed with younger people in mind, and be fairly straightforward, although still interesting and educational. This way the fun of exploring our universe could be made available to those who don't want to spend a month in the process.

The process of learning about the universe is definitely fun. I really enjoy knowing some of the basic laws and principles that shape our universe. It is nice to be knowledgeable about what is going on around the universe. And I always tell myself that I might as well memorize these laws, like the constant speed of light and the Einstein's theory of special relativity, because they're not likely to change anytime soon. I like knowing in general, and the structure of the universe is a great thing to know about.

A classmate asked me a question about the universe that I could not answer: Are four-dimensional objects in the cosmos? My first reaction was "yes," followed by "no," then "sometimes." I thought that maybe four-dimensional objects could move in and out of our three-dimensional cosmos at will, like a three-dimensional object passing through a two-dimensional plane. Do you know the answer?

Also, could you please recommend some books for further reading on the subject of universal laws and the fourth dimension and the other subjects covered in *Cosmos*? I want to learn more specifically the laws of the universe, and I thought you would be a good person to ask.

Please write back as soon as you can. I have enclosed a self-addressed, stamped envelope. Thank you for your time.

Sincerely,

Patrick

Patrick

Figure 1–3 cont.

asking him for author recommendations), while looking for ways that I can help him grow as a writer. Ways that get him writing. Writing that makes sense to him.

One day Mark showed me mistakes he'd found in the map section of *Writers Inc.* "I can't believe a professional publisher could be that

CORNELL UNIVERSITY

Center for Radiophysics and Space Research

SPACE SCIENCES BUILDING
Ithaca, New York 14853-6801

Telephone (607) 255-4971
Fax (607) 255-9888

Laboratory for Planetary Studies

January 5, 1994

Dear Patrick

Thanks for your recent letter. I was most impressed with your writing ability, the maturity of your judgement and your interest in science. I think the best way for your to pursue the interests you describe is with a modern introductory college textbook. I'm taking the liberty of enclosing one with my compliments.

With warm good wishes,

Cordially,

Carl Sagan

P.S. Your question about whether four-dimensional objects are in the cosmos is not a matter of physics, but a matter of words. It depends on what our definition of the cosmos is. If it's defined as I do, as everything that is, then by definition the answer to your question is yes.

CS:jmb

Enclosure

Figure 1–4. *Carl Sagan's response.*

sloppy," he said. "Maybe you should let them know what you found," I suggested. After a bit of prodding, Mark wrote to the publisher (see Figure 1–5).

The publisher responded (see Figure 1–6).

Because Mark was taken seriously as a geography sleuth, he took his communication with *Writers Inc* seriously. In Mark's first letter I was unsuccessful at convincing him that a business format was necessary. When he knew he was being taken seriously, he took what he did seriously and made sure the letter was in a correct style (see Figure 1–7).

Mark has been "working" for *Writers Inc* for more than a year from Utah. Because someone needs and respects what he knows, he works carefully and thoroughly.

Nahanni, Jay, and Sarah taught me to take all the work my kids do seriously. When their artwork, a large mural in response to the book *Night* by Elie Wiesel, was stolen, unbolted from our cinder block walls, and disappeared without a trace, Sarah asked, "Do you think it was the same robbers who emptied out that museum in Boston?"

October 17th

Dear Editor,
        A few weeks ago I received <u>Writers Inc.</u> from my teacher. That night I took it home and I looked at themap section, on the map of Europe I noticed two things that struck me as odd.
        The first being that much of the former Czechoslovakia was north of Germany and Holland, covering much of Denmark and northern Germany.
        The second was that Slovakia was the color of water, light blue, which makes it look like a very large lake in the middle of Europe, with its capital being a wharf.
        I hope next time you do not make this mistake again.

                                Sincerely Yours

                        Mark

Figure 1–5. *Mark's letter.*

WRITE SOURCE
EDUCATIONAL PUBLISHING HOUSE

Box 460, Burlington, WI 53105   Telephone (414) 763-8258

November 11, 1993

Mr. Mark
Geography Department
Oyster River Middle School
47 Garrison Avenue
Durham, NH 03821

Dear Mark:

So you found one--an error in the handbook, that is!   Congratulations on the great detective work, Carmen. It takes a skilled, well-trained eye to spot such mistakes. We appreciate it too, and you should know your "find" has led to a change in the next printing.

I'll explain to you what went wrong, but first, let me tell you who I am. My name is Tom Gilding. I have been a middle-school language arts and social studies teacher for seventeen years in Lake Geneva, Wisconsin. Now, I am a writer developing instructional material for students. Each of us at Write Source do many things, but my primary focus is developing classroom writing workshops for cross-curricular instruction in language arts, social studies, science, or wherever writing, thinking, and learning takes place.   One of my favorite projects is contributing to the "Almanac" or "Appendix" sections of the handbooks, keeping our maps up to date.   And that "ain't easy" these days!

Let me explain the procedure that goes into the production of our map section. First, we do some good ole' detective work ourselves, looking through newspapers and magazines, keeping our eyes open to new developments in the world. Since we like to have new countries included as quickly as possible, this, as you may imagine, is an ongoing process. (The Hammond maps we formerly used were never current enough for us so now we draw our own maps freehand on Macintosh computers using an altered version of MapArt by Micro Map Software.)

In major decisions such as adding new countries to the maps there are always many considerations that need to be made: Do we have proof positive that it "officially" is a new country? Are the borders in the right location? Do we have the correct or definitive spelling?   Considerable debate, for example, occurred in house about "The Union of Myanmar" before it was officially included in the map of Asia. We kept receiving conflicting reports about the official use of the new name. Myanmar is in fact the official name now, but you might still read some sources incorrectly referring to it by

Figure 1–6. *Tom Gilding's letter.*

its old name--Burma. Another example of a recent "find" that led to a major change on the map of Africa is my discovery of the new country of Eritrea carved out of Ethiopia. A Milwaukee Journal newspaper article caught my eye one Sunday morning about an upcoming vote in Ethiopia that would allow a portion of the country to secede. I followed the story closely for the new few days waiting for the results of the election. In less than a week the vote was final and the northern province of Eritrea did in fact break away, but before we could literally put this new country "on the map," we had to check at least two different sources--Facts on File is a good one--to be sure it was official.

After we "know" a country is official, the next step is the drawing of the borders on the computer. Sherry Gordon, our extremely talented graphic artist, draws the new map and prints it onto a laser printer. The map is then shipped to Arcadia Printing in Kingsport, KY, where a new laser copy is made and then turned into a "film" copy. The printers then "output the film" onto a four-color "final copy." At the printers in Kentucky, is where the error--now called "The Webster Debacle"--occurred in the map of Europe. During the output process, for some unknown reason, the outline of the former Czechoslovakia ended up north of Germany.

Now, even though the mistake was made in the final printing in Kentucky, that doesn't let us off the hook in house here in Wisconsin, because the "proofs" of that final copy were shipped back to us for a final, final check. I have to confess that on this final check we simply, honestly, missed it. We goofed. We screwed up. Dropped the ball. Fumbled in the final seconds on the one-yard line. And so that is why Slovakia has a capital that is a wharf and a giant land mass big enough to be the lost continent of Atlantis now extends out into the North Sea a good 300 km northwest of Hamburg, Germany!

By the way, Dave Kemper and I loved your use of the word "wharf" in your letter and both felt it was an excellent word choice. It brings to mind Mark Twain's words, "The secret of writing is using the right word. The difference between the right word and the almost right word is the difference between the lightning bug and lightning."

Anyway, you should be assured that in the new printing of the handbook maps Slovakia is represented on the map in a dark-blue "land" color. Unfortunately, however, we will have to wait for the next printing date to submerge "the newly-surfaced Atlantis" back down into the North Sea.

Again, Mark, thanks for the letter. We appreciate your input, and I hope I have sucessfully explained what happened to the map of Europe. But, wait a minute. Since you brought this up, and since I still have your attention (You are listening, aren't you?), I'd like you to know we are not content with your finding of that one mistake. Oh, no, we want you to find more! "There's gotta be more mistakes in them there maps some'eres and maybe Mark there is just the hombre who can find 'em." At least that's what the publisher, Pat Sebranek, and I thought after discussing your letter. (Yes, we actually think in cowboy dialogue like that sometimes.)

Figure 1–6 cont.

We further thought, "And maybe we have indeed found the right person, the right 'cartographic editor' for the job?"

"What job?" Well, since you asked, and since you "already have a title," we would like you, and perhaps a team assembled by you (their new-found leader), to edit the whole map section of *Writers INC* and *Write Source 2000*. We figure it will take a super geography sleuth such as yourself to find border lines that should be more "crooked," latitude and longitude coordinates that maybe "don't add up," and cities that might actually be miles from their true location. Your first order of business might be to check on the new country of Eritrea. I'm a little suspicious about its southern border; I think it should go north more toward the capital before it turns southeast and heads toward the Red Sea. What do you think?

Anyway, let me know if you wish to get involved, or if you wish to pass this information and job on to others--classmates, your geography class, teachers, friends, Romans, countrymen (countrypeople)--who might be interested.

And what's in it for you? Well, I can't promise all the gold in the Yukon, or all the diamonds in Africa, or even all the tea in China, but if you can trust a former geography teacher--Have I lied to you yet?--I guarantee it will be something worthwhile, something you, as a fellow cartographer, just...might...like. In addition, you could grab the initiative on this and ask your social studies teacher for a little extra credit. Probably wouldn't hurt.

So, there's the deal. Take it or leave it. But either way, we at Write Source want you to know we appreciate the input of students everywhere who take an active interest in our material, contributing ideas and making the Write Source writing handbooks the very best--North, South, East, and West!

Sincerely,

Tom Gilding
Enclosures

P..S. - Mark, I'm sorry this letter is so long, but as Mark Twain once quipped in a letter to his friend Andrew Carnegie, "I apologize for the length of this letter; I would have made it shorter, but I didn't have the time."

Figure 1–6 cont.

Matt taught me to stop giving senseless assignments, those things I already know the answers to, when he responded to an essay test "Mac-Beth and Lady MacBeth, the Perfect Marriage" (see Figure 1–8).

Pat taught me patience when he handed me this piece in March—his first piece for the entire year—with the words, "Thank you for not yelling at me [for taking so long to write]." There wasn't a whole lot about

December 3, 1993

Write Source Education Publishing House
c/o Tom Gilding
Box 460
Burlington, Wisconsin 53105

Dear Mr. Gilding:

Thank you so much for your letter; it was greatly appreciated and
quite exciting.

I am very flattered that you have offered me a job as your cartography
editor. It seems like the perfect job, and I enthusiastically accept.

But, in less than a month I am moving from Durham to Salt Lake
City, Utah, which means I may have some trouble establishing a team
until late January, or as late as early February. But if your
publication deadline is earlier than that, I will attempt to finish it
myself. Please let me know as soon as possible.

I found another error, or three! (I think). The capital of the Ivory Coast
is Abidjan, not Yamoussoukro. And isn't the capital of Western
Sahara called El Aaiun now, not Laayoune? And I've never heard the
Baja Peninsula called Lower California before. Eritrea's capital is
much further inland, which is probably the reason for your confusion
with the south eastern border of that country. The neutral zone
between Iraq and Saudi Arabia is green, which is the same color as
Kuwait, and it looks like a newly ceded territory to Kuwait. (I think a
separate mid-east map is a good idea, it is kind of squashed in there).
Did Montenegro leave Serbia too? I didn't hear of that, but you're
probably right.

I look forward to working with you.

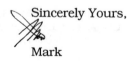

Sincerely Yours,

Mark

Figure 1–7. *Mark's second letter.*

school that made sense to Pat. His mom had committed suicide three
years earlier (see Figure 1–9).

Lindsay taught me never to go back to the way I was taught when she
handed me the following poem. She wrote the poem in her journal, out
of frustration with the teacher in a high school class who went into the

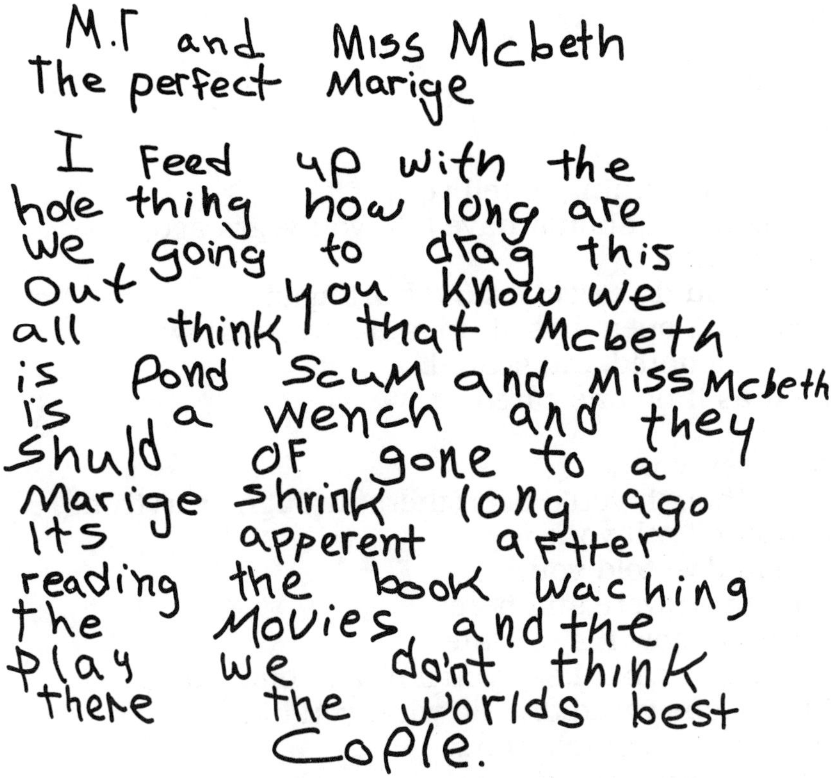

M.T and   Miss Mcbeth
The perfect Marige

I Feed up with the
hole thing how long are
we going to drag this
out you know we
all think that Mcbeth
is pond scum and miss Mcbeth
is a wench and they
shuld of gone to a
Marige shrink long ago
Its apperent after
reading the book waching
the movies and the
play we don't think
there the worlds best
Cople.

Figure 1–8. *Macbeth essay on marriage.*

same poem for what "seemed like days". "She went into that poem like there was no bottom to it," Lindsay said (see Figure 1–10).

And I've learned that the relationship that is created between my students and me is a key element to keeping them learning and growing.

Decades ago Haim Ginott said, "I've come to a frightening conclusion that I am the decisive element in the classroom. It's my personal approach that creates the climate. It's my daily mood that makes the weather. As a teacher, I possess a tremendous power to make a child's life miserable or joyous. I can be a tool of torture or an instrument of inspiration. I can humiliate or humor, hurt or heal. In all situations it is

It's Hard to Say

Hi, Mom,
It's me.

I have something to tell you,
Something I should have told you years ago,
But couldn't.
I just couldn't risk getting hurt again.
I couldn't open myself up and let you know.
I felt alienated and scared.
I felt as if no one cared.
No one.
Not even you.
Even though you'd been there through everything,
I couldn't tell you.
I should've told you,
When you were still here,
Because now it's too late.
No matter what I say you'll never come back.
I just hope you didn't do what you did
because you didn't know,
That through everything
I've always
Loved you.

Figure 1–9. *Pat's poem "It's Hard to Say".*

my response that decides whether a crisis will be escalated or de-escalated and a child humanized or dehumanized" (Ginott, 1972, p. 13).

    I know that still holds true today.

    My stance as a teacher is tied to all I am as a human being. Who I am and how I am permeate the classroom. No matter what subject we teach, we teach and live what we value. What we value is woven throughout the textures of who we are as human beings, and who we are as teachers. We are the curriculum. Our students are the curriculum. None of our students remember the innumerable times we reminded

An English Teacher Dies of Analysis Poisoning

Her stomach
when pumped
was found to contain ten times
the legal limit. Enough
nouns and verbs
in there for a whole
university, she drank them down
as fast as a fraternity
rush.

The authorities said she hadn't eaten of
prose
in two week's time,
and the lack of nutrients
caused a buildup of poetry
in the blood.

And she dragged her disciples down
to the depths
of analysis
with her, a small army
scanning pentameter,
categorizing sonnets, recounting
the syllables of haiku.
If only they had seen themselves
dying
with each flash
of her blood-red pen, this mass
suicide could have been prevented.

As of yet, it is unknown
the number of casualties
taken, in this
war on words.

Figure 1–10. *Lindsay's poem "A Teacher Dies of Analysis Poisoning".*

them, and continue to remind them, that *a lot* is *not* one word; or wrote out for the umpteenth time the difference between their, they're, and there; or how they felt as they read some innane passage on a standardized test and filled in the blanks with a date or a part of speech. What they do remember are the times we were honest with each other as human beings, because in those moments of showing honest emotion we formed relationships.

I'm sure an entire class of eighth graders remembers a writing conference with Nate who asked me if he could be honest in a piece of writing about what would happen to a fourteen-year-old boy if a blonde-haired, blue-eyed Swedish "babe" were saving a seat for him on the bus. When I said "of course," a little too quickly, he read, "When Trevor sat down next to her, he got a hard-on the size of Florida . . ." A room normally filled with talk became silent, everyone waiting to hear what I would say. I sat speechless. We all burst out laughing when Greg filled the silence and mimicked me from across the room, "Wow, great detail. I can really see it."

Scott and Brad will never forget certain parts of speech "taught" to them on a canoe trip on the Saco River. I had thirty students and parents in ten canoes. The weather turned. Rain poured down in torrents. The temperature dropped into the forties. Two kids were throwing up. I beached the canoes and left the parents with most of the students while Scott and Brad paddled me down river to find a phone in the woods to alert the canoe company that we needed to be picked up early. I was soaked, miserable, and a nervous wreck about something happening to anyone. We nearly careened over a waterfall in our attempts to land the canoe. As I stepped from it, I sank knee-deep in the soft muck of the embankment. "Shit!" I exclaimed. Scott and Brad exchanged surprised looks. "Is that a *noun* or a *verb*?" Scott asked. "*That* is a noun *and* a verb," I said. "And here's the adjective. This is the *shittiest* day I've ever had." On the way back to the other canoes, Brad blurted out, "I don't suppose we could make that into a gerund!" We proceeded to twist the word into every part of speech we could think of.

Just this week I read the students an excerpt from *Harris and Me* (1993, p. 130–32) by Gary Paulsen (see Figure 1–11). They howled with laughter, recreating the images in their heads over and over again. What I'll remember from that reading, though, are Cody and Joe, the next day—two full-grown eighth-grade boys racing into the room to read the book again, landing simultaneously in the wing-backed chair, squishing together like Velcroed twins, reading to each other and crying with laughter.

Erin came into class a day later saying, "I kept thinking all night, when you write the newspaper with seventh graders and ask, 'Who wants

"I've got them."

"Let me see."

I raised my shirt and showed him the pictures, lowered it. "So go ahead—pee on it."

He unbuttoned the fly on his bibs and took his business out, then stood there, frowning.

"What's the matter?"

"It don't work. Nothing's coming out."

"Push a little."

"I am. It's scared. It don't want to do it."

"If you don't pee on the wire, the deal is off," I reminded him, thinking it would prompt action.

"I know, I know. It just won't work." His frown deepened. "It's like it knows what's coming and don't want to do it."

"Two pictures . . ."

"I'll have to lie to it."

"Lie to what?"

"My business. I'll just have to lie to it and start peeing over here, then swing it around, make the dumb thing think everything is all right."

He turned sideways, aimed away from the fence, and in a moment it started.

"So turn," I said. "Before it's done."

"It ain't that easy. Something in me won't let it happen . . ."

"Ahh heck, you're going to run out."

"No, I'm holding her back. Here, now . . ."

He turned slowly until the stream of urine was only inches away from the wire, hung there for a second, then hit the wire.

"There," he said, "now are you hap—"

He had crossed the wire between pulses, when the electricity wasn't moving through the wire, and the pulse hit him halfway through the word *happy*.

Later I would come to know a great deal about electrical things. I would understand that water is an excellent conductor of electrical energy but that urine, with its higher mineral content, is even better and what Harris did amounted to hooking a copper wire from his business to the electric fence.

The results were immediate, and everything I would have hoped for from a standpoint or scientific observation, not to mention revenge.

In a massive galvanic reaction every muscle in Harris's body convulsively contracted, jerking like a giant spring had tightened inside him.

He went stiff as a poker, then soared up and over backward in a complete flip, arcing a stream that caught the afternoon sun so I swore I could see a rainbow in it.

Nor did the spectacle end when he hit the ground. He landed on his side, both legs pumping, then sprung to his feet, running in tight circles holding himself and hissing:

"Oh-God-oh-God-oh-God-oh . . ."

All in all it was well worth the investment and when he finally settled, leaning against the barn wall holding his business, panting loudly, I reached under my shirt to give him the two pictures.

Figure 1–11. *From* Harris and Me.

to be on *business* and advertising?' no one will be able to say it, because all they'll think of is you reading that book. As a matter of fact, I'll never be able to use the word 'business' or read it or hear it again without hearing you reading that book."

I have to recognize though that all kids will not take to reading and writing as passionately as I do. If I surround them with the structure, with tools, with irresistible models, and with my passion for reading and writing, I stand a better chance. If I'd brought a keyboard into the classroom, and if I'd surrounded myself with music, I might have sustained my desire to learn to play. At least I would have stood a better chance.

Despite all I do, there are some kids I never reach.

Ryan taught me that there are some students I can't seem to make the connections with to build those relationships, no matter how hard I try.

Ryan came late to every class. He never looked me in the eye. His long hair covered his face until one day he appeared with his head shaved. On the last day of school I handed back portfolios. Ryan grabbed his, swaggered over to the wastebasket, did a one-handed leap into the air like Michael Jordan and slam-dunked his portfolio into the basket. He turned and looked right at me for the first time. "And that," he said, "is what I think of you and this class."

I have to remember that there are kids I will never be able to forge relationships with, and I have to stop feeling guilty about it. There are things in their lives that I cannot control and I cannot fix.

In fourteen years of teaching, I've learned that I can't sacrifice the learning of twenty-four other students in my attempts to reach the student who is passionately dispassionate about everything connected to school—especially reading and writing. I learned that from Ryan and Gary Paulsen and from Jim, a seventh grader.

Several years ago at a National Council of Teachers of English conference in Seattle, a teacher asked Gary Paulsen, "What do we do about the student who refuses to do anything?"

"You're looking at that kid," Paulsen said. "And there was nothing you could do until I was ready, and I wasn't ready 'til I was in my twenties." He urged teachers to reconsider the amount of time and energy they give one student at the expense of all others in a class.

Paulsen's words followed me back to New Hampshire. I returned to school and Jim, the student I had spent three months sitting next to each time his class had language arts. The boy who took all fifty minutes of class time, while twenty-five other students worked on their own after a few hasty directions from me.

On this day in late November I slid into the empty chair next to Jim. "So what the fuck are you doing?" he asked, pulling his journal closer to his chest, cupping his fingers around penciled lines. The counselor's words rang in my head. "We suspect Tourette syndrome, although doctors have never formally diagnosed it as such. Deal firmly but calmly with his outbursts. He can't help them." I read all the articles I could find on Tourette's. Nothing Jim did seemed *unintentional.* But I had been patient for three months. Patiently ignoring every student but Jim.

"Jim, I would appreciate it if you did not use that language or that tone of voice," I said. "I'm sitting here because I need a place to sit and write, and this chair was empty."

"Fuckin' convenient, ain't it, that the chair beside me is always empty."

Amanda, all sixty pounds of blonde hair and blue eyes, blushed with Jim's words, and she hunched down further into her chair directly across from him. I bent down into my journal and wrote: "Linda—be patient—be understanding—remember what Joanne [our counselor] said—he swears intentionally to cover up all he might do unintentionally—I'm having a hard time believing that—I'm . . . "

Kaile screeched as she grabbed for the back of her neck. "There, he did it again. Oh gross, oh sick . . . somebody get it off my neck. Disgusting! Mrs. Rief, do something—he did it again!"

I turned quickly toward Jim. In one practiced motion, he dropped his head back into his writing, clenched his jaw shut tight, and covered his mouth with his hand. I looked closely into his right hand. He was "writing" with an empty pen casing. A plastic baggie was secured with electrical tape to his notebook. Tiny wads of paper floated in this bag filled with spit. I reached out with my left hand, continuing to write with my right. "Give me that please!"

"What?"

"You know what."

"For cris'sake, go sit the fuck next to someone else."

"I prefer sitting next to you. Hand me the pen casing, *and* the entire bag of spit balls, *or* you are out of here!"

"Who gives a shit if I'm outa here. All we do is read an' write. Who needs it!"

"Hand it all to me."

"I ain't handin' you nuthin'."

I swivelled in the wooden chair, full-face, inches from Jim's face, my back to the rest of the class. I was enraged. "My son nearly died of spinal meningitis contracted by swallowing someone's spit in a hot spring. Hand me that bag and shooter!"

Looking straight into my eyes, Jim stripped the bag from the notebook, and chucked it and the shooter under the table. "Go get 'em!" he said.

I used my foot as a fishing line, never taking my eyes off him, and pulled the bag toward me. I picked the bag up, turned, and bent back into my writing. I heard gurgling to my left. I turned slowly. Jim's hand was moving across the page in scribbles while saliva bubbled from the corner of his mouth. He let the froth drop slowly to his T-shirt, slowly, and deliberately. I felt like I was watching a character from a Stephen King movie.

I stood, walked slowly to the intercom on the wall and pressed the button. "This is room twenty-three. Please send the assistant principal up immediately. I have a student who needs attention."

Jim stood, shoved his books to the floor, kicked the chair over, and swaggered slowly to the door. He slammed it open so hard a chunk of plaster fell to the floor as the doorknob struck wall. "Fuck you!" he said, and left.

I've learned to take a stand for *all* my students. Whether Jim truly had Tourette syndrome or not, I could not function alone with him. I could not solve his problems. He wouldn't allow me to teach him or anyone else. No individual student, no matter what his or her needs, has the right to be in the classroom *if it is at the expense of all our other students.* We need to reexamine our role as public school teachers. I demanded an aide for Jim. If an aide did not appear with him, then I would call the parents of every other student in that class and explain why it was impossible to teach their children. We can no longer be reluctant and timid about voicing our opinions about what's working and not working with our students. We are the ones in the classrooms day in and day out. We need to stand up for what's best for all of our students.

I write and read and speak about what matters to me. I encourage the students to write and read and speak about what matters to them.

Dennis, on the second day of school this year, his first year out of a self-contained classroom, wrote for all of us when he wrote this passage in his log (see Figure 1–12).

Gillian was one of my students in 1985. I still remember that first writing conference with her. It was a piece about the day her father left

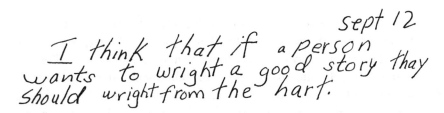

sept 12

I think that if a person wants to wright a good story thay should wright from the hart.

Figure 1–12. *Dennis's entry.*

the family. He tore down the driveway in a pickup truck with Gillian running after him. She burst into tears before she got to the end of the piece. She raced into the girls' room. All I could do was hug her.

Last November Gillian left a piece of writing with me. She had just returned home from college and was on her way to teach at an alternative school in California. She had stopped in to visit, and we ended up talking for hours. I hadn't seen her for six years. This is an excerpt from that piece:

> There is a rose bush on the west side of the community garden that I planted in October. It was a rainy, warm, and windy day. I had been teaching at Wildwood School all morning and although I was exhausted, I knew I wanted to plant. I could taste and feel the rich, soaked soil on my skin. There is a magic I feel with children and with gardening. The growth and potential excites me. Sorting the roots of the thorny rose plant and pressing them into the soil with my fingertips soothed me on that afternoon.
>
> I have sat up many nights with my housemates talking about the speed of our earth, migration patterns of whales, or the many wonders of corn. I often fall asleep and wake up thinking of certain children we have spent time with. Their faces and ideas stay with me, dancing in my mind. My life has been consumed. I admit, I've fallen for it.
>
> I have learned how to listen to children in ways in which I wish people listened to me. The way I tilt my head, the tone of my voice, the lift of an eyebrow can bring joy and empowerment to a child in ways I had never imagined. It is a fine balance, some interactions can make or break a child's self-esteem and I never know when those moments will be. It is so delicate.

I learned long ago from my own example that many children seem to be happy and are not. I learned that pain can be hidden so deep that it hides in behaviors and actions that are unidentifiable. For me, writing brought me to rest with my childhood in many ways. It wasn't until I was away from home, the source, that I was able to come out of my journal and transfer my pain and desires into a strong support system and open myself for children. . . . I teach and learn from my heart. . . . I may look like I'm talking about composting, but I'm very aware who I'm composting with.

During our earlier conversation, Gillian mentioned she had never received the copy of *Seeking Diversity* (Rief, 1992) I had sent her when it first came out. Her writing was a significant part of that book. I packed up a copy and delivered it to her before she left for California. The next day there was a note in my mailbox:

I read your book last night until my eyes hurt! I don't think it's too bad that I never got the copy you sent—this is the perfect time for me to be reading it.

In so many ways it is an excellent guide for me. I question some ideas: the notion of 'gifted', how do you give attention to everyone? In particular I wonder about when some students are doing a real spectacular art/writing project and others are reading Sweet Valley High—how do you give attention to both? Most of my questions I can/will/do answer on my own, but I really value the motivation you give me to continue questioning.

Let's spend a year together so we can just talk and write and read . . . oh, and color, too!

Tom Newkirk, in his introduction to a writing conference held recently at the University of New Hampshire, said that we too often forget what's at the center of the craft of teaching—the students— and they are what keep us "off-balance and alive." The students and the relationships we develop with them should be what matter the most.

Yes, Gillian, let's spend *another* year together, talking, writing, reading—*and coloring.*

P.S. Do you have a keyboard?

References

Ginott, Haim. 1972. *Teacher and Child.* New York: Avon.

Paulsen, Gary. 1993. *Harris and Me.* San Diego: Harcourt Brace.

Rief, Linda. 1992. *Seeking Diversity: Language Arts with Adolescents.* Portsmouth, NH: Heinemann.

Sebranek, Patrick, Verne Meyer, and Dave Kemper. 1992. *Writers Inc.* Burlington, WI: Write Source.

Wiesel, Elie. 1960. *Night.* New York: Bantam.

Dear John (Dewey, that is),

Judith A. Fueyo

Dear John,

I've been wanting to write because you had it right way back then. But still, some among us just don't get it. Literacy and evaluation, that is. The profession is still straddling two paradigms—one for purposes of classroom practice, the other for purposes of evaluation. And even for those whose evaluative practices more closely match classroom endeavors, few have a grip on how to see composing in alternative symbol systems like art and drama even if we believe these expressive forms suit literacy endeavors. I "believe" because many of us know intuitively that art, even play, contributes to verbal language development, but we are less sure of naming and evaluating these contributions. I am invoking your spirit, John, that your vision will contribute to ours at this precise juncture.

You'll be happy to know that the conditions for literacy acquisition and learning have never been better in schools, now that holistic learning principles guide classroom practice more and more. Children's purposes drive literacy encounters in these classrooms where desks are moveable, if there at all. Remember your frustrating search through the supply houses in Chicago for moveable desks for your lab school? No one understood why any teacher would want desks that moved! In these new literacy classrooms, children have choices of what to write and read, how to respond, with whom, for whom. Spaces are cleared for dramatic performances in response to story writing and reading. Art materials such as clay, collage-makings, paints, Styrofoam chunks, woven cloth, and beads compete with pens, pencils, computers, and magic markers near the writing table. So, John, we're shaking up narrow views of what constitutes educative experiences in English language arts.

Because of this expanded notion of literacy, many are struggling with standards or outcomes for literacy growth. Notice I didn't say *objective standards,* John. Thankfully, we are not locked into mechanical notions of objective standards—things like the meter for which a bar deposited in Paris sets the accuracy of the judgments so that ambiguity is minimized. Schools have come a long way, friend, from mandating numerical grades in literacy. Still, we are myopic on assessment.

In *Art As Experience,* (Dewey, 1934, p. 37) you discerned between objective standards and objective judgment. Judgment involves the qualities of the human mind at work balancing intuition, empirical facts, and human histories of both evaluator and evaluated. Judgment calls on all those culturally and socially grounded human abilities we can use to discern what is good and what is not. Yes, judgment is subjective and interpretive, but these subjectivities and interpretations are continually being shaped within informed communities of good folks, and that, according to rhetorician Richard Weaver, is the best we humans can do in search of the good. In short, you helped validate teachers' unique positions to offer professional judgments concerning literacy growth.

Still, we are at a crossroad concerning assessment.

Paradigm schizophrenia suggests a rethinking of terminology, especially the term *whole language.* Though not all of us subscribe to that name, most of us share common ground. For example, Harste, Short, and Burke (1988) envision a model for a literacy curriculum that they call "The Authoring Cycle" (see Figure 2–1). Harste, Short, and Burke explain that in their model the situational contexts in which instances of authoring are embedded are inside the oval and the various culture-specific contexts or forms in which literacy events can be enacted are outside the oval. Any author may crisscross between alternate symbol systems to expand potential meanings (Harste et al., 1988, pp. 10–11). Notice the variety of expressive modes invited into the curriculum.

In Pennsylvania the document known as the Pennsylvania Framework for Reading, Writing and Talking across the Curriculum recommends the following expressive modes in response, for example, to reading: discussions, enactments, presentations, writing, and other media (Lytle and Botel, 1990, pp. 32–33).

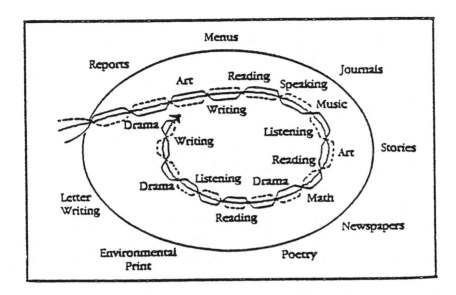

Figure 2–1. *The Authoring Cycle.*

The Framework states that "all of these formats or activities involve some form of composing, whether oral or written, and may take place before, during or after reading" (p. 33). Note, John, that even this document remains verbocentric at heart: For example, "other Media—artistic (e.g., drawing, sculpting, constructing), musical, audiotape, video or film" come last among the composing options (p. 32). What's worse, the framework leaves teachers on their own to translate the relationships across children's work in alternative media and literacy. Still, the Pennsylvania Framework does suggest that work in alternative media is permissible, even desirable.

Of course, you knew, John, that transmediation—crossing media boundaries—has always distinguished children's meaning-making ventures. But did you know that the array of forms children spontaneously employ—drawing, pasting parts, making sound effects, talking, playing, and gesturing, for instance—suggest compelling influences on language and literacy development? Margaret Donaldson (1978), whose work, I think, you'd like, argues for an eclectic conceptualization of thought and language development, one where "the learning of language may be bound up with nonlinguistic concerns more inextricably" (p. 33) than language arts typically has appreciated.

Clearly then, philosophically and practically, the new literacy folks endorse alternative experiences within English language arts. Our intentions, John, are good. However, what ends up counting for language growth is mainly, if not exclusively, what ends up in words, especially print. Composing in alternative symbol systems, if it is not validated for its contributions to literate sensibilities, threatens to be none other than "a frill."

I remember that morning a school administrator stopped to observe Chris Gaudet's first-grade classroom where I spent two years researching the range of symbol systems young children use in early writing. It was language arts time, and the children were interpreting the Thanksgiving story in mime. The administrator said, "Oh, you're just playing. I'll come back when you're doing language arts." It's easy to be defensive, John, even though you know in your gut, that for some children, alternative expressive modes are their access routes to literacy. It'll come as no surprise to you, then, that aesthetic experiences that might well contribute to thinking are invited into our classrooms cautiously, if at all. We're no fools when it's us being evaluated. So, John, the Kuhnian notion of paradigm shifts in numerous disciplines is neither here nor there for us in language arts if we cling to evaluative schemes that are out of sync with new understanding of language growth and new classroom practices.

What's in a name? A lot. The very name *whole language* bedevils us. Instead of whole language, once we understood how contextualized languaging is, we should have called our venture *whole experience*. Such a shift of terminology would better honor the full range of semiotic options that linguist Michael Halliday claims is essential for "meaning potential." You, John, however, were able to break free of paradigm identity crisis when you conceived of art as experience. We who share holistic language sensibilities should do similarly: reconceive language arts practices—the whole gamut from verbal to nonverbal composing processes and products—as whole experiences that contribute to meaning making in general and to verbal literacy in particular. Then, and this is a critical distinction, John, we would be positioned to nurture and receive whole new meaning potentials.

Halliday's (1975) vision of meaning potential forces us to ask, not what the child knows here and now, but how many ways to make meaning are available to him. Clearly, the dynamics between meaning-making options and meaning-potential are fundamental. But to invite multiple forms for meaning making into curricula, we need ways of seeing, new ways of naming the features of experience within, for example, creative movement. By exploring new evaluative lenses we will not only open doors to art experiences, but possibly inject powerful insights into what's fundamental within language experiences. You, John, described "experience" best by insisting that all experience has a unity that is emotional, practical, and intellectual. To strip experience of any of these features threatens its meaning potential.

In the spirit of such experience, then, John, guide these proposed "new basics," for English language arts classrooms. I'm taking cues from Goodman (1968) and Langer (1953)—Nelson Goodman and Susanne Langer, both philosophers of art. Their search to understand the nature of aesthetic processes and products has a closer affinity to what we're about in these new literacy classrooms than any verbocentric evaluative schema I've yet seen. It is that aspect of language arts that inquires into the 'nature' of the thing that deserves our attention. The highest form of dialectic, that transaction in which you, reader, and I are presently engaging by virtue of participating within this community of language arts readers, is one that inquires into the nature of things. It is with a question of nature, then, that we might begin and Weaver (1970) can lead the way:

> There is a branch of dialectic which contributes to "choice or avoidance" . . . involving questions of policy . . . and the dialectic which precedes it will determine not the application of positive terms but that *of terms* which are subject to the contingency of evaluation. There dialectical inquiry will concern itself not with what is "iron" but with what is "good." (p. 72) (emphasis mine)

That literacy evaluation has been myopic is evident in our jargon: back to basics, competency testing, minimum competencies, functional literacy, and survival skills. Worse, the tail wags the dog, so they say; thus, minimum competencies too often are the programs. Analogically then, these minimums' mentalities seem to be asking what is "iron" instead of what is "good."

Traditionally, the spoken and especially the written word monopolized the conversation in elementary and secondary English language arts classrooms. That was not inappropriate, given the nature of exit expectations in the past, a past when speech and print dominated school culture in particular and the larger information culture in general. In the past, the basics in primary language arts classrooms meant concepts like sound-symbol correspondence, phonemic segmentation, the word, story grammar, and so on. My perceptions of the not-necessarily-linguistic are what I'm calling the *new basics*, or qualities of experience in the sense you meant "experience," John, qualities that have been scantily articulated, underexploited (if not disallowed), and undervalued. The new basics do not ignore the old basics. Rather, the new basics may be more fundamental, more democratic, and perhaps even more complex.

To reason about anything, we must first discern—as nearly as we are able—its nature. If we underconceptualize the nature of this literacy venture, if we rush to words too quickly, we threaten what is possible to mean. If we are to invite children to engage the array of forms and meaning that surround them, we need to temper our proverbial passion for the basics and do none other than reconceptualize them in our classes.

Louise Rosenblatt (1978) may help set the tone for a changed literacy mental set. She distinguishes between efferent and aesthetic reading, that reading one does to take information from texts as opposed to living within the text. Both stances may be taken on any test: the quality efferent or aesthetic is in the reader's stance, not the text. Much literacy instruction in classrooms reeks of an efferent stance, doggedly pursuing old basics like sound-symbol correspondence and punctuation precision at the expense of the more aesthetic stances.

Yet, aesthetic stances are crucial to many literate transactions, and children do wrestle with them. For example, when children write they discern what is worth writing about: with whom this book might be worth discussing, what effect to create for this audience, how to "let the music" into a story's illustrations, why Mairin's Halloween mural is like Ezra Jack Keat's collages in *The Snowy Day* (1962), why Stacy's shadow play "felt like the story with words," why the Thanksgiving mime was "harder than acting out with words," why Shaine needed real holes on his story to show the explosions, why Erin spent a whole day testing titles for her story about one special day, why Kenny needs to enact play fights while he's composing battle scenes, why Shalala stands by her desk, hands on hips, experimenting with "how my mama would really say that," before she adds dialogue to her story.

Aesthetic sensibilities or stances that characterize work in the arts might prove powerfully informative for literacy. Many problems with welcoming art/play into our language arts curriculums lie in our failure to conceive of our discipline as *art*—a distinctly human process in which we, in community, create and are created by. Concerning writing in particular, Janet Emig (1983) begged us way back in 1978 to find out what is organic. She even had her doctoral students following premed students on their hospital rounds! Now, in 1995, because we know that writing is in a synergistic relationship to reading, speaking, and listening, how might other symbol systems participate as well? We need to wonder, John. We need to find out.

Here at Penn State as I work with preservice and in-service teachers in language arts, the teaching of writing, and emergent literacy, something continues to happen. Each semester I toss out my new basics for the students to try out on their own literacy growth (and they compose in multimedia during the semester). The resonance of these new basics, with both preservice and in-service teachers, appears to lie in the power of naming elusive, even virtual features—things that are real but intangible, like one's image in a mirror—of student work that previously were apprehended only intuitively, if at all. Frequently, teachers report back to me that they've managed to "get some of 'the new basics'" into their districts' literacy evaluative schema, and that they're "working to change more of the old language into the new because it fits!"

Now, John, hopefully you see how all this leads to a best shot at naming comprehensive, largely aesthetic qualities that can describe multimodal work within a literacy curriculum, be it called English or language arts. Chris Gaudet and I spent two years reconceptualizing the literacy curriculum and its evaluation for her first-grade classroom. There we struggled to name and give credit to the children's varied expressive acts, not only those that involved spoken and written language. We worked to develop a literacy curriculum to include creative dramatics, movement, drawing/painting, collage, sculpture, dance and music, just as whole language experts recommend. We knew that we had to evaluate children's work in these expressive modes and had to make the connections to literacy visible to outsiders—school administrators for starters.

What did matter, then, as we watched and documented the children's meaning-making ventures three mornings a week for two years in that first-grade classroom in northeastern United States? What did the children's writing and reading, videotapings, anecdotal records, interviews, and photographs allow us to see? What follows are the characteristics of meaning making—the new basics—we learned to see in action.

So, John, what began with Chris's and my dissatisfaction with existing evaluative criteria for language arts was the result of a paradigm identity crisis: we were trying to fit our vision of what could constitute language arts curriculum into an outdated, verbocentric vision that valued mainly, if not only, words. So we broke out of old evaluative routines and designed our own. What we were doing, clearly, was jumping paradigms, moving from a more linear, language-saturated one to an arts one: one that was frequently non-linear, affective, subjective, and still rigorous. Best of all, now we were able to honor children's ranges of expressive work as they contributed to literacy growth in our language arts spaces.

Below is the working list of the new basics, John. What do you think? Can you envision these descriptors naming, thus validating, so much of what we know children know?

- Initiative: Does the child take responsibility for beginnings?
- Problem Posing: What is the child trying to do? What is the nature of the problem the child initiates?
- Expressiveness: Does the work convey emotion/mood for either maker and/or receiver?
- Repleteness: Does the work exploit the potentials of the medium, for example, the *blockness* of blocks, the *poetryness* of poetry, the negotiability of talk?
- Problem Solving: How does the child envision possibilities? Does the child follow through in some way?
- Transmediation/Media hopping: Does the child express the idea in different forms?
- Risk Taking: Does the child try new things beyond his conventional repertoire?
- Collaborative Nature of Invention: Is the child growing aware of the contributions, however tacit, that others have made to his work?
- Evaluation: Does the child evaluate own and others' work in light of developing criteria?
- Care/Passion: Is the child invested in the idea, the process, the product?
- Time/Effort: Does the child appreciate that time/effort are intrinsic to much good work?

Chris and I have many stories to illustrate the above, but heck, John, you were with us all the way. And truly it's not the new basics per se that I'm championing (though I'll hang on to them until I find a more congruent fit). Rather, it's the spirit of the new basics—their virtual fit for all those expressive processes and products that students demonstrate in our midst.

Admittedly, these basics take a wide circle around literacy development. They explore influences on thinking and language development that transmediation—meaning making in various media—can offer under the umbrella of language arts. The pursuit of meaning is more basic to the pursuit of verbal literacy than words. Literacy *basics,* if indeed one accepts *fundamental* as a synonym, need first and always—to mean—the intention to discern and express meaning. Because the teacher, Chris Gaudet, and I knew that words do not represent the totality of thought, even for that fifteen percent of persons who are highly verbal, we urged children to generate and represent thought in any form. Teachers frequently notice children showing what they know, exploring what they don't know, playing with ideas in nonverbal ways. Still, for all the flexibility implicit in new evaluative frameworks like the portfolio, what counts in most English language arts assessments is what ends up in print, no matter how much attention or lip service is paid to alternative expressive modes. The new basics, however, appear to free teachers by providing names for real things that matter.

Annie Dillard characterizes a seeing that captures the essence of what I'm suggesting here. In *Pilgrim at Tinker Creek* she distinguishes between two kinds of "seeing." The first kind of "seeing," she claims, "is of course very much a matter of verbalization. Unless I call my attention to what passes before my eyes, I simply won't see it. . . . I have to say the words, describe what I'm seeing. . . . I have to maintain in my head a running description of the present" (Dillard, 1974, pp. 30–31). Another essentially different kind of seeing, she notes, "involves a letting go. When I see this way, I am transfixed and emptied. The difference between the two ways of seeing is the difference between walking with and without a camera. When I walk with a camera I walk from shot to shot, reading the light on a calibrated meter. When I walk without a camera, my own shutter opens, and the moment's light prints on my own silver gut. When I see this second way I am above all an unscrupulous observer" (p. 31). Dillard admits that she can't "go out to see this way. I'll fail, I'll go mad." She simply tries to "gag the commentator, to hush the noise of useless interior babble that keeps me from seeing. . . . I cannot cause light; the most I can do is to put myself in the path of its beam. It is possible, in deep space, to sail on solar wind. Light, be it particle or wave, has force; you rig a giant sail and go. The secret of seeing is to sail on the solar wind. Hone and spread your spirit 'till you yourself are a sail, whetted, translucent, broadside to the merest puff' (pp. 32–33).

John, I've quoted Annie Dillard at length to breathe the spirit of a new way of "seeing" into questions of development in English language arts. Instead of traveling with traditional camera lenses—scope and sequence charts, unit tests, to mention only two parts of our discipline's older assessment repertoire, or even portfolios, new forms that too often house incompatible old and new repertoires—we as professional "seers" must be cameras. We, not the unit test, record children's meaning in whatever forms they appear on our own "silver gut."

Wish you were here, John. Thanks for your continued support.
Sincerely,
Judith Fueyo

References

Dewey, J. 1934. *Art as Experience.* New York: Putnam's.

Dillard, A. 1974. *Pilgrim at Tinker Creek.* New York: Harper & Row.

Donaldson, M. 1978. *Children's Minds.* New York: Norton.

Emig. J. 1983. "Hand, Eye, Brain." In *The Web of Meaning: Essays on Writing, Teaching, Learning, and Thinking.* Portsmouth, NH: Boynton/Cook.

Fueyo, J. 1991. "Reading 'Literature Sensibilities': Resisting a Verbo-centric Writing Classroom." *Language Arts* 68: 641–48.

Goodman, N. 1968. *Languages of Art.* New York: Bobbs-Merrill.

Halliday, M. 1975. *Learning How to Mean.* Wheeling, IL: Whitehall.

Harste, J., K. Short, and K. Burke. 1988. *Creating Classrooms for Authors.* Portsmouth, NH: Heinemann.

Keats, E. 1962. *The Snowy Day.* New York: Viking.

Kuhn, T. 1970. "The Structure of Scientific Revolutions, 2nd ed." *International Encyclopedia of Unified Science. Vol. 2.* Chicago, IL: University of Chicago Press.

Langer, S. 1953. *Feeling and Form: A Theory of Art.* New York: Scribner's.

Lytle, S., and M. Botel. 1990. *The Pennsylvania Framework of Reading, Writing, and Talking Across the Curriculum.* Harrisburg, PA: Pennsylvania Department of Education.

Rosenblatt, L. 1978. *The Reader, the Text, and the Poem.* Carbondale, IL: Southern Illinois University Press.

Weaver, R. 1970. *Language Is Sermonic.* Baton Rouge: Louisiana State University Press.

Willinsky, J. 1990. *The New Literacy.* New York: Routledge.

Share What You Love: An Interview with Katherine Paterson

Jack Wilde

I wish there were some way to infuse this written interview with Katherine Paterson's laugh. It's a laugh that disarms with equal parts soul-searching honesty and simple humility as she accepts the responsibility her storytelling gift carries. This laugh erupts wholeheartedly as she considers the vicissitudes of reading, writing, censorship, parenthood, education—life. It's a laugh that invites us all in, that certifies that the going is hard but that that's precisely where joy and satisfaction are to be found. As Trotter says near the end of *The Great Gilly Hopkins*: "Did I say (life's) bad? I said it was tough. Nothing to make you feel happy like doing good on a tough job, now is there?" It's a laugh that celebrates, that values life.

Two important places of value are reading and writing. But where exactly does the value reside? Certainly, we transact business, communicate ideas, process information, and entertain ourselves, but are these the most important riches reading and writing bestow? In this interview Katherine Paterson locates her mother lode, presenting ways to think about and mine the riches in reading and writing; not the fool's gold of *Hooked on Phonics,* standardized test scores, basalized trade books, or writing to form, but the nourishment of the poem to soul and eye that tremors the body, the story that caresses the lips with joy, and the phrase, written just now, that scents the air with freshly mown hay. She asks that we treat reading and writing no less seriously or playfully than life itself.

I hope as you read you can hear Katherine's laugh, and smile in return at the task before us each day: to teach reading and writing.

Comfort and Passion: Valuing Reading

JACK: Why do we read?

KATHERINE: Did you see *Shadowlands,* the life of C.S. Lewis? I thought it was wonderful, and in it they say we read to know we are not alone. I think that's certainly a reason. We do read to know we're not alone. I started to read very early. I couldn't stand not to read. My older brother and sister read and the family read aloud, so I read. I really can't remember not reading. I even read when I ate; it was that important. When we moved to the States (from China), life was crazy. Initially, I had no friends; books provided companionship and comfort.

JACK: How do we get the schools to move beyond decoding and comprehension to the riches of reading like the sense you just described?

KATHERINE: Decoding isn't reading, it's decoding. We must never see decoding as an end in itself. Therefore, we should never be moving from it. We should start with story and with poetry . . . with things that enhance and enlarge life. You learn along the way the skills you need to manage the reading. The decoding will come in large part from the child's desire to participate in this language feast. My son John taught himself to read before he went to school. His school librarian commented that he was the only child she'd seen who walked by the library like he was walking by a candy store with his tongue out, eyes wide. But in class the teachers were worried. He'd finish his work sheet in a minute and want to read, but he wasn't supposed to know how to read yet, so they wouldn't let him. One of his teachers wanted to give him medication to help him focus. I said, "Wait a minute, I think his powers of concentration are pretty good." Always, as he went along, they would complain to me about his reading. Along about the fourth or fifth grade, his teacher worried again about his reading. I went into school and said, "I don't see the problem: he can read anything I can read and understand it." "Oh, sure, he can read," was her reply, "but his skills are weak." "His skills are weak. I thought the purpose of the skills was so you could read anything you wanted to and understand it." Apparently, he couldn't put the diacritical marks over the words. He could read the word, pronounce the word, and understand the word. But because he couldn't put the marks in correctly, his skills were weak. We really can get ourselves balled up in some kind of craziness.

Teaching Like a Librarian

JACK: In almost all of your books, one or more characters has an important relationship with books. Why?

KATHERINE: It's interesting to me. I guess the first time this was remarked upon was in *Bridge to Terabithia* because that was my first contemporary book. In it a child, Jesse, is learning about the world of books. Therefore, actual books are referred to. Even my wonderful editor said to me she thought it was lovely that this child was reading but wondered what would happen to readers who hadn't read those books. I said, "Well, they'll go out and read them."

It was astounding to me how many people commented that they thought it was wonderful that my characters read. I just thought in my experience people read, and characters are people. In books we're trying to portray the whole person. In my life, reading is an important part of the wholeness. It would be hard for me to write a book about a child without reading being a part of it.

JACK: But in your books all the important reading takes place outside of school. Must it?

KATHERINE: That's not quite correct. The school librarian in *Come Sing, Jimmy Jo* recommends *Ramona, the Brave,* and that's very helpful to Jimmy Jo. But mostly you're right; they read outside of school. Probably because it was my secret; it kept me sane. Looking back on my elementary school experience, it was the librarians, not my classroom teachers, who made life bearable for me. I didn't have terrible teachers all the time, but mostly they didn't open up the world for me. The librarians did. The first library I remember was at the Calvin Wiley School. It was the sheer number of books that were available which overwhelmed me. It was like falling heir to a fortune. I just didn't know there were so many books in the world and they were free. I could take any of them

I wanted to. I just remember going up and down the shelves. The librarian may have helped us; I don't remember. What I do remember is what a safe place it was and that she trusted us. I also remember she had me read aloud to younger children, and I mended books and shelved them.

Testing and Learning

JACK: What do tests have to say about what we value?

KATHERINE: So many teachers are slow to make real books a part of classroom experience that it's hard to measure. And when they do use trade books in the classroom, something hideous often happens. Let me give you an example. I have a friend with an adopted son. His grand-father died, and he became more anxious and concerned about his adoption. Adoption and mortality are linked, so the death increased his struggle. Just at this point his mother, who's a good person, gave him *Tuck Everlasting* to read. It came to be his book. The book brought his feelings and experience together. He just loved that book. Now that happened in fourth grade. The following year *Tuck Everlasting* was part of the fifth-grade curriculum. He was thrilled initially because that was his book. The teacher was heavy into symbolism, emphasizing what things in the book stood for. On the final test the boy got a C, which meant it wasn't his book. He didn't know this book. Obviously, he was just average or below average in understanding this book, so how could he love this book? It's just so sad because here was a book which was seminal for him, and the teacher convinced him that he didn't know anything about it. It's a crime. I wish teachers could understand.

I go through this with textbook people who want to incorporate trade books into their curriculum material. They can't understand when I ask, "Will the students hate the book by the time they've finished; has the book just been turned into an exercise?" So I have to see the questions they're going to use before I say yes. So many still have this textbook mentality which they're now willing to apply to my book. And I know what happens from firsthand experience: A friend of mine has a son who was reading *Bridge to Terabithia* in school. She asked him if he loved the book. His reply: "I used to." I don't want kids talking about my books that way.

JACK: Is there any way to value reading as long as there are standardized tests in the classroom?

KATHERINE: As long as there are standardized tests with four alternative answers and you scratch your answer in the box . . . no. This has nothing to do with true reading or learning. It says how clever you are about scratching the marks. It doesn't have anything to do with how wise you are, even how informed you are, or how compassionate you are. Standardized tests came into existence solely because they're easy to grade. Anything that is machine scorable should automatically be suspect; it can't have anything to do with real learning. Can it?

Standards: Needs and Ways

JACK: Serving on the board of the Standards Project for English/ Language Arts (SPELA), did you feel you were moving toward ways to effectively value and evaluate literacy?

KATHERINE: I only actually attended one meeting. I had two polarized experiences at that session. We met in a small group. I was very impressed with Maureen [Barbieri] and her group. The encounters were thoughtful, intense, wonderful really. And then we went back to a whole group meeting, and I got frustrated. We were trying to come up with a writing standard and it seemed to me the harder we worked the more watered down the standard became. So we were saying almost nothing by the end. The standard seemed to me to be an insult to a child. Everything that some of us proposed that would strengthen the standard was challenged by the other half of the group. They said we would offend this group or that. So we ended up with a weaker standard even though our charge had been to strengthen it. I thought, there's something wrong when we can't set a meaningful standard.

I don't think it's a good thing for a child to think anything goes. I mean I think it's wonderful to begin with invented spelling and all that, but everyone wants to end up proud of what they've done. If a child compares his writing to the writing in a book, he sees the distance. Now he doesn't want his declared the ultimate. He wants to know how he can get better and better so he can love his as much as he loves the book.

You don't get there by laying down rules. We may have gone about it in ways that are killing more than nourishing. Kids always ask if you have to be a good speller to be a good writer. I say, "No, I'm not a good speller." But I don't want to send anything to my editor that I'm not proud of. Because I'm a poor speller, I have to spend more time looking up words. I know it's a weakness of mine, so I know I have to be more careful. If I'm not proud enough of my work to be careful, then who else will have respect for my work? Grammar, spelling, all those things aren't the ultimate, but they are a part of constructing a piece of writing. Learning rules is probably not the best way to do it. That's really taking things apart instead of constructing, but it doesn't mean it's not important to know. If I break a certain rule, it's for a certain effect, not because I'm stupid or ignorant.

What I've observed in my four children is that for John, who was an early reader and read widely, writing came easily, almost naturally. The other three children had more of a struggle. Because he read so much, he was immersed in the language; he knew how the language worked. He didn't learn by observing the rules of grammar. You learn to write by reading, and reading different kinds of writing. And I don't think imitation is a bad thing when you're learning to write. It's an apprenticeship. If you apprentice yourself to a carpenter, you imitate that carpenter. Eventually, you're going to take off and figure out things on your own, find better ways of doing things, but initially you find a master and copy. Now you need to know what you're doing, so you don't just copy Robert Frost and say it's your work. But you can read Frost, absorb his style, then write in the style of Frost—try it out. I don't think that's a bad thing.

When children are at this stage when they should be copying and experimenting, that's when we start giving them prizes. I think it's a mistake that at the very time they should be imitating effective ways to use language, we have them enter contests. That's not the time for prizes. Usually they're given for the wrong reasons, and besides, only one person wins; everyone else loses.

Another form of the problem is when we say or imply that everything goes, and then we treat the product as if it were the ultimate. What really bothers me is when a teacher comes to me and says, I have this really bright eight-year-old who I think should be published. And I say, I'm sure she's a great writer (occasionally there are great child writers who do get published, and there are magazines that publish children's work), but . . . And the teacher interrupts me to say that this child's picture book is so good it should be published by a major trade book house. Now maybe the book is as good as an adult's. But it's a very, very, very exceptional eight-year-old who is ready to take on Steven Kellogg or Chris Van Allsburg. And I'm not sure it would be good for them. I think sometimes teachers get carried away in valuing their students' work. I think it's wonderful that they do value the work, but that doesn't mean they should place the child in an adult situation.

You have the whole example of child actors. They're wonderful as children, but few of them mature gracefully into adult actors, even into adulthood. It's very hard to be put into a spotlight when you're so young. Of course, winning a contest is minor compared to that. But it's not minor to the child who's learning to write; it carries a lot of responsibility at a time of experimentation.

Teaching Practice

JACK: Maybe one of the teaching tools the teacher has is to share his or her way of reading a text. Could that be of more help than offering a specific interpretation?

KATHERINE: One thing I often say to children is to use the image of music. I ask how many play a musical instrument. A few hands go up. I say when someone hands you a sheet of music it's just little black squiggles on a white page. It doesn't become music until you pick up your instrument and start to play. The same thing is true of a book; the black squiggles on a page gather dust on a shelf until a reader picks it up. It's the reader's imagination, and the reader's experience and skill that turn it into a good story. Now there's something there—Beethoven is Beethoven—but he can't be Beethoven without a musician. There's no novel without a reader. The work is to get the reader to play the book. And the more skill and wisdom, the better the playing. I can remember trying to talk to my college professor about Ursula Le Guin's book *Tombs of Atuan*. Of course, he would tie it into all kinds of mythology. It was wonderful the way he could read. You have touchstones in other literature that enrich the book you're reading. And I'm always embarrassed when someone says, "Of course, that's what they're referring to" when I don't see it. I never claimed to be a gifted reader. But I am a reader, and I read a lot.

JACK: Are there gifted readers?

KATHERINE: There are gifted readers, and once again it starts in childhood. I think my daughter, Mary, is a gifted reader; she reads with such understanding. It's a gift and like all gifts lays a burden on you. She reads and rereads for deeper understanding. Sometimes people stop after childhood, but I know people who continue. For instance, Sara Schmedman, a professor of children's literature, . . . has said that she can't comment on a book she's only read once. What she means is she hasn't given the book a chance. She doesn't reread everything, but if the book has promise, she will.

JACK: Can aspects of reading that we value be a part of school experience or are those aspects learned outside of the school structure?

KATHERINE: I go around to schools a lot, and I certainly see a lot of children who are the kind of child I was. Many of them are much more comfortable in school than I was, simply because they have teachers who value them for themselves; the teachers aren't trying to jam them into some kind of preconceived mold. Now maybe that's rarer than I like to think, but I see a lot of teachers who are open to their students. Maybe that's because they're the kind of teacher who invites me into their class. From my observations I have a positive view of schools.

I've seen deeper readings come out of discussions by children of a single book. Each of them has had a different experience, and they come to the book from a different point. They enrich each other's understanding, and that's without an adult perspective. I think that's one of the values of having books in the classroom and as a part of the curriculum —you can have that kind of discussion. The teacher needs to be skilled enough and know enough to entrust the discussion to the children. Real deep understanding of a book can come from a discussion that is not the teacher trying to extract information from the children which will let the teacher know whether the child has done the reading or not. I think, with a real discussion, children will read because they want to be part of the discussion, and they can't unless they've read carefully.

I remember this school I visited in Missouri. They had a wonderful book discussion program. They decided they would bring parents in for a family book discussion. What they found out was that the kids who had been in book discussions for years knew well the methods of discussion and listening. You couldn't, for instance, add to the discussion until you had repeated the previous point. I've seen tapes of these; they were wonderful discussions. But the parents would jump in and not listen, and they would ask questions trying to see if their child had read the book. Finally, the teachers realized that they had to train the parents. With practice, the parents learned how to do it. Once they caught on, the parents would be overwhelmed because they'd suddenly find themselves in this group weeping over a book. Fathers who'd never cried over a book in their lives would tell about something in a book and burst into tears. They might have been moved by a book before but never in an intense community of readers.

It's in this community that questions about the book should be asked and answered. The author is the last person who should be asked questions. Some teachers make part of the reading work to write to the author and ask questions. The author doesn't know the answers; that's not the author's job to understand the book—the understandings come from readers. So the children and the teacher should discuss the questions. Now it may be that no one can come up with a satisfying answer to a question. That should tell the readers that the author has let them down, not done what needed to be done. Writers are often doing that; it's hard to keep the same high standard throughout a book.

Value in Story

JACK: What is of most value to you in writing?
KATHERINE: Story; story is paramount. If the story doesn't work, nothing else will matter. The second thing is that the writer asks only genuine questions; you're writing the book to answer a genuine question of your own. If you have the question answered ahead of time, there's no point in writing the book. If you do, the book will be a polemic because you already have the answer. So the book represents the struggle with the deepest questions of your life. That means, for one thing, that the book is below the surface. It means it's very much the deepest part of you reaching out or reaching in. And because you are a storyteller you answer it by means of a story. Others answer it with a mathematical formula or

a science experiment or a poem. I'm a novelist so I answer it with a story. The question tells me to tell this story, and I'm wondering all the time if I've got it right. By the end I may or may not have a satisfactory answer. The struggle is the story.

JACK: Did your reading influence your writing or your desire to write when you were a student?

KATHERINE: Maybe, I'm not sure. A lot of my life was secret. I played by myself even though I was one of five children. My brothers and sisters paired up and I was left to myself. So I made up stories for play. A lot of my life was fantasy, and I think my writing was an extension of that. I remember being overheard once and feeling humiliated and embarrassed. My fantasy life was a secret, private thing.

What I wrote in school was what I thought they wanted, which was really stupid. So no one ever thought I had any writing ability, because I was writing what they gave me to read and, therefore, what I thought they wanted. I didn't think it was natural for me, just a school thing. My own reading was quite apart from the reading and writing in school.

JACK: In writing a story, do characters only express and embody values the writer holds?

KATHERINE: No, you have to be true to characters. The minute you start approving or disapproving of characters you've lost it because you're not a judge. And if you are, you're not going to have a true story. You have to love your characters but not lean on them. You have to let them be who they are. If they're perfect, if there's nothing to criticize, then you have no story. For the reader's sake, too, a perfect character offers the reader no comfort. A perfect character has nothing to do with human experience. There are adults in Virginia who want me to clean up Gilly. They want her cleaned up so she'll be acceptable to them, but then what comfort would she offer children?

Fantasy can draw a clearer line between good and evil. All good can be placed in one character, all evil in another. In realistic fiction, good and evil are mixed together in each person. Every reader should have a rich diet of books, read widely. I was nourished most by those books that let me know I was not alone. I didn't know somehow that it was all right to be mad—that other people do it too. Books let me know it was all right for me to be mad. Fantasy didn't give me that deep comfort; it was too different from experience; realistic fiction let me read to know I'm not alone.

Often my characters do things which I disapprove of, but which I deeply understand. In some way they are part of my emotional experience. Not my literal experience; very few of these things have I actually done.

Teaching, Not Explaining

JACK: What is the teacher's work in trying to value reading and writing?
KATHERINE: I think it's up to the teachers and the school librarians to broaden the children's experience. The children's experience is too narrow. I mean they don't know what's out there; how can they choose what will be of most help? The mature adult can offer the wider world to the child.

In college I took a seminar on nineteenth-century writers. Each one of us had to study one writer in depth. Now the only writer I knew was Charles Dickens, and I wasn't about to do him because there'd be too much reading. So I chose Kipling and went to meet with my professor. He said, "No, no don't do Kipling, you should study Gerard Manley Hopkins." So I agreed. I hadn't even heard of Hopkins. I went over to the library, took out a book of his poems and started to read "The Windhover." I didn't understand it at all. I read it over and over; I read it aloud; I looked up just about every word and still didn't get it. I realize now that it's one of the greatest poems I've ever read, but I didn't know that then—I was too ignorant. Even when I started to get it, it seemed too hard for me. But because my professor had said I would like it, I had to keep working to figure what there was about it that I would like. And I think that's the teacher's role; to expand the student's experience, the sense of what there is. It's not the teacher's role to explain it, to sit the student down and say this is what it means. No, the teacher has the wonderful role of pushing the student into discovering new possibilities and exploring them first on their own. Of course, my professor and I talked about the poem endlessly, but only after I'd struggled with it. Otherwise, he would have just been telling me things.

I also think that a teacher doesn't need to feel that they have to do everything for their class. No, what you should do is share what you love. Other teachers love different things, and they'll share that with their students. Your value for a particular child is your passions. When you share them, that opens up a whole different thing. You're working at a different level. I've had people say they have to teach a certain book of mine. I say don't do it; don't teach it unless you love it. Only teach books you love; don't teach them because you think they'll be good for your students or any other reason. I know there are curriculum problems; schools sometimes dictate what book must be taught. I think that's terrible. I think teachers should have the leeway to choose among a number of books.

The more passion you have about something, the more likely it will translate into a passion in the student. Everyone develops a passion because someone shared a passion when that person was young.

References

Babbitt, Natalie. 1975. *Tuck Everlasting*. New York: Farrar, Straus & Giroux.

Cleary, Beverly. 1975. *Ramona, the Brave*. New York: Morrow.

Hopkins, Gerard Manley. 1970. *The Poems of Gerard Manley Hopkins*, 4th ed. Oxford: Oxford University Press.

Le Guin, Ursala K. 1971. *Tombs of Atuan*. New York: Macmillan.

Paterson, Katherine. 1977. *Bridge to Terabithia*. New York: Crowell.

————. 1978. *The Great Gilly Hopkins*. New York: Thomas Y. Crowell.

————. 1985. *Come Sing, Jimmy Jo*. New York: Lodestar Books.

Confessions of a Reader

Carol Wilcox

Almost spring.
A spider
Stakes a claim
On a corner
Of the eight-foot window
In our living room.

Each morning
I admire
Taut guidelines
Carefully placed spokes.
Dancing gown threads,
Architecture unrivalled.

My mother
Would not tolerate
Such slovenly housekeeping.
She would get a broom
And knock down
This errant squatter's palace.

I do not.

I am waiting for Charlotte
To leave a message.

4

School's Cool When It Comes Down Real

Mary Mercer Krogness

An English composition paper lies hemorrhaging on the floor of a corridor in our middle school. Misspellings and grammatical problems, mostly, have been slashed and circled in red pen. I bend down to pick up this paper to which a teacher has awarded an ambivalent F+/D-. It is no wonder to me that the writer of this composition crumpled and tossed the wrinkled story carelessly to the floor as he ambled out of his seventh-grade skills English class. What sense could the paper's owner make of an evaluation like this? What could an F+ over a D- possibly mean to him? What good or harm could a plus or a minus do in this case? (Maybe the teacher wanted to encourage the boy by adding a plus?) What is a high F over a low D, anyhow? Does this grade mean that Donald, the writer of this composition, didn't fail as well as other low-achieving students in his class? Or does it mean that he didn't fail as miserably? Perhaps this grade means that Donald did a terrible job, and he should do better. Might the teacher have wanted Donald to know in no uncertain terms that he was hovering between failing and passing English? Or by giving him an F+/D-, was the teacher trying to gently warn his student to get busy in this course?

The hazards of giving letter grades intensifies in my mind as I stand in the school corridor staring at all the red marks made by an English teacher, a colleague, who obviously held a sharp instrument while grading his students' compositions. As I hold Donald's paper in my hands, questions that I'd asked myself a thousand times whirl through my head. I ask myself what possibly could this student have learned from getting back a paper that was assaulted twenty-nine times?

But I realize Donald *has* learned something after all: his story isn't worth much. What the teacher found wrong with the boy's plot, characters, story development, transitions, focus, or lack of voice was not conveyed, because there's no note of explanation or encouragement, not even of exasperation or futility; there are only red circles and slashes. The little nuggets, the few moments of hope or promise that might lie buried in Donald's story, went unnoticed by the only evaluator in this class. Like countless students who have grown up in classrooms where letter grades are the standard, Donald is likely to be harmed by receiving letter grades. Letter grades tell him daily that he's not making it in school; he probably won't make it out of the seventh grade unless miracles happen between now and June. Bad grades tell him he is worthless. The F+/D- on Donald's story tells him everything, yet it tells him nothing.

As I consider Donald's crumpled paper, I think about the meaning of *to evaluate*; its root is *to value*. Evaluation is, then, a question of valuing. Each day I set out to show my students that above all, I value them; I accept them unconditionally. I demonstrate my intellectual and artistic values each time I acknowledge my students' self-conscious, perhaps new, interest in writing poetry; praise the questions they are learning to ask; appreciate their fresh insights in literature; or admire their cautious or even fleeting understanding of a novel we are reading. But I know that while I am endeavoring to help the young people in my charge build stamina for learning and guide them to see themselves as students—maybe for the first time—many have serious doubts about the fare I offer them, as well as about my standards for excellence. After all, my students have learned that school places a high premium on tests (teacher-made or standardized), scores, letter grades, and percentage points.

Likewise, my students have learned to value tough teachers who give the most homework, the hardest tests, and the lowest grades. Jewel-Ray, a bright African-American girl with flashing brown eyes and an eighth grader at our school, had wonderful moments academically, when she wasn't being shipped off to ATS, our alternative to suspension, or shipped out—suspended—for fighting or otherwise causing mayhem in most of her classes. This fourteen-year-old was best known for the trouble she brought with her to class, certainly not for her intelligence and rich imagination. Although she could be unruly, provocative to the extreme, and behaved outlandishly, she more often than not simmered down in our class. Jewel-Ray threw herself into improvisational drama; she held us spellbound each time she cast herself in a role, usually playing opposite a willing classmate or me.

Her original poetry puzzled her classmates, while it pleased me no end. The language she used was spare, hard-driving, and fresh; her images were original. Words awakened this eighth-grade girl's imagination, and she, in turn, infused the language with her spirit.

Just Sittin'
by Jewel-Ray

I like just sittin' in school.
It safe and clean and quiet and it
give me time to think
about how my life gonna be
when I am grown.
I see a average looking young woman
with long brown legs,
a mind of her own and a head
full of ideals walkin' downtown
going to look for a job.
Not just any job. A BIG job
at 9th and Euclid Ave.
The building look
like a castle.
She walk through a pair of swinging doors,
look up at the beautiful carved ceiling,
then she go to the elevator.
She push the button for the 13th floor,
the one for good luck.
And she wait.
The elevator ride give her
a roller coaster feeling.
If she get the job, she can

get this feeling every day.
And get paid too.
They said so in the paper—

"Custom Cleaning Service needs
experienced custodian. Minimum wage
to start."

Maybe she don't like just sittin'
in school picturing her life
when she is grown after all.

Jewel-Ray didn't see anything poignant or perceptive or imaginative about the words she'd set down on paper. She told me how easy "talking on paper" was for her. And from her point of view, anything easy didn't count as learning. Although she enjoyed reading, writing, and performing poetry in class, she didn't consider it an important part of the language arts curriculum.

"You can't get no good-payin' job writin' poetry," she grumbled.

"But through poetry, you can learn about—feel—the power of language," I said. "And in the world of work, using language powerfully counts!" I took this opportunity to lead Jewel-Ray to consider a broader perspective; I was showing her what I valued.

When we read YA literature, it was Jewel-Ray who could get to the heart of it, offering all sorts of reasons why a character behaved as he did, or explaining how the author let readers imagine a scene. I considered my students' moments of reflection, insights, vision, whimsy, and fresh use of language as harbingers of what would—could—eventually develop; I valued these moments as much as, if not more than, I did the traditional means of evaluating students—with tests and quizzes. By my enthusiastic comments and questions that usually asked them to say more, I told them what I valued most.

Jewel-Ray relished our classroom fare; she flourished in our midst. But a comment from her told me she didn't yet consider what we did in class as bona fide learning. "Mrs. K., I don't want to hurt your feelings or nothin', but we don't do what the rest of the English classes do. We just do improv, read, write, talk, and have fun. And you such a easy teacher."

Flustered and defensive, I asked her to clarify what we didn't do that other English classes did. Jewel-Ray turned to her cohorts in my skills

English class and said, "It true—them other classes, they have tests; them teachers—they hard. They make their students read so many pages of a book every night. Them kids have to do book reports, too." Jewel-Ray paused. "And all we do is talk and write about books we read in class. We always talkin' about our writing, readin', doin' drama, and pickin' out which pieces of writing we like best to put in our portfolio."

"Yeah," another girl agreed. "That's true, Mrs. K."

I spoke slowly, "So, do you think you're not learning in here? Just having fun and enjoying yourselves?"

Jewel-Ray again took the lead in this conversation. "I'm not sure. We doin' different stuff in here, so I can't tell if what we doin' is as good as what they doin'." Jewel-Ray obviously was struggling to figure out what she valued, what she considered authentic school work and learning. Her attitude and active class participation plainly told me she liked and benefited from the kinds of experiences offered in our class, but she was questioning the worth of intellectual conversation about stories, poems, and articles we read and the writing she and her classmates were doing in here. Jewel-Ray wondered if so much classroom conversation added up to learning. (Maybe she'd heard that talk is cheap!) She expressed doubt about the value of doing improvised classroom drama, an active and interactive way of making meaning and connecting story characters' motives with her own life and the lives of her classmates. Like many students, (regardless of whether they were in accelerated, regular, or skills classes) Jewel-Ray believed that if learning wasn't hard, arduous, didn't come in large quantities, and was not delivered by a tough teacher, it couldn't be real learning. And furthermore, learning surely wasn't valid if it was fun!

"Learning, Jewel-Ray, comes in many different forms," I told her. "The hardest thing you'll ever have to learn you accomplished by the time you were two years old," I said feeling more relaxed than I had when this conversation began.

Jewel-Ray looked puzzled as did a number of her classmates who, by this time, had tuned in to this conversation about values.

"An' what did I learn when I was two years old that was the hardest thing in my life?" Jewel-Ray demanded to know, in a voice tinged with skepticism.

"You learned to use words; you learned to talk; you learned to use the language. That's the most difficult, most complicated, the most puzzling intellectual challenge you—any of us—will ever meet." I paused again.

"And you know something else?" I asked. "You learned to talk long before you came to school and before you learned to read and write." I paused. "Did you use a workbook or a study guide to help you learn to talk? When you were two, did you ever take a test on your ability to talk?"

She looked serious but still skeptical. I explained further. "What I'm saying is this: We learn all the time and in many different ways. We learn when we're in school and out of school; we learn when we're least aware of learning. We even learn when we're mad at the teacher and don't want to learn, because a person can't stop her mind from working, from thinking.

"Now, about my being an easy teacher. Maybe I make learning easy for you. Maybe I help you find success in our class so that it's easy for me to give you good grades. Maybe for the first time you're seeing that being a successful school learner is possible. Maybe learning is easier and more fun that you thought. Learning can and should be fun, I mean satisfying to students."

At that moment, Jewel-Ray looked as if she were seriously considering what we'd spent the better part of a forty-two-minute class period talking about. Speaking of values, that's what I call a rich and important classroom conversation; that's what I call spending school time well. I find that showing young people what I consider important in my daily practice can help them expand their notion of what learning is, what excellence is, and who they as learners are and can become.

My goal, however, is not to inculcate *my* values, but rather to help my seventh and eighth graders learn to value themselves by discovering over the course of time that they can be able learners. I invite them into language learning. During class, we play with words, engage in improvised drama, generate ideas, raise evocative questions, make important decisions about our writing, try out ideas by talking, and practice the gritty technical skills of reading and writing according to need. I help my students find their stories, poems, plays, and then I show them how to hone their writing. Together we read and respond to novels, write and perform poetry; our family folklore project offers us an opportunity to conduct taped interviews of our relatives and get in touch with our own history. All, of course, are avenues for evaluating students' academic work. In these ways, I help them find and develop their talents and multiple intelligences that often go unnoticed and unappreciated.

In my classroom laboratory, I help the young people in my midst, mostly African-American boys and girls, who are often overaged and underprepared, gain a fresh vision of what constitutes excellence. Mainly I try guiding them to develop one that is broader than school's usual definition (doing well on tests), which usually excludes them. By actively engaging my students—immersing them—in many and varied language experiences that apply to *their* lives, yet lead them forward, I aim to stretch their perception of what learning and academic accomplishment really are. From my perspective, the magic moments—when kids use the language surprisingly, when they ask remarkable questions, or offer insights—equal excellence. Students' growing ability to be prime movers in the classroom rather than empty receptacles who passively sit waiting for the teacher to fill them up; or their decision to take charge of their own learning and therefore their lives—these manifestations of desire and personal growth do, indeed, demonstrate accomplishment. I want my students' new definition of academic excellence to embrace *their* talents, intelligences, and their courage to take hold of life; I want it to include them!

True to my values, I actively and purposefully seek alternative ways of engaging my seventh and eighth graders in language learning. Knowing that there is no one way for them—for anyone—to become accomplished readers, writers, and thinkers, I feel free to be inventive. No one, best way for engaging kids in learning exists either.

For one particularly resistant and obstreperous class of eighth graders, assigned to my language arts/reading class because they read at or below the local third stanine in reading comprehension and vocabulary on the Stanford Achievement Test, I decided to try hooking them on language and helping them harness their energy (or jar them loose from their own inertia) by making a film with them. They'd told me in no uncertain terms they hated to read. They didn't like to write much either. By making a film with these kids, some of whom wandered into class late and then did everything in their power to derail it, I imagined that together we could weave talking, listening, speaking, reading, writing, and viewing—all of the language arts—into a splendid fabric. I reasoned that while working on a promising class project, I would have the opportunity to help them learn how to work together peaceably and productively. And for this group of teenagers, such a goal was worth achieving. All of us would be working on an exciting project that everyone had a stake in accomplishing. Film-making would cause each of us to be more self-reflective, too. Because this particular class was transient (ten students entered and exited this class between mid-October and late May), making a film (with the help of our library-media specialist, Pat Fagel) would allow us to regroup each time a new student joined or left us.

One day early in October, I said, "From what I observe, this class is pretty smart and creative. (I *had* observed these qualities!) I've always wanted to make a film with a class. I think this is the class to do it." Little response. I pressed on. "What do you think we could make a video about?"

One boy retorted, "Who said *we* wanted to make a film?" Undaunted, I reminded them of the striking metaphor Ladell (who now slouched low in his chair, his hooded eyes nearly closed) had just made while we'd discussed a novel we all were reading: "It's funny how some people have to make U-turns in their lives," he'd said in an offhanded way. Bells rang and lights flashed in my head when I'd heard Ladell's dramatic use of language. People's lives taking U-turns certainly invited more conversation; I fancied that we might use street signs as the hooks on which we'd hang scenes for our film. "Let's talk more about Ladell's interesting symbol—people's lives taking U-turns. What *is* a U-turn in life? Have any of your lives taken U-turns?", I asked. At that moment, I'd expressed my interest and pleasure with Ladell's symbolic language, and I demonstrated my commitment to capitalizing on *students'* rather than *my* ideas.

My kids and I spent the rest of our class period that day generating a long list of street and road signs: Stop, School, Yield, Detour, Under Construction, Caution, Slippery When Wet, One-Way, Dead End, and so forth. While interest still lingered, I began the next class period by using the familiar stop sign, an evocative symbol, as a point of departure for both generating and discussing a list of teenagers' concerns. "What are the real-life stop signs that teenagers need to pay attention to?" I asked.

"Hanging with the wrong people, and getting in trouble," Rachel called out. "Not doing your school work, then failing in school and droppin' out," Alicia added. "Runnin' the streets all night, and runnin' from the cops," LaShawn offered. After more students became modestly invested in generating ideas which they tied to the familiar street signs, and when this classroom conversation had gathered more momentum, I organized the students into small groups to briefly generate and jot even more ideas. One group imagined joining gangs and then going to prison as a one-way street—a dead end; a group of girls equated teen pregnancy with a detour; for another group, doing and trafficking drugs called for the caution sign.

During the weeks and months that followed, I deliberately engineered more sustained and intense group work, encouraging my kids to decide upon and more fully develop what we called the "street-sign scenes," by sketching the vignettes on newsprint and blocking possible scenes for our film. Just as one group of girls had fleshed out a mother-daughter scene, intentionally omitting dialogue, librarian/media specialist Pat Fagel suggested we film then view it. Rachel played the teenage girl who works up enough courage to tell her mother, played by Amisha, that she's pregnant. The two girls improvised this emotion-packed scene that we captured on film, the first of many takes. Everyone sat riveted to the TV monitor. For the first time since we'd begun this long-term project, even the most disengaged kids felt energized by what they saw. And so it went: sometimes we'd meet all together, while at other times we'd gather in small groups or individually to map out scenes that we wanted to film, not once but maybe a half-dozen times. During the class periods that were devoted to making our video (from October through mid-June), we practiced reflecting on our work by asking each other and ourselves questions such as these: What part of this vignette works? What doesn't work? What's original, fresh, convincing? What is lacking, lagging, lackluster? What about a scene isn't authentic? Or as the young rap artists in our class said: "It comes fake and phony." Which scenes work together? Which ones don't fit? Each time we asked questions like these and made artistic decisions, we were developing a system of values and standards of excellence.

While we engaged in the stop-start process of making "One-Way Streets," our film about the tough decisions that teenagers face, the young people and I found out how talented they were, the many gifts they had to offer. While they talked in small student-made groups to plot, plan, and improvise each dramatic scene or vignette, they began to take themselves more seriously as learners. We witnessed certain classmates gradually open up to new possibilities and assume leadership roles while we cast characters, learned to operate the camera, or decided on particular audio or video sound effects.

From my perspective, the implications of this collaborative, creative project cannot be underestimated. Making a film accomplished what I'd hoped for and more: it brought discordant young people together for a common purpose. In a safe setting, my students had the opportunity to deal with important issues that greatly concerned them: getting pregnant or making someone pregnant, dropping out of school, joining gangs, doing or selling drugs, being the perpetrator or victim of violence. Making "One-Way Streets" provided a forum for discussion and debate, a valid reason to do research (reading newspaper and magazine articles, locating statistics on teenagers, viewing other films), and a vehicle for creative expression. While this project allowed all of us to become deeply immersed in language-using and making, it motivated my eighth graders to make excellent intellectual and creative decisions—to evaluate and value—what they were creating.

On one warm June night, the world premier of "One-Way Streets," our families and friends met in the school library to view our twenty-minute film, the culmination of a nine-month project. My students' personal testimonials—self-evaluations of our language arts project—spoke volumes. With pride and confidence, Rachel spoke first: "This film was made from scratch. We didn't get our ideas from a book or magazine. They were our own ideas that we brainstormed in class." The petite eighth-grade girl talked animatedly about working with her peers to shape the various improvised scenes: for example, when the teenage girl tells her mother that she is pregnant, the distraught mother declares, "But I already raised *my* kids!" There's the vignette of the little three-year-old boy, exposed to violence, and who, ten years later, at thirteen, is sentenced to five years in DH (Detention Home) for committing a crime. A courtroom scene follows. The three young rappers, who wrote and performed their original raps, tell it like it is (drugs, violence, and death) for an increasing number of America's teenagers.

Alicia decided to write a dream speech for "One-Way Streets." She looked majestic as she talked to the appreciative audience about the effect that creating and reciting her speech had on her: "This dream speech has not come from a book, but from my heart." Alicia said she would never forget this speech, and that she would think about and practice it forever. Here is an excerpt: "I am here to talk to you about dreams. What are dreams? Dreams are wanting to succeed and accomplish. I want to see all of you having dreams. I want your mind to roar with questions and answers. Knowledge is power. Knowledge is power. Be a dreamer—there is the magic. Let your light shine through the darkness. What this world is desperately in need of is a dreamer and her dream. That's what the world needs—a dreamer and his dream. I say to you, my brothers and sisters, get the power. Dream the dream."

Another girl, Amisha, who, through filmmaking, had gained confidence speaking in front of a group, talked about her improved attitude toward language arts and reading; she explained that by working on this film with her peers, her reading comprehension and writing had improved. By no stretch of the imagination had Amisha become a proficient or voracious reader, but she had learned to assert herself, to generate ideas and discuss their merits confidently; Amisha read with more insight and wrote with greater clarity and conviction. Clearly, she enjoyed language learning more than she had earlier.

Raj noted that he (who had earlier felt uncomfortable with his peers) gained confidence in working with these new friends in authentic ways. Curtis, who'd originally been placed in a class for students with serious behavioral problems because he'd patently refused to do any school work, was transferred into our class late in January. He found filmmaking a wonderfully liberating and creative experience. Curtis told our guests that he'd worked hard to outline a scene, film, act in more than one vignette, and play the background music for our movie on the piano. This was the first academic work he'd agreed to do for nearly two years. His mother expressed great pleasure when she told me that school had never been so rewarding for her son.

Curtis said: "It [filmmaking] was a wonderful experience."

Rasheem and Steven, two rappers, who wrote and presented, live, their original raps about gang-banging, doing drugs, and being fathers to children—one-way streets—benefited from making the film, because this kind of schoolwork, they declared publicly, was real and therefore had meaning.

Steven confessed: "Sometimes I came to school *just* to make this film."

5

We Know Because We Asked

Mark Milliken and Steven Tullar

Abe sighed and shook his head as he said, "I'm not good at it. I haven't learned how to work well in a group. I'm better at independent work. Like in the bird study group other people wanted to do things differently. People would never agree. My ideas always get voted out. My ideas are better! I want to learn to communicate without getting mad."

Abe shared these comments during his midyear progress interview. His response to group work situations provided insight and information Mark would not have learned if he hadn't asked. Abe made clear his frustration along with his genuine desire to change. After this interview, Mark knew Abe better as a member of a study group: where he was in his development of group skills and where he hopes to be. In the midyear narrative Mark wrote: "Abe's earnest desire to accomplish tasks leaves him with little patience for peers who do not contribute as much as he does. As a result, Abe feels he is not very effective at cooperative group work. His goal is to try to communicate his ideas and feelings without getting overly emotional and to demonstrate more self-control when difficult group scenarios arise. This is especially hard when Abe feels his ideas are best, yet the group sees things differently. Abe works better by himself, but wants to work on effective cooperation skills required for group work."

We are elementary teachers, and the student interviews we conduct give us a closer look at what we value in classrooms and help us to report student progress more accurately. The Oyster River School District in Durham, New Hampshire—where Mark teaches fifth grade, and Steve teaches a four-five multiage classroom—now uses narrative reports as the primary communication tool in the elementary schools. We base these narratives about our students' growth and learning on our observations, anecdotal notes, day-to-day student interactions, portfolios, and interviews. The interview clarifies what we know about the learner and their learning, which makes for more accurate report writing.

When we first reported student progress in a narrative format, we told parents what *we* saw, what *we* thought, and how *we* planned to proceed; we portrayed the learner through our eyes, those of the teacher. Student work helped to highlight our statements of observation. Our increased use of portfolios helped us include student work in the reporting process. Yet, our narratives remained a detailed communication between adults. The students went home, carrying their "report cards" and asked their parents, "What did my teacher say about me?" It remained a mystery to be unfolded and solved.

No matter what we said, how we said it, or how much we said, the narratives lacked the reflections of the learners. We wanted information closer to the source. We finally settled on one way to add this valuable component: ask. Although simply put, the bottom line was to just ask the learners about their learning. The student point of view we wanted to include in the narratives required individual interviews. The discussions that evolved from the asking heightened our awareness of our students' learning and in turn enhanced our written narratives.

The interview:
- Takes an in-depth look at student learning, growth, and challenges. We and our students can explore and learn together, valuing all learning. We ask, "What are you comfortable with in your learning? What do you do well? What are you working on?"
- Includes setting student goals from the perspective of the learner. "What are you planning? How will we keep track of this?"
- Allows students to reflect on learning experiences and to reconstruct learning experiences. Reflecting on and talking about specific work and past learning experiences help students clearly see their growth

and areas that need change. "Can you tell me about what you did? What did you learn? Would you expect that again?"

- Provides interactions between us and the learner that clarify what the student understands what the teacher knows. During the interview, students sometimes demonstrate their understanding of math concepts through manipulation of concrete objects. "Can you show me how this works? How do you use this in your life? How could you?"
- Identifies areas of learners' interest. "What would you like to learn about? What do you wonder about?"
- Enables responsive teaching. We learn. We look at ourselves through the eyes of the learners in our rooms. Their evaluations help us evaluate our own teaching and help us respond to their expressed needs. "How can we change to meet the needs we see in our students as individuals? as a whole class?"

Where to Begin

The design of our classrooms helps our students become independent workers, know where their resources are, take responsibility for their time, and work within the classroom structure. We spend time setting up the workshop, response groups, and individual conferences early in the year. Students work independently, in small groups, in pairs, and with other adults. When we begin the report card interviews, students are well accustomed to a classroom where they control their own time and learning, where they go to each other for help, where we will intervene to offer students support in decisions, and where our time is distributed among all the learners in the class. The interviews happen with a minimum of interference and interruption. Students know they will get their time and often come to the interview prepared to talk.

We begin interviews by asking students what they are comfortable with in school. We want to know what they feel good about, what they are "good" at, where they have improved since the beginning of the year. The interview then follows their lead. If they talk about math, we ask questions related to math learning. We developed a checklist based on the district progress report to help fill in holes that the students may not touch on. It also works as a focus point to ensure that the interview moves (see Figure 5–1). When students reach a stopping point, if they are unsure of what else they have to say, we wait. Then we nudge them a little, asking questions. If they are talked out on a topic, we allow them time before switching to other areas. We take care not to fill the silence with our agenda.

The interview process works because we are truly interested. The questions asked are genuine; they are about topics we are interested in and want to know more about. Questions follow the students' lead. We look for their comfort in the dialogue and listen to them push the edges, then we help. The interviews extend our interactions with students. The students talk about learning experiences and, as they talk to us, they begin to hear themselves.

When beginning the interview with an open question, we have learned to be prepared for the students to go in any direction. They start with personal interests, areas of confidence, areas of improvement, or even areas of dissatisfaction. In the following example, Sharon begins by talking about herself as a writer. She mentions past writing habits, dependency on the teacher to begin pieces, and her lack of editing for publication. She recognizes how her lack of practice starting her own stories has interfered with her growth as a writer. She is now comfortable and excited about her writing. As she talks about her writing improvement this year, she becomes animated and then grows serious as she discusses goals:

> Last year I was not a good writer, I never wrote stories to publish. The teacher always gave us story starters. This year I'm a much better writer. I still have a hard time thinking of stories. But the story I wrote about the two girls and the two ghosts is the best thing I have ever written. It has more details, is more understandable, and is realistic. And it has a believable ending. I dreamt part of it. And response group has helped me to add to it.
>
> I don't always use capitals and punctuation. When I edit on the computer it sounds better. My goal is to publish this story and a future goal is to think of topics I like more.
>
> I haven't changed as a speller. It's easy for me to remember words. I usually study one night and get hundreds. My goal is to spell bigger words like words in science . . . photosynthesis. I want to go through all my work and enter words I have misspelled into my dictionary.

Oyster River School District Checklist

Science, Social Studies, and Health
Includes:
Gathering and organizing information
interpreting and applying information
demonstrating an understanding of skills and concepts

Mathematics
Includes:
understanding and using the language of mathematics
recognizing relationships among different mathematical operations and
    procedures
estimating and checking reasonableness of solutions
using appropriate problem solving strategies
computing accurately with appropriate number combinations
applying skills and concepts

Language Arts
Reading
Includes:
selecting books at appropriate level
using a variety of strategies to identify unknown words
demonstrating an understanding of what is read
locating and using reading materials to find information

Writing
Includes:
expressing ideas clearly in writing:
        revising
        editing
        exhibiting growth toward standard spelling

Learning Behaviors and Attitudes
Includes:
attending to classroom discussions and activities
contributing to classroom discussions and activities
following directions; working independently in a group
working cooperatively in a group; organizing time and materials
assuming responsibility for assigned work
demonstrating self control
understanding and complying with classroom and school expectations
respecting the needs and property of others
assuming responsibility for own behavior

Figure 5–1. *Oyster River School checklist.*

In this example, Sharon moved from what she was comfortable with in writing to an area where she was unsure, editing. Then she went back to a comfort area, spelling test scores, and then finished with an area of need, spelling challenges. This information translated into the following writing portion of her narrative:

Sharon has experimented with a few different writing topics this year. The impressive quality about Sharon as a writer is her willingness to listen to readers' feedback. Her latest piece is a fiction story that involves a ghostly apparition. Sharon is trying hard to keep her story believable and uses her small response group's feedback to reach her goal. Her writing is clearly expressed, has a nice flow, and shows an impressive sense of detail. These are qualities we have worked hard on in class, and it is rewarding to see them appear in Sharon's writing. Sharon feels this is her best writing ever! Sharon has the desire to self-edit, and we will be working on more effective ways for her to do so. She does tend to use punctuation appropriately. Sometimes in her printing she misuses capitals. Sharon's drafts do have misspelled words in them. I would like to see her continue to work on circling these words so that she will edit them out of her final work. She could use some work on recognizing the spelling differences between homonyms such as "their" and "there." Her spelling test average is an impressive 93 percent.

When we give students the lead, we find they start not just with different areas of comfort, but different perspectives. Some students share from the negative, their personalities dictate the direction of the dialogue. Anthony started with, "I don't know what I'm doing well in, but I know what I'm not doing well in." (Mark listened to him talk.) "I get the easy stuff wrong and the hard stuff right. Like last night I got the subtraction problems wrong and the decimal problems right." Mark kept listening and Anthony talked about decimals.

Mark asked him to tell about something that was going well. Then after a long pause, Mark asked "What do you think about yourself?"

He replied, "I'm good," sounding as though he were trying to convince himself as well as the teacher.

When he talked about reading, Anthony said, "I haven't changed as a reader since third grade. I learned how to read slowly, my mom read *Zoobooks* to me."

Stopping him at this point, Mark asked him to look at his reading more closely, "What did you read in third grade?"

Anthony then talked about his reading in more specific terms. "I read Garfield . . ." Once he looked at the specifics, it dawned on him that he had indeed changed quite a bit since third grade. "Yes, I have changed as a reader. Now I'm reading *Goosebumps*." This negative first approach was consistent throughout the whole interview. The interview is a very honest interaction between student and teacher.

Mark wrote about Anthony as follows in the reading and mathematics sections:

Anthony feels particularly unsure of accomplishments in math. He feels he frequently makes silly mistakes. He has a better understanding of place value; however, he still needs to check the reasonableness of his answers. I feel with more concrete manipulative work Anthony will learn to trust his eyes and not feel there is some magical formula that he doesn't know."

Anthony loves to read *Goosebump* books. This year he is more aware of the author's use of detail and character description. He is very good at independent reading. When he comes to unknown words, he tries to figure them out by rereading and using context clues. He doesn't usually look any words up. Anthony is aware that he is not challenging himself and expanding his reading repertoire. For this reason I have asked him to read more of a variety of books. I have nothing against the books he currently reads, I simply want him to grow as a reader. I would like to help Anthony find other interesting genres and authors. We are beginning to read historical fiction books about the Revolutionary War time period. Hopefully, he will find he enjoys some of these books."

An overall observation I want to share is that it is much easier for Anthony to tell of his weaknesses than it is for him to speak of his strengths. I am aware of this and am working on helping Anthony be aware of this tendency and to help him recognize his strengths.

Part of our job in the interview is to help the learners look at themselves specifically, to use real work and to see real outcomes. Part of the art of the interview is getting the students to look at their opinions of themselves in the light of specific work and to ask them to see if their opinions hold water. Whether it is an underinflated or an overinflated view of self, we give them time and a structure for growth. We learn about our students and then are able to take action. One of the results of this interview was to involve the parents, the counselor, and Anthony in a discussion about how he views himself as a person.

In the classroom, Mark helped Anthony recognize his growth and encouraged him to begin his self-assessment with strengths. We deal with knowledge, issues of self-esteem, areas of need, and we acknowledge accomplishments. When students talk about themselves they will give examples, repeat important thoughts, and self-correct when they misspeak. They hear themselves talk. They work to communicate their knowledge effectively and accurately.

Establishing Comfort Allows Risk Taking

After students feel comfortable in the interview process, they often bring up a problem that needs work. They don't always choose the easy route. When students choose to openly discuss a difficulty, no matter if it is a teacher issue, the fact that the student expresses the concern is bigger than the specific subject they are addressing. The skill being worked on is that of honest evaluation and self-reflection, growth and self-development. When students displays this type of self-awareness, we feel a sense of accomplishment and a need to affirm and acknowledge their growth. That is not to say that we hesitate to extend their goal areas and to help the students refine and expand goals. When Steve asked Joel, "What do you do well in math?"

He responded, "I love math. I know most stuff. But I don't know much division."

STEVE:: What do you know?
JOEL: Well one divided by two means one-half, by three means one-third. Like twelve divided by three equals four.
STEVE: How?
JOEL: There are two sixes in twelve. And two threes in six so three goes into twelve four times. Well, four means one-fourth. Four groups of three. And twenty divided by four is five. Five in a group.
STEVE: So what do you need to work on?
JOEL: I need to know more division.

STEVE: Where would you start?

JOEL: I need to practice what I know. Then I need to spend time doing it.

STEVE: How do you suggest you'll practice?

JOEL: Well, the ones I know I'll use a division sheet. The others I just need to figure out. . . . I'll use paper.

STEVE: Perhaps we could work with some of the math stuff. Have you used the tiles?

So, together they talked about how Joel could improve his comfort with division. They considered numbers, physical things in the room, and in life. Steve went on to show a way to use tiles to build rectangles. Later, Joel worked on basic division concepts, counting out groups, building the tile rectangles, recording information with diagrams and in conventional form, and just dividing a variety of manipulatives. The interview leads to new learning, reinforcement of past experiences, new teaching methods, and reaffirmation of student sense of learning.

In writing the narrative, Steve was able to include Joel's perspective on math:

> Joel loves math. . . . In computation, Joel is comfortable with the concepts of addition, subtraction and multiplication. He sees these processes as abstract. . . . He occasionally forgets to apply problems to real-life objects in order to make sense of what he is doing. Increasing Joel's real-life uses of these concepts will help him ground his understanding.
>
> He explains division as breaking something into equal parts; he can picture the process. In working through any computation, Joel has difficulty in checking for reasonableness of answers. He forgets place value, has trouble keeping numbers in order, and varies in which direction he works. (Sometimes he subtracts left to right and other times he will begin with the ones.) He has trouble revising his answer. One strategy for him is to start over when he becomes confused.
>
> Joel understands fractions as parts of the whole. He sees how they build upon each other and fit together. Joel can talk about fractions with comfort and confidence. He can find equivalent fractions and add fractions with common denominators. He knows the denominator communicates the number of parts and numerator names the number of parts present. He uses the numerator for clues in adding.

He was able to see two-thirds as two parts of three with one missing. He could also figure how to add in two-sixths in place of the third.

When asked, learners are able to talk about their learning, their choices, and their plans. We often found out the "why" behind an observed action. Students shared their decision-making processes by giving specific instances of when they realized growth. Sometimes the growth occurs during the conversation, as it did with Teresa in talking about computation. This dialogue is condensed; for every operation Teresa used concrete materials, paper-pencil methods, and talked through her process; the discussion of math computation took time. Steve and Teresa touched on the four basic computation operations.

Midway through the interview Steve asked, "What about math?"

"Like what?"

"Addition?" (Something Steve had seen her use with confidence.)

"I can do it really good in my head."

"How?"

"I count tens on my fingers and the rest I do in my head."

"Ninety plus forty-two?"

"Ninety is close to one hundred so I take ten off forty-two and then add thirty-two to one hundred."

"Subtraction?"

"It's harder, but I can do it. Sort of the same way . . . on my fingers."

"Multiplication?"

"That's hard. I know 'two' doubles the number and 'three' triples it. 'Four' quadruples it."

"What's that?"

"Well, four times four equals sixteen, eight times four equals thirty-two . . . sixteen plus sixteen . . ."

"Division?"

"I can't do it; well, not very good. Two splits in half. Divides it even."

"Fractions?"

"I'm learning more. I didn't know it, but now I do. See, if you have one-fourth it's the same as two-eighths. When the top number and the bottom number are the same the fraction equals a whole . . ."

In talking about fractions, she used concrete manipulatives to demonstrate her knowledge and to discover the depth of her understanding. She continues to use the manipulative Fraction Stax during math time.

Teresa is an example of a student who grows in confidence during the interview. She had certain ideas about herself as a math learner which she changed as we talked.

Steve wrote:

> Even though Teresa lacks confidence, she is math able and works carefully. She has strong conceptual understanding of operations and can compute a variety of problems mentally. She has developed strategies which allow her to keep place value straight when adding large numbers (up to three digit numbers). When subtracting, she has a bit more trouble computing mentally, but is successful when writing down problems. She can independently name and write place value into the hundred thousands, and has a sense of how zeros keep values in place. With help she can go into the millions.
>
> In multiplication [she says, 'It's hard'], she can compute numbers through five independently. Although she needs some assistance with "fours," she understands how to do repetitive addition to get answers.

Students Know

We understand more about where the learning takes place in our classrooms during interviews. Students demonstrate learning by sharing specifics from their reading and their writing. They talk about what they know and what they are using. Their strengths are evident, and they know what needs work. They often identify next steps.

During his interview, Ben asked Steve to help him choose a book. Steve knew Ben was an avid Gary Paulsen reader. The two had shared many of the adventure stories Paulsen had written. Was Ben interested in another Paulsen? He responded, "What I would really like is a Stephen King." While several students in the class have read King (which they brought from home), Steve hesitated to support the choice. He told Ben that he wouldn't recommend a Stephen King, but that they could look at other choices together.

When the two sat down in front of the bookshelf, they pulled off books by John Bellairs, Susan Cooper, Avi, and Lois Duncan. Steve also grabbed *Canyons* by Paulsen, to show how Paulsen writes books of varying difficulty. As they talked about the books, all of which contained some of the adventure Ben was looking for, along with a higher degree of difficult language and story, Ben was drawn to the books by Avi, and soon was reading *The True Confessions of Charlotte Doyle*. In this exchange, Ben's needs were met; Steve introduced him to a variety of authors and a supply of books, and, most of all, Ben explained how his reading had improved. Ben said, "Reading *Willow* changed how I read. It was a different choice. It taught me I could read long books, not just the short ones I usually read." Steve used information from Ben's interview in the narrative to show Ben's understanding of his own growth:

> Ben is most comfortable reading. He enjoys making choices about what he reads and feels satisfied with his progress as a reader. He enjoys the freedom to choose his own reading material. He varies his reading challenges from book to book, by reading 'way hard' books than 'easy ones' and then finding books that he feels are 'just right' for his enjoyment. Recently, he finished reading *Willow*, a book he felt was a challenge and a new choice. It was a mystery-adventure-fantasy, and now he is seeking other ones which are similar. It was also quite long, which taught him he could read longer books and sustain the effort necessary to focus on longer stories.

Students discover specifics connected to their own processes and actions. In the next example, Steve asked Joel about his writing. Joel began, "I like to write about mice, rats, and other animals having adventures. I like to choose what I am going to write about. In fiction I let my mind go, anything can happen."

Joel gave specifics from his writing; he left the interview table to grab his folder and pulled out a story on his return. He flipped pages of a long draft. "See, I frame my fiction; I tell a background. I like to do this thing when I say seventeen years later, then that's the real story. I tell a little before, then I jump ahead."

"So, what influences your story ideas?"

"I read Brian Jacques. I got from him to write about mice myself. Now, I am reading *Rats Of Nihm*."

Joel understands the books he reads, the writing styles of authors, and shows how his imitation of what he has seen improves his writing process. He is able to talk about his writing and reading, demonstrates a strong connection between reading and writing, and uses his writing to illustrate what he says about himself.

Steve wrote in the narrative:

Joel makes strong connections between reading and writing. He is an avid writer of fiction using personification, modeled after his reading. He writes using many of the styles he prefers as a reader. He talks about how he sees his story in his mind before he writes; he thinks about the characters in the books and uses them for his stories. He also writes fictional personal narrative where he takes things that happen to him and expands them. He adds things that might happen in situations he has been in and develops the humor part of the characters further.

Response Teaching

The better we know our students, the better teachers we become. The interview is perhaps the single most important tool we have for truly understanding learners and their learning. Through the interview, Mark discovered that many students learn from demonstrating a concept on the overhead, or that they enjoy using Fraction Stax, which is helping them learn about fraction relationships. He knows that students are benefiting from his occasional read-aloud interruptions, when he stops reading to marvel at a professional author's style. He thinks about Anthony's self-image and the fact that Sharon may have a hard time getting started in her writing.

Steve learned that computation concepts need to be continually reinforced as students move from the concrete to the abstract and back from Teresa and Joel. Steve's ideas about ownership and goal setting for readers were reaffirmed by Ben. A reading-writing connection was made so very clear by Joel.

We know our students, we know the curriculum we teach, and now we are better able to help them in their learning. We know because we simply ask; we listen and learn during the half-hour interviews with our students. The student interviews prepare us for writing report card narratives, help focus our teaching, and help students reflect on their learning experiences.

References

Avi. 1990. *True Confessions of Charlotte Doyle.* New York: Avon.

Davis, Jim. 1992. *Garfield.* New York: Scholastic.

Jacques, Brian. 1986. *Redwall.* New York: Philomel.

London, Jack. 1903. *The Call of the Wild and White Fang.* New York: Bantam.

Lucas, George. 1988. *Willow.* New York: Random House.

O'Brien, Robert. C. 1975. *Mrs. Frisby and the Rats of NIMH.* New York: Aladdin.

Paulsen, Gary. 1990. *Canyons.* New York: Delacourte.

Sharmat, Marjorie Weinman. 1972. *Nate the Great.* New York: Dell.

Stine, R. L. 1993. *Goosebumps.* New York: Scholastic.

Wexo, John Bonnett. 1986. *ZOOBOOKS.* San Diego: Wildlife Education.

6

Postcard

Kathleen J. Mahan

"*Mrs. Mahan, could* we talk to you for a minute?" Their words caught me by surprise as I rounded the corner heading for the copy machine. It was early. "They shouldn't even be in the building," I thought as I considered whether to even acknowledge I'd heard them. If I stopped to talk, someone might get ahead of me, and you never could tell how long that would take. I was a busy person.

So no, I really didn't have the time, and that's exactly what I wanted to say. And I was even a little annoyed Mario had the nerve to ask. He'd been such a pain since he'd come into my class midway through the year. He was tall, handsome in a boyish way, and had managed single-handedly to find everyone's vulnerable button and push it at will, making someone's bad day even worse. "Hey Jeff, you must have really felt stupid last night, scoring the only goal for the wrong team. The coach puts you in the final quarter, the score's fifty-one to zippo, and you manage to run the wrong way. Man, I can't believe you even had the nerve to come to school today."

And beside him stood Joe, never-making-waves-Joe, his short dark hair always clean, brushed naturally into place; doing what was asked, never more, almost "robotical." Never seeming to ponder or engage or care about anything other than guns and getting through school. "I hate reading," he'd say. "I never finished a book in my life, and I don't see any reason to break that record now." And his pat answer to any question began with a shrug, and if pushed, his words were, "I don't know and really don't care."

And now before school, on *my* time, they wanted to talk to me. I really wasn't in the mood. But mustering as much interest as was possible, and in a relatively polite voice I said, "Hi guys, what is it?"

And as I said this, Mario reached into his back pocket and shoved a wrinkled postcard toward me.

"We got this yesterday, when we were in Washington," Joe said. "Me and Mario."

"How'd you get this?" I asked as I looked at the card, immediately recognizing where it had come from. This place hadn't been on their class trip itinerary.

"Me and Mario went there. We asked the bus driver where it was and he told us, so us two just left the group. We must have walked two miles. It was hot."

"But that wasn't part of your trip. Did you ask if you could do this?"

"When I spend twenty-three dollars of my own money to go somewhere, ain't nobody going to tell me what I have to see," Joe said matter-of-factly.

"Yeah, the other stuff was boring. So we just walked off and did what we wanted to do."

"So how was it?" I asked, still not believing what I was seeing.

"It was kind of hard to get into," Mario said.

"Yeah, we didn't know you needed tickets."

"So what'd you do?" I asked.

"We went to this one lady, and she told us we couldn't get in, but I guess we sounded pretty good, and she must have felt bad for us, so she told us we could go talk to another lady. I don't know who she was, but I guess she must have been higher up or something. You know . . ."

"Yeah, so we had to tell her our whole story again, and she said we needed tickets, but we told her we didn't know that and about how the rest of the stuff we were supposed to see was real boring and this was our twenty-three dollars, and we really wanted to see this place, and finally she said okay. I guess she got tired of listenin' to us. So she gave us this special paper that we had to show to this guy. She told us we couldn't see it all, because we really did need a ticket, but she let us see some of it."

"How was it?" I asked again, now not believing what I was hearing. Were these the same boys who'd sat in my classroom, day after day, complaining? Making rude comments? Acting disinterested?

I could still picture their class, a chunk of eighth graders seated on the floor, squeezed around the edge of the carpet so we could all fit. It had been December, and I'd read them the short story, "It happened on the Brooklyn Subway." It was about a miracle, not the one many of us think about, but one involving a photographer who'd met a woman at the home of friends and who'd listened to her story. . . . How she had survived Auschwitz and was shipped to America after the war and had never seen her husband again. And later, how this same photographer rode a subway he had never taken before, sat in the only available seat, and listened to a man's story. How this man had survived the Holocaust, returned to his home after the war, and was told his wife had been killed at Auschwitz. And how this photographer asked questions of this man, and then persuaded him to get off at the next stop with him. How he made a phone call to this woman he'd remembered from his friend's house . . . to this stranger's wife.

And when I was finished reading, I had expected sensitive responses. Instead I heard silence and then questions. "Why was this such a big deal? What was Auschwitz? And what was the Holocaust? And as I tried to answer some of these questions, I realized that I didn't know nearly enough, and these students seemed to know nothing, except for one boy who said, "Mrs. Mahan, I really think there's another side to this story. My grandfather said there was."

"And, what might that be?" I had asked, trying to imagine what he could possibly say that would justify or make sense of this horrible time.

Chris, a bright boy, an avid reader of fantasy, able to retell a story and analyze the author's underlying meanings—never willing to risk responding about how he felt about *anything*—continued, "I don't know exactly, but he was German, and he said there was another side. Hitler was just trying to do what he thought would be best for Germany. His intentions were okay."

"Who's Hitler?" another student asked. But my mind was still spinning from Chris's comment. How could *anyone* possibly justify what Hitler had done? Especially this boy. He was obviously bright . . . probably from a very intelligent family.

We would study this time period. They needed to know. I needed to know more.

Months later when I told the class we were going to study the Holocaust, I remembered their responses. "Why do we have to study about something that happened fifty years ago?"

"It doesn't concern me," Joe had said. "I don't care nothin' about it. It's just about a lot of dead people."

And then the clincher, the words that burned, "It's just about a lot of damn Jews. Who cares about them anyway?"

We began with a journal write, responding to the question, "What do you know about the Holocaust?" And then we continued by reading, "A Walk Through Horror," a journey, via *READ* magazine, through the U.S. Holocaust Memorial Museum. The walk seemed real as we read and then studied the picture of two interwoven triangles filled with old tattered shoes—a Star of David, behind barbed wire, the barbs made of swastikas. What did this mean? We needed to investigate. We had questions. Where was Germany? What was it like? How could a man like Hitler come into power? And who was he anyway? What had he been like as a child? Authentic research we needed to do in order to make sense of this world that seemed so far away.

And then we read the play, "Daniel's Story"—a short glimpse into the life of a Jewish boy who'd had his head measured by his teacher and been told he was inferior because it was too small around. A boy who'd been shipped to a concentration camp.

"Mrs. Mahan, did this really happen? Could a teacher really do that?"

"I wouldn't let anybody do that to me. I'd punch him in the face."

"That must have felt awful. . . . I'd have been so embarrassed."

"Why didn't their parents stop this? Why didn't they just move away?"

Their reactions were varied. Some were asking questions. Some were feeling. Some were not. Some appeared bored. "This is so-o-o-o dumb! Can't we do somethin' fun?" Mario would ask.

I read poetry from *I Never Saw Another Butterfly*.

They read the play, *The Diary of Anne Frank*. "Can I be Anne today?" "No, it's my turn." "I haven't had a big part yet."

"Not this again," Joe said as he laid his head down on top of his book. "I ain't going to read nothin' today."

I read them excerpts from her real diary. The language was rich. "Can I read the real book?" "I want to read something else about this time. Can you recommend something?"

They watched, "Auschwitz: If you cried, you died," a video about the impressions of two survivors returning fifty years later.

"Who cares about what two old men have to say?" Mario asked. "Why would anyone be stupid enough to go back?" And these responses, which happened daily, became as predictable as the outcome of the play.

Yet, here they were with this postcard from the U.S. Holocaust Memorial Museum, a photograph of the thousands of shoes taken by the Nazis from men, women, and children—gray and empty and haunting—concrete evidence of their journey. And in the split second it took me to recognize what it represented, I realized that if I hadn't taken the time to listen, I would never have known that they'd learned anything or made the connection—or cared. That I'd almost been too busy to experience one of those teaching memories that will always be a treasure.

And as I started to return the card, Joe said, "No, Mrs. Mahan. We got it for you."

References

1994. "A Walk Through Horror." *READ* 43(16): 6–11.

Matas, Carol. 1994. "Daniel's Story." *READ* 43(16): 12–25.

Deutschman, Paul. 1993. "It Happened on the Brooklyn Subway." In *Read All About It!* ed. Jim Trelease. New York: Penguin.

Goodrich, Frances, and Albert Hackett. 1976. *The Diary of Anne Frank.* In *COUNTERPOINT in Literature*, eds. Edythe Daniel, Edmund J. Farrell, Alfred H. Grommon, Olive Stafford Niles, and Robert C. Pooley. Grandview, IL: Scott, Foresman and Company.

Moore, Martin J. 1991. *Auschwitz: If You Cried, You Died.* Indianapolis, IN: Impact America Foundation. Videocassette.

Volavkova, Hana, ed. 1993. *I Never Saw Another Butterfly: Children's Drawings and Poems from Terezin Concentration Camp, 1942–1944.* New York: Schocken.

Believing Makes a Difference

JoAnne Rains

When I was a small child, three or four years old, my mother read me the Bible, paraphrasing as she read. This was one of my favorite storybooks, telling gruesome stories of lions' dens and fiery furnaces. One afternoon Mama read several stories and put the book down. I began to cry. My daddy, who was sixty-four years old when I was born, rushed into the room and demanded to know what she'd done to make me cry. When she told him, "She's crying for me to read her another story from the Bible," Daddy was furious and shamed her with, "I can't believe you'd let that baby cry to hear a story."

Daddy always "read" the funnies to me. When there weren't words, it didn't matter to us. Daddy always made up the dialogue complete with the appropriate voices. Daddy told me, "You'll soon be reading the funnies to me." I believed him.

Mama and Daddy liked to read in their big, old bed all propped up with pillows, spotlighted by the bed light clamped to the headboard. As a young child, I must have intruded on their personal reading time. Time that, I now realize, was as necessary as breathing to them. That year they bought me a huge four-by-four-foot blackboard and propped it against their bedroom wall. From their bed they taught me the alphabet by directing. "Draw a line straight down—now draw another line across the top. Good! That's a T. Now, draw a circle beside it." On and on we went. Mama and Daddy read for information devouring the daily newspaper. I sensed their enjoyment of the detective stories, best-sellers, and poetry they read into the late nights. However, Mama and Daddy made time to read to me, and I developed a passion for letters, words, books, and poems. I remember Mama reading me "The Wreck of the Hesperus." I can still envision that little girl tied to the mast—all frozen, but still so beautiful. They told me, "It won't be long before we buy you your own bed light to read by." I believed them.

My passion was separate from the school world. I could hardly wait for the school day to be over, so I could get home to my well-worn chair and the book in which I really lived. I once overheard my teacher talking to a colleague. She said, "What am I going to do with that JoAnne? She just does enough to get by. I can't imagine how she scored so well on those standardized tests. She doesn't seem that intelligent to me." I believed her.

I unconsciously carried that negative memory of school for many years. However, I didn't allow those feelings to interfere with my voracious appetite for reading. I borrowed books from anyone whose bookshelves I could get close to. All through high school, I was the clown, the dreamer, the girl who could please no teacher. Beta Club, 4–H Club, class plays, merit scholarships, SATs—still no one believed. The years passed. I was married, divorced, and raised my children. Many years later, I married again, this time a teacher. I went back to college. I reveled in the college courses, and over dinner I'd tell my husband what I was studying. He listened carefully and said, "You'll be a wonderful teacher." I believed him.

Most of the sixth graders I teach don't have parents who invent dialogue for comic strips and read in the bed until all hours. These students are fragile readers and writers who require as much care as a newborn baby. I must, as their teacher, allow them a clear view of my love for literacy. So I stop children I don't know in the hallways, and we discuss the book they are carrying. The students who desire some personal attention know where to find me on the playground to share some special passage. I have, early in the year, overheard students say, "Yeah, she really reads to us. You know, just like in the first or second grade." Hilarious laughter usually follows this remark. But in a short time, these are the same students I catch holding their breaths when Travis saves Little Arlis from the she-bear in Fred Gibson's *Old Yeller* (1956) or writing in their journals, "My Mama better not leave me," as we read Patricia MacLachlan's *Journey* (1991). By midyear these students have no doubt about what I believe is important. They realize how I feel about listening and speaking, because we have spent numerous class periods conversing and discussing. They also know that reading and writing are important to me, because I read during silent reading time, and they've seen me cry when I read Robert Munsch's *Love You Forever*. They have caught me resetting the timer for five more minutes when my own writing flowed too well to stop on time. They have seen the hairs on my forearm stand on end in response to a piece of writing well done.

Teaching middle school is hard work. Some days I'm tired, and the students are inattentive or disruptive. But just about that time, some tall boy who sits in the back of the room and seldom speaks, slides into the chair beside my desk and hands me a poem he has written. I read it with him looking on. When I hold up my arm to the light, he sees the hairs standing on end. With my tiredness forgotten, I say, "What a fantastic writer you are! Promise me an autographed copy when it's published." He looks at me, smiles, and grows taller and stronger. His eyes say, "I believe her."

References

Gipson, Fred. 1956. *Old Yeller.* New York: Harper & Row.

Longfellow, Henry Wadsworth. 1922. "The Wreck of the Hesperus." In *The Complete Poetical Works.* Boston, MA: Houghton Mifflin.

MacLachlan, Patricia. 1991. *Journey.* New York: Delacourte.

Munsch, Robert. 1991. *Love You Forever.* Ontario, Canada: Firefly Books.

7

Evaluation: Making Room for Robbie

Carol Wilcox

Eight-year-old Robbie is a researcher, a scientist, a storyteller, a poet, and an artist. He loves nonfiction, adventure, technology, creating diagrams, and performing or sharing his work with an audience. Robbie, however, is also an eccentric, a nonconformist, and a rebel, and his strengths are not easily captured by typical school evaluation tools, which measure not only students' ability to perform, but also their willingness to conform to the expectations of others. How do we, as educators, evaluate Robbie in ways that emphasize his strengths and help him to grow? In a world that values conformity, how do we make room for the Robbies?

"I'm a real disgrace," announces Robbie during his first week in third grade. The sandy-haired rebel, clad in black Harley Davidson T-shirts, begins establishing his image as class eccentric almost immediately. During a cooperative math activity in September, he announces, "Karen, guess what I'm going to do this weekend? I'm going to get a tattoo." Karen eyes him with disbelief as he continues, "I might get a heart or an anchor. But I don't know if I can take the needle."

By the end of the first quarter, Robbie's position in the class is well established. No one will lend him a pencil, because he eats the erasers.

No one wants to sit with him, because he makes rude noises. His class-mates groan in disgust when he crawls around the floor eating broken potato chips and cookie crumbs during snack time. In December, my stomach rolls when Robbie tells me that the gum he has been chewing all day came from the wastebasket in the music room.

In Robbie's classroom, children have many choices about their learning. Each morning, students participate in an hour-long writers' workshop, choosing topics and genres that range from personal narrative to nonfiction, poetry to plays, signs to letters. Writing time is often followed by a share session, in which children read their pieces aloud and receive response from their peers. After recess, they have a readers' workshop: a minilesson, followed by thirty minutes in which children read and occasionally share self-selected novels and picture books. Several times a week, the children respond to their reading in journals, which are then answered by Sue, their classroom teacher, or by me, a university researcher.

Even though he has many choices, Robbie is not particularly fond of school. In a note explaining one of his many behavioral digressions, he writes, "I hATe The schooL RooLes Becuaes the YeAR StoPeD" [I hate the school rules because they are stupid]. In "The Haunted House," a horror story he writes in October, he decides he will put "a kid's worst horror—teachers" in the bottom of a pit. Robbie hasn't, however, given up on schools entirely, and in January, he shares his plans for school restructuring (see Figure 7–1).

Robbie's priorities rarely match those of Sue or his classmates. "I don't want anybody to know I'm smart," he says. Telling me he is "only going to do the important stuff," he completes about half of the class assignments. He rails against the segmented structure of the typical school day, choosing to stay in from recess or skip whole group activities to work on his own projects. "This is my working day. Once I start writing a story, I never stop, unless it's important work." To Robbie, even the simplest class routines seem made to be defied.

Sue makes many exceptions to accommodate Robbie's uniqueness. She is kind and warm and laughs often. She supplies a steady stream of books like *The Stinky Cheese Man* (1992) and *Horrible Harry in Room 2B* (1990), and searches out nonfiction titles from the school librarian and reading specialist. Because Robbie's handwriting is atrocious, Sue provides extra computer time so that he can produce quality finished products. She

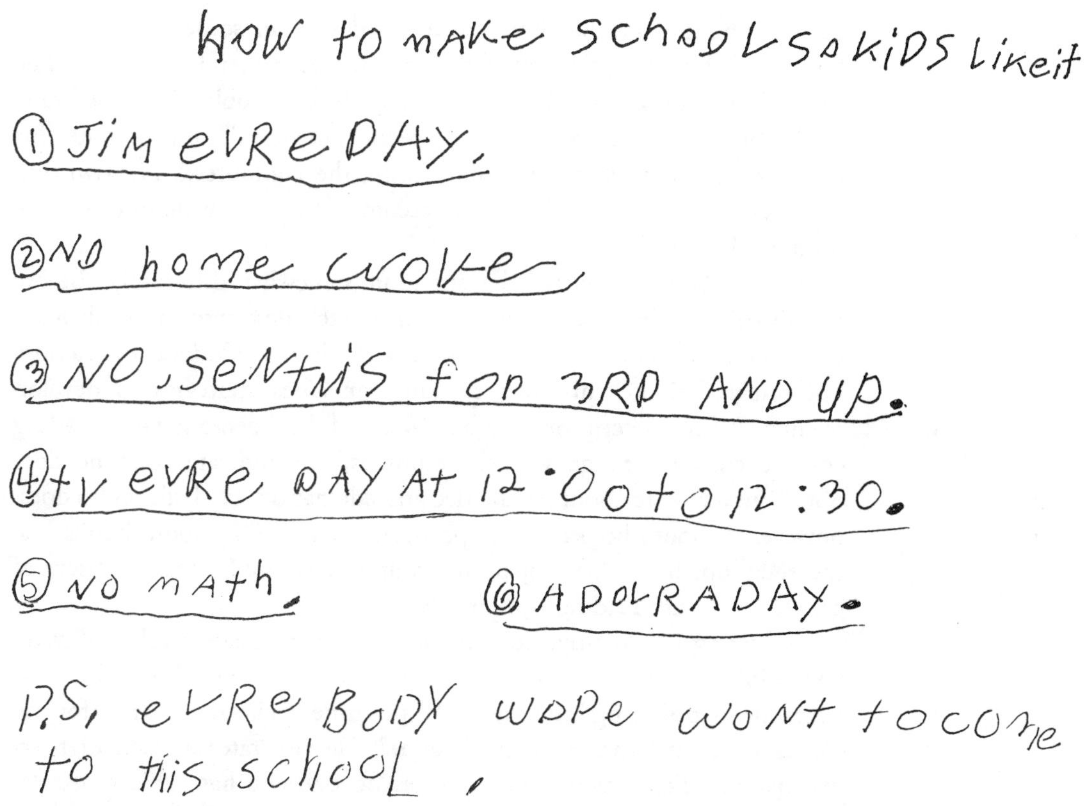

hOW to mAke school so kiDs Likeit

① Jim evRe DAy.

② No home wolie,

③ NO, seNtuis for 3RD AND Up.

④ tv evRe DAy At 12˙0 o to 12:30.

⑤ vo mAth,   ⑥ A DoLRA DAy.

P.S, evRe BoDY woPe woNt to come
to this school ,

Figure 7–1. *Robbie's list "How To Make School So Kids Like It".*

interrupts classroom routines to allow him to share his learning and ignores many of his inappropriate behaviors, intervening only when he interferes with learning or endangers someone's safety. She also makes use of the school guidance counselor and other available resources. Still, Sue faces huge dilemmas when it comes time to evaluate Robbie.

Robbie Is Evaluated

Robbie's January report card is bleak. Although he reads at grade level, his performance in over half of the subcategories in reading is unsatisfactory. Sue comments, "Robbie spends a lot of his reading time working with nonfiction. He has been encouraged to read some 'easy' chapter books, but he doesn't follow through with recommended books." The evaluation of Robbie's writing is similarly dismal. Robbie is below grade level, does not "write responses to specific activities," and "initiates his own writing only when he is able to use the computer." Handwriting and spelling "need work!" He has "accomplished very little in class time for several weeks."

Robbie, however, views the situation somewhat differently. Before Sue distributes the report cards, I explain each descriptor and ask Robbie to evaluate himself. He tells me that he is at grade level in reading, but rarely "initiates his own reading" or "uses strategies to develop meaning" [my descriptors]. When I ask if he "demonstrates reading comprehension through written responses," he indicates that he does not. "I never write about it," he declares adamantly. He believes he does, however, "choose books at an appropriate level" ("I choose books like the encyclopedia"), "participate in group discussions," "read a variety of genre," and "use reading time wisely."

Evaluating his writing, he tells me he is above grade level, "Why do you think I have so much stories in my files?" When asked if he "initiates his own writing," he says, "All the time; I choose to draw for my stories to see if I can get better stories." He also rates himself high on originality, "That's why I have stories no one else has." He especially enjoys sharing his writing with me, and tells me that he "revises and edits his work," but "the teacher checks it sometimes too." He thinks that he demonstrates an understanding of mechanical skills and also grammar. He also believes that he "uses his writing time wisely." Again, Robbie's evaluation is very different from his teacher's.

Robbie's assessment of his work habits and social attitudes also reveals discrepancies. When I ask about following directions, Robbie says, "Almost always, except when I misunderstand." Asked if he "works independently," he says, "In math, I have Bill help me, and I help him." He tells me that he always "organizes his time and materials," "requests help when needed," and "practices self-control." He "respects the rights and property of others . . . except my sister's." He is usually attentive. Only when asked about whether he is courteous and considerate does he indicate that he might have questions about behavior. In response to that question, he says, "We'll talk about that later."

But Robbie Is a Learner

Robbie, however, has strengths that cannot be documented on the typical report card. He is an avid researcher and spends reading time under a table examining old *National Geographics.* When I ask if he can read them, he says, "I can't, but I look at the pictures, and they tell me a lot. . . . I like them because they tell me lots of information." When he's not reading *National Geographics,* he's often in the back of the room, "picking up a few facts" from the pictures and charts in the encyclopedias. He mulls over these facts, analyzing and synthesizing. "Miss Wilcox, you know how people are usually called airheads? . . . I think they should be called waterheads, it says in this book that our brains are made up of 80 percent water. . . . Your brain is 80 percent water, that gives you twenty percent dry. I usually use the right side. You use the right side when you play music, draw a picture, or invent things. The whole paragraph says your brain is divided into two halves; you use the left side of your brain when you speak or solve problems in mathematics."

Robbie rarely reveals such depth in his written work, which is often messy and incomplete. Indeed, Robbie's writing is largely functional. He writes to his grandparents, who are wintering in a warmer climate:

Dare Grandma and Grandpa
    I hope grandpa get's his cast off soon When are you coming home to stae.

He passes notes to me. "Dare Miss wilcox, Me and Bill like you cuz you help us."

When I inadvertently crack my knuckles, Robbie, who wants to be a doctor or scientist, decides a little medical advice is in order. "You shouldn't crack your knuckles purposely." I am conferring with Jill and don't respond, so he repeats himself. When I still don't respond, Robbie decides the issue is serious enough to warrant a written reminder and tears the corner from a piece of paper sticking out of his desk.

"YoU ShoD NoT CRAK yoUR NuKLS PRPiLY [You should not crack your knuckles purposely]," he writes.

"Why not?" I write back.

"It cooD BRAk yOuR NucLS [It could break your knuckles]", Robbie responds.

I write again. "You think so? Who told you that?"

Robbie decides to draw on a higher authority. "The inEnCyCLoPe-DiA DiD."

I write again, "Oh yeah? I don't believe it!"

Robbie is insistent, "LooK foR yoURSeLf."

I write again. "Is it under K for knuckles, or H for hand?"

"K," Robbie writes, but then he runs out of paper, so he turns to me and says, "Actually it would be under B, for break knuckles."

Robbie goes to get the B encyclopedia, but can't find "body." "How come it's not in here anymore?" he asks. I suggest he try the H volume. He carefully peruses information on the human body, identifying which bones would be part of the hand, and specially, which would be the knuckles. I push him a little, and together, we look up hand. Unfortunately, knuckle cracking is not mentioned. Robbie, undaunted, launches into a diatribe on the evils of this vice. Then, unsure that I am convinced, he draws an elaborate diagram (see Figure 7–2).

In late February, Robbie writes a persuasive letter to Sue. He wants to buy a bike speedometer, and concludes that shoveling snow would be more profitable than doing homework. "Dare mrs. w," he writes, "could I please have one day off of homework if i lose my recess for a day, to finish up." He hasn't quite mastered cursive, so his letters loop and curl and march crookedly across the page. At the bottom, in Robbie script, appears

CRRKL yeS OR NO
yeS/No
FRom. Robbie

Occasionally, Robbie's letters are in response to class assignments. Surprisingly, but perhaps because of the communicative function, Robbie takes these notes seriously, and abandons his usual messy, half-capital, half-lowercase print for more conventional handwriting and spelling. A thank-you note to a dentist receives careful attention. Robbie painstakingly uses a ruler to write "THANK YOU" in block letters on the front of the card, then makes five dark, smudgy, slightly angled lines about three inches long on the inside of the card. He copies his note and creates a beautiful diagram of the tooth, seemingly from memory, then pulls *Body Facts* out of his desk. "Let's see if I got it right." Satisfied with his picture, he begins labeling and color coding the parts of the tooth. "I

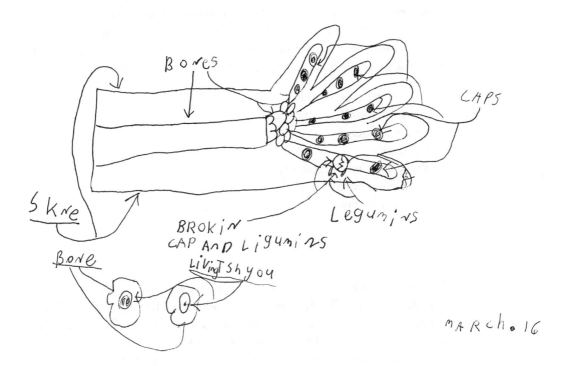

Figure 7–2. *Bone and hand.*

gotta look," he says, "because I don't know how to spell the words." Proud of his accomplishment, he signs his name in the beautiful cursive reserved for his most special efforts.

Surprisingly, Robbie's interest in writing extends into poetry. In mid-November, he announces that he is going to write a poem and sits at the computer through writers' workshop, story, snack time, and recess. Finally, almost two hours later, he is finished. Having watched Robbie play with language for three months, I expect a masterpiece, but I am disappointed. "Dieing," by Robbie L., is better known as "Don't Ever Smile When a Hearse Goes By," a song Robbie has copied from Alvin Schwartz's book, *Scary Stories* (1984).

In March, however, Robbie writes a "real" poem, almost by accident. As part of a multiage unit on weather, Karen, the second-grade teacher, asks the children what would happen if there were no clouds. Robbie writes, "If there were no clouds, There wouldn't be any water. And no water, no trees, Then there will be no air, no life on earth. It would be just another lonely planet in the solar system." When Karen shares the writing with me, I am stunned by the beauty of the language and tell him it sounds like a poem. That night, I type the poem.

> If there were no clouds,
> There wouldn't be any water,
> And no water,
> No trees,
> Then there will be no air,
> No life on earth.
> It would be just
> another
> lonely planet
> in the solar system.

Delighted with his newfound talents, Robbie writes two more poems the next day and proudly glues all three into his booklet of finished writing. He also passes out copies to all available audiences. His favorite is Bob, the school custodian, who also writes "in poet style."

Robbie draws on his love of science to write in his favorite genre—the research report. Robbie's special interests—space, the human body, and the ocean—are not topics in the third-grade curriculum; and the third graders do not study report writing until fourth quarter, so Robbie's early reports are self-initiated. His first report, composed on the computer, consists of one sentence, "Erth has a poling forc coled gravity. [Earth has a pulling force called gravity]." Turning to me, he grins mischievously and says, "This story is true, but they have changed the names to protect the innocent." Then he returns to the computer, deletes his words, and types a new fact: "Mars was discovered in 1966."

In February, he writes "The Great Experiment," a much longer report:

> Take a double a battery and take a flash light's light.
> Then take some wire.

Then take the bottom piece of the wire and attach it to the bottom piece of the battery.

Then take the light and attach it to the top piece of the battery on top of the wire and then go to a dark room and hold the bottom piece of the wire against the bottom piece of the battery then push the wire against the top of the battery and the light on top of the wire and it lights up.

In March, Robbie writes about the human body:

"Blood and Skin"
When you cut yourself, blood rushes to the cut or injured area. When the blood gets there, the blood gets sticky, and when it is done, there is something that is called a scab there.

"Bones"
Bones are made up by living tissue. Bones keep you from being clay. Bones protect your body.

"Organs"
I am going to tell you about your organs—heart, stomach, bladder, flesh, lungs, and living tissue.

I admire Robbie's descriptive language and his use of paragraphs and encourage him to expand his report. For days he's been barraging me with facts about the human skeleton—the number of bones in the body, which are the biggest and smallest, how bones are connected—and I suggest that he might want to include some of that information in his report. I tell him that he could do research on the heart, stomach, bladder, and skin, and have separate paragraphs on each organ. I show him diagrams of those organs and ask if he'd like to draw some of his own. I bring pamphlets other third graders have created and type Robbie's report on my computer, so he can see what it would look like. Robbie, ever the rebel, resists all of my suggestions.

What Do We Learn from Robbie?

Conventional evaluation systems, which view the child as a "finished product" who "shows reading comprehension through written responses," "demonstrates mastery on weekly spelling tests," "is attentive," and "works independently," emphasize Robbie's weaknesses. In March, he didn't write in his reading response journal even once, failed almost every weekly spelling test, lost his homework book and several notes requiring parent signatures, and interrupted classroom instruction and routines innumerable times with inappropriate behaviors. During that same time, however, Robbie produced three poems, three daily newspapers, a labeled diagram of the hand, a thank-you note with another labeled and colored diagram of the tooth, and a research report on the human body. Certainly, those accomplishments should be acknowledged. How do we, as educators, highlight Robbie's strengths? How do we delineate between issues of conformity and issues of competency? How do we make room for the Robbies in our evaluation systems and our classrooms?

Expanding School Concepts of Literacy

We begin by expanding our concepts of literacy. For Robbie, literacy will probably never be about fiction or personal narrative, genre typically endorsed in the schools. Robbie's texts will come from the world of science and technology. He will probably always read informational books, newspapers and magazines, computer handbooks and car repair manuals, and write letters, reports, memos, diagrams, maybe poetry on the side. A sense of audience is critical in encouraging Robbie to produce quality finished products. Only when he is writing for others—filling out a form to enter his light shoes in the school Invention Convention, creating a flier to invite children to a play he is writing, editing a daily newspaper—does he take the time to apply the conventions of written language. When we narrow the purposes, functions, and audiences for literacy in our classrooms, we exclude children like Robbie from the "Literacy Club" (Smith, 1988).

Expanded understandings of literacy should also include expanded understandings of how written text is produced. On the computer, Robbie overcomes his difficulties with handwriting and spelling and creates multiple drafts of stories, reports, newspapers, letters, and signs. He experiments with a variety of fonts and graphics and produces quality finished products. These real-world uses of the computer are skills children will need in our increasingly technologized society. It makes sense, then, that they should begin learning to use them now. How might we begin to provide our children with greater access to high-quality, up-to-date technology? How might we allow our students to use computers in the ways that we, as adult writers, use them every day?

Closely related, perhaps, to expanded understandings of literacy, might be expanded understandings of how knowledge can be demonstrated. Increased emphasis on written language has resulted in the devaluation of oral language and performance—recitation, debate, poetry, and plays—in our classrooms. Some children do not learn or demonstrate what they have learned, through the medium of written language. Robbie's written work is often less then adequate. Allowed to talk or perform, however, he eagerly demonstrates a vast knowledge of the world around him. Some of Robbie's classmates—David, Joe, and Eric—demonstrate that same knowledge through art. Does the written word always have to be the medium for demonstrating knowledge in our classrooms? What if we allowed children to demonstrate their learning by writing a script and producing a play, or drawing and labeling a diagram, rather than completing a written assignment?

Expanding School Concepts of Time and Space

Robbie's literacy development is affected not only by narrow understandings of literacy, but also by narrow views of time. Robbie would prefer to settle himself and work for two or three hours, or an entire day, uninterrupted. "Once I get going," he says, "I don't stop." The twenty- or thirty-minute segments and the constant interruptions of the typical school day prevent Robbie from immersing himself and creating the quality finished products—newspapers, diagrams, posters, and plays—that he loves. Perhaps we should reconsider our use of time in school. Maybe children could begin the day with a goal-setting session and then work the entire morning writing a play or creating a brochure without interruptions. The next day, or the next week, they could immerse themselves in math.

School conceptualizations of space also limit Robbie's literacy development. For Robbie, a twenty-by-twenty-foot classroom, bounded by walls and a closed door, is not large enough, and he challenges us to open our doors and push back the walls of our classroom. Why can't he go next door to share his weather poem or upstairs to view the fourth graders' life-sized diagrams of the human body? Why can't he go to the library, or the guidance counselor, or the bathroom, whenever he needs to? Better still, we push the boundaries even farther to include the outside world.

How might we use the telephone or newspaper, or electronic tools like Internet, to move children beyond the confines of our classrooms and into the larger community? What outside mentors might allow students to visit their worlds? Robbie challenges the institutional need to control, limit, and manage, and emphasizes the need to help children develop into responsible, trustworthy individuals, capable of functioning in a larger society.

Expanded space would also allow Robbie exposure to a wider variety of people. Children like Robbie entertain and challenge, but also drain the energy of classroom teachers. Perhaps it's time to push away from schools where each adult is responsible for twenty-five children and move toward learning communities where all of the adults care for all of the children, and where each child has someone—an aide, an administrator, a custodian, a cook, a university researcher, a community member—who views him as hugely worthwhile and interesting.

Expanding Concepts of Evaluation

Most importantly, we must reconsider the purposes of evaluation in our classroom. Do we assess students so that we can label or sort—good/bad, fast/slow, smart/dumb? Or do we assess students for the purposes of helping them identify their strengths and become increasingly competent? How do we evaluate in ways that enable all children, and not just those willing to conform, to be viewed as successful and capable learners?

We begin by changing the focus of our evaluative systems. For too long, especially in the case of children like Robbie, we've thought in terms of weakness or deficiency. If we are ever going to make room for our Robbies, we need to begin emphasizing learner strengths, speaking in terms of possibilities, of what children can do, or what they might be able to do with extra support or time. We need to talk not about weaknesses or deficiencies, but rather about goals for growth. We need to recognize children's approximations not as mistakes, but rather as signs of progress.

Robbie's literacy portfolio, for example, provides me with a great deal of information about his learning. When he shares it with me in late March, the portfolio contains approximately ten different artifacts, most with reflections. These include:

- "Terror in the Woods" story: "I think it is the best one in third grade. Because it is the longest one I've written." (Robbie's oral reflection, however, is somewhat different. "This is my haunted house story. It says 'Haunted House' by Robbie. I wrote it. The date when I finished with it was October 23, 1993. The best one that Mrs. Wilcox likes is, the best part that Mrs. Wilcox likes is 'Mayday,' the witch cried.''

- Earlier draft of "Terror in the Woods," [on which I have written a note to Sue.] "This is in here," says Robbie, "because you wrote on this and I like you."

- Diagram of the hand: "I think it's neat how I drew this."

- School rules: "I like this. It says how to make school so kids like it. . . . I figure it's kind of funny, I gave it to the principal."

- Poem: "One day we were in multiage. We had to make a story called 'If There Were No Water' so I wrote this story."

- Spelling scores: "I got my spelling scores. . . . It might tell people how good I am at this." [Because Robbie struggles continually with spelling, I am surprised at this comment. He, however, resists all of my efforts to pursue this discussion.]

- Reading genre chart: "My first one in reading is realistic. I got one for that, so I'm not very much realistic reader. But fantasy I'm real big on fantasy, so I've got three on fantasy, those are the ones I finished, four of 'em. One goes to realistic, three go to fantasy. Nothing for mystery, folktale, humor, adventure, historical fiction, science fiction, realistic fiction, oh no, no, not realistic fiction, and he pauses, p-p-p-pot-tree [poetry]."

- A booklist from third grade: "And these are the books I've read, *Camp Big Paw, In a Dark, Dark Room, Clues in the Woods, The Scary Book.*"

- Book reflection: "And then I have, like something I read, a little journal, that I put into my folder. It says *Bony Legs* by Joanna Cole and Stephanie Chameleon. It says, [he reads] '*Bony Legs* is a book. It is about a girl who goes to borrow a needle and thread, but she got captured and she gets out. I like the book because it is the best one I've read in the third grade, cuz it is very good, one that I've read. I like the beginning of this story and I am now finished.'"

- Diagram of the light shoes: "'Things we are proud of.' My invention that I invented. It is light shoes, they are neat."

In reviewing these artifacts, I see a child who reads and writes in a variety of genres, loves science and technology, demonstrates his knowledge through diagrams rather than words, uses rich and descriptive language, can retell a story, has a good sense of humor, and has strong connections to at least one, literate mentor. This knowledge allows me to work with Robbie to set reasonable goals. For Robbie, such goals might include reading a chapter book, becoming a more proficient speller and editor, or taking on an extended research project. Adult input would ensure that such goals were realistic and achievable.

After Robbie has set goals, we need to help him achieve them. First, we encourage an increased awareness of his accomplishments, growth, and efforts. "That letter you wrote in cursive is beautiful, Robbie; your handwriting has really improved." "I was really glad to see you get the dictionary when you didn't know how to spell the word animal." "You're trying to use apostrophes, that's terrific. Could I show you where they go in plurals like 'snakes?'" This feedback should help Robbie see himself in a historical context. Robbie responds especially well to "remember when" comments. "Remember when you couldn't write cursive, and now you can." "Remember when you used to use a *t* at the end of words like *walked* and *stopped,* because you didn't know the *ed* ending? Today I see that you used *ed* correctly." "Remember when you couldn't sit through a silent reading period? Today you were completely involved with your book for thirty minutes."

Our responses must also enable Robbie to see new possibilities in his writing, speech, and thinking. "What you just said sounded like a poem. Can you say it again, and I'll write it down?" "Wow, you chose to make a diagram to show what you know about the hand. Maybe you'd like to put your diagram in a pamphlet, with some words." This feedback should not only support, but also challenge Robbie. He must be held to the same high expectations as his classmates. "It's great that you chose to make a diagram. Now can you give it a title, so people will know what it's about." "If you want to hang your poster in the hall, we're going to need to edit it, so that the spelling will be correct."

Anecdotal notes provide a more permanent record of Robbie's progress and efforts. My anecdotal notes about Robbie, for example, indicate that he is, in fact, becoming more aware of the conventions of spelling and mechanics. When he and Matt collaborate to write a play about aliens, he reminds Matt repeatedly to spell things right, so that people can read it. Writing his class newspaper, he consults several different sources, including wall charts, his portfolio, and me, to make sure that his spelling is correct. He carefully divides his snake report into paragraphs according to subject—kinds of snakes, sizes of snakes, snakes' kidneys. All of these events indicate growth and progress, and all should be acknowledged. These notes, as well as the drafts and finished products included in Robbie's portfolio, can then be shared at quarterly conferences including not only Robbie and Sue, but also his parents. Such conferences could be a time for recognizing accomplishments, assessing progress, and making plans for future growth.

Measured by real-world standards, Robbie could be extremely successful. He's bright and creative. He analyzes needs and initiates projects to fill those needs. He immerses himself in his work, going for hours without a break. He draws on a variety of resources, including books, periodicals, and instruction manuals. He consults colleagues. He uses technology and adeptly solves problems. In the world of school, however, Robbie is an anomaly, a misfit. We need to rethink our evaluation practices so that there's room for kids like Robbie.

References

Cole, J. 1983. *Bony Legs*. New York: Four Winds Press.

Cole, J. and S. Calmenson, comps. *The Scary Book*. New York: Doubleday Book and Music Club.

Cushman, D. 1990. *Camp Big Paw*. New York: HarperCollins Children's Books.

Drew, D. 1989. *Body Facts*. Crystal Lake, IL: Rigby Inc.

Kline, S. 1990. *Horrible Harry in Room 2B*. New York: Puffin.

National Geographic Magazine, a publication of The National Geographic Society. Washington, DC.

Parish, P. 1968. *Clues in the Woods*. New York: Macmillan.

Schwartz, A. 1984. *In a Dark, Dark Room and Other Scary Stories*. New York: Harper & Row.

———. 1986. *Scary Stories to Tell in the Dark, Collected from American Folklore*. New York: HarperCollins Children's Books.

Sciezska, J., and L. Smith. 1992. *The Stinky Cheese Man and Other Fairly Stupid Tales*. New York: Scholastic.

Smith, F. 1988. *Joining the Literacy Club: Further Essays in Education*. Portsmouth, NH: Heinemann.

8

The Value of Blabbing It, or How Students Can Become Their Own Go Yows

Douglas Kaufman

"*Jon,*" *I asked,* as we discussed his portfolio, "are there other ways to learn and communicate other than reading and writing?"

"Yes," he replied, emphatically. "Use your mouth. And hand language."

"What do you use?"

"I use the mouth. I like to *blab it.* . . . I like to *talk.*"

I, too, like to blab it. I remember myself as a grade school student, tempting my teacher with questions designed to pry her from the subject at hand. It was on those rare occasions when I intrigued her enough to stop the lesson and initiate a really good, meandering conversation that I learned the most. In those conversations, the teacher allowed us to link classroom information with our own experiences and opinions, framing academic knowledge in an understandable context and rendering it personally relevant.

Looking back at my own teaching, I was uncomfortably aware that my sixth-grade reading and writing classroom had been short on blab. My students and I had certainly spoken. We all had lectured and given lessons to one another. We had conferred—exchanging necessary information about a line of prose or a troublesome rhyming scheme. But we had not often sat down together to just blab it. Now, working with the Manchester [New Hampshire] Portfolio Project as a researcher in Jon's fourth-grade classroom, I found myself in a similar position: asking students a series of dry questions about their portfolios, which they dutifully answered and I dutifully recorded in a notebook. I was filling pages, but the essence of each student was missing.

Jon's garrulity prompted me to alter my approach. Instead of a question and answer format when discussing portfolios, why couldn't we just blab it? I decided that the next time we discussed portfolios, I would let the conversation go wherever it wanted to go.

The portfolios in Jon's class, which the student's began on the first day of school, were perfect for initiating good blabs. They did not hold just written work waiting to be evaluated, they also contained drawings, family photographs, tests displaying good *and* bad marks, photocopied covers of favorite books, basketball trading cards, comics, shiny pebbles, copies of birth certificates, notes from grandmothers and classmates, and a flower from a dead brother's grave. For each artifact, the students wrote an accompanying reflection explaining its importance. This is the material—the *it*—from where good blabbing comes.

One day, abandoning my notebook and arming myself with a tape recorder, I began our first blab session. The participants were Steve, Millie, Jon, Tan, and myself. We brought our chairs and portfolios out into the hallway, so as not to disturb the class by our talk. Before we began, I told them that each of us would share one artifact.

I started by sharing a black and white photograph of my mother reading to me and my brother when we were small children. In it my brother and I rest our heads on our mother's shoulders and suck our thumbs. Sammy, our fat dachshund, sits alertly in my lap.

The students pounced on me with questions: Which one are you? How old is your brother? Do you still have your dog? What's your mom's name? Is she still alive? Where did you live? To this last question I answered, "This was taken in Texas, I was in El Paso, Texas, at the time."

JON: El Paso?
DOUG: Yep. Like "Old El Paso." Have you ever seen that in the supermarket? Old El Paso beans?
MILLIE: E-e-w-w . . . My dad eats sauerkraut.

Here Millie made the first foray into a new topic. She had recognized a connection with her own life: food that she found unappealing. Beans reminded her of her father's sauerkraut-eating habit. I was to learn that this was how all blabs operated. The participants continually probed the conversation for new instances of group connection. When at least one other participant identifies with the new topic, a new avenue of conversation begins. In this case Millie might have led us to blab about "the grossest foods we ever ate," but no other participant picked up her thread. Steve steered the conversation back to my picture by asking, "How old was your mother when [this picture was taken]?"

The group absorbed my photograph, intrigued by this peek into my personal life. Answering their questions, I described my love of books, how my mother read to us every night, the death of Sammy. Eventually, Millie recognized that my father was not in the picture:

MILLIE: Was your dad in the . . . where your city was? I forget where.
DOUG: Well, when this picture was taken my dad had already died. My dad was in the Vietnam War.
STEVE: He was?
JON: He was?!
TAN: Why he was? Did he . . .
DOUG: He was in the Vietnam War. Do you know anything about the Vietnam War?
JON: That's where she [Tan] comes from!
STEVE: She was there.
DOUG: I know. . . . My dad died when he was in the army.
TAN: [My dad was] in the army, too.
DOUG: He's in the army, or he was in the army there?
TAN: He's the biggest in the army.

A revelation of sorts had occurred—a connection between my life and Tan's. Instantly, naturally, Tan began to eye me with an invigorated interest. Perhaps my life was not so foreign and incomprehensible. Jon steered the conversation away, asking me, "What street did you live on?" Others asked about my house, whether it had spiders, whether tarantulas lived in Texas. But Tan's curiosity had been piqued:

TAN: Did your father know how to speak Vietnamese?
DOUG: No, but I have some letters, and he wrote some things in Vietnamese that people taught him when he was there. [He] talked about . . .

some Vietnamese friends he made there. They used to make him these feasts where they'd make all this food and . . .
JON: I like Mexican food. It's nice and *spicy*!

Jon again connected the topic with personal experience and diverted attention to the discussion of everyone's favorite foods. But almost immediately Tan expertly manipulated the conversation to include that which was so important to her:

TAN: [Vietnamese food] is a lot, lot more gooder than the things you eat here.
JON: I never ate Vietnamese food. I bet I'm never gonna unless I'll go to Vietnam.
STEVE: You'll go to Vietnam. Yeah!
DOUG: People are going there now. It's a beautiful country. I've seen pictures. And it's like . . . it's like beaches and palm trees and jungles.

Compulsively, I had assumed a traditional teacher's role and began to lecture on the beauty of Vietnam. I knew little about Vietnam except from what my father's yellowed letters and a small, brittle stack of black and white photos revealed, but here I was benevolently doling out my perceived wisdom while a true expert, a native daughter, patiently listened to me. Catching myself, I sheepishly locked my lips. Steve saved me from further embarrassment by altering the topic a bit:

STEVE: You know why [the Vietnamese] gave up the Vietnam War? . . . Because, umm, they didn't want to fight no more. They just wanted to be friends with the Americans. They just wanted to have fun. Did you know that?
DOUG: Yeah, I did.

I was learning quickly. Although I might have disseminated some of my knowledge and opinions about the war and its end, I decided that now was not time to lecture. Instead, it was time to learn about one another. It was a time to build a foundation upon which all future teaching could rest. Facts could be worked out later.

Vietnam fast became the topic around which all talk revolved. The Vietnam War reminded Steve of the troops in Somalia. He and Jon speculated that the people of Vietnam had "turned on us . . . when we were trying to help them, like in Somalia." And, as conversation shifted to my dog, Sammy, Tan focused in again:

TAN: In Vietnam they go bicycle to go to buy store. Bicycle and other stuff. They don't go like car like us do on the American. They go on the, umm, motorcycle.
JON: They have motorcycles?!
TAN: Yeah.
JON: Yeah! That's where I'm goin'! . . . I'm gonna live in Vietnam if they mostly got motorcycles.

On we blabbed. Different topics of interest gave rise to one another, weaving in and out of one another, connecting the conversants through mutually shared experiences and interests. Steve was the next to share an artifact. He showed pictures and an article he had cut out of *Sports Illustrated,* and we learned of his love for football. His reflection: "I like football. I like the Buffalo Bills." He and Jon argued about who would win the Super Bowl. Jon shared his drawings and tracings of cartoon figures. When he was done he held up a piece of paper and read it: "'I like to draw.' That's my reflection. That's why I drew it. . . . We're going to put these in my portfolio, and they'll say, 'You are gettin' to be an artist!'"

When Tan shared, her artifact was not about Vietnam, but about an experience in the United States. It was a certificate that said, "Tan, The Friendliest Camper Award. July 23, 1993." She read her reflection:

I get this paper. It's American. I went to the camp with my favorite friend, and me and my friend only went a week. In camp we get a lot of fun. We get to go [swimming], making a lot of things, like make a coat out of sticks, and we play games with a lot of people. And we sing a lot, too. . . . Me and all my friends get to go pick berries, and when the party's done, each person got a paper, a different paper, like this.

As Tan spoke the words "It's American," I realized I had never heard her speak about Vietnam. Her portfolio contained only a few artifacts relating to the first seven years of her life, and she had never chosen to share them. Tan was a model student. She listened to her teacher intently. She worked with unparalleled diligence. As a result, she quickly had become intimate with all the demands and expectations of the American system of education. It occurred to me that perhaps she had spent the last two years working so hard to learn a new way of life that she had not had the time, nor saw the need, to incorporate her past experience into her present life and share it with others. As her classmates had not inquired about it, she simply had not told. But today, through a tiny social connection that had been revealed through our portfolio conversation, Tan's life in Vietnam had forged new interests among us all:

STEVE: Excuse me. Um-m, Tan. Can you say something in, um-m . . .
JON: . . . In Vietmanese? (sic)
TAN: Like what?
JON: Anything.
STEVE: Anything.
JON: Like, say, "My name is Tan. I live in Vietnam."
TAN: Okay. (She speaks in Vietnamese. Steve, Millie, and Jon all laugh in delight.)

The others flooded Tan with questions: Can you say "teacher" in Vietnamese? Can you read in Vietnamese? Do you speak Vietnamese at home? "Tell us something in Vietnam," said Millie. "Like the teacher poem," suggested Steve. Tan had written a poem (see Figure 8–1) in English about her teachers. Steve remembered it and wanted her to translate:

TAN: Wait . . . (She searches for her poem)
JON: She's gonna read it in Vietnam!
TAN: (Translates her whole poem from English to Vietnamese. Each line begins with the sound "Go yow" [Cô giáo].)
STEVE: (Whispering) What's "Go yow?"
DOUG: (Whispering) Maybe we can find that out after she shows us in English. Maybe we can figure it out.
JON: What does "Go yow" mean? "Teacher"?
TAN: Yeah!

The group, revelling in the ring of the word, repeated "Go yow" over and over. "I hate my 'Go yow!'" sang Millie. Steve played with the sounds, chanting, "Go yow-w-w! Go yow-w-w-w! Meow. Meow-w-w! Yeow, yeow-w-w! Yow! Yow! Go yow! Go wow-w-w!" Jon, connecting Vietnamese with his knowledge base, suddenly blurted out, "Adios, amigo!"

Cô giáo xinh xắn, Cô giáo sáng láng
Cô giáo thông minh, Cô giáo làm việc chăm chỉ?
Cô giáo vĩ đại, cô giáo thích cái hồ
Cô giáo tốt, Cô giáo nhìn giống cố gái Khăn đỏ
Cô giáo tử tế, Cô giáo đúng giờ
Cô giáo mạnh khỏe, Cô giáo là của tôi

Poem

The teacher is nice, the teacher is bright
The teacher is smart, the teacher works hard
The teacher is great, the teacher like the lake
The teacher is good, the teacher look like Redriding hood
The teacher is kind, the teacher is on time.
The teacher is fine, the teacher is mine

Figure 8–1. *Tan's poem.*

JON: Okay, I wanna ask Mr. Kaufman a question. If I asked you something in Spanish, would you think you'll know what I mean?

DOUG: Maybe.

JON: Yo comprende Espanol? (sic)

DOUG: Un poquito.

STEVE: Oohh!

JON: I don't understand that!

DOUG: It means "a little bit."

JON: I just asked you, "Do you understand Spanish?"

DOUG: And I answered you. I said, "A little bit."

STEVE: Cool! (Making up his own words) Trdrdum. M-m-m . . .

JON: Wow! I can learn Spanish!

STEVE: Heeder mareener!

JON: I'm gonna be a translator!

MILLIE: Uno, dos, tres.

DOUG: (To Jon) That's a good job.

STEVE: Jon! Jon! "Tdrdum! Guhro!"

DOUG: (To Millie) Uno, dos, tres? Cuatro, cinco, seis! Siete, ocho . . .

STEVE: (Referring to the sounds he has been making) Do you know what that means?

JON: No.

STEVE: Chinese! Chinese. Chinese.

JON: Uno, dos, tres, cuatro, cinco, seis, siete, ocho, nueve, dies.

STEVE: Dherow-w-w. Cherow-w-w! Jow. . . . Yeah! Do you know what this means? "Cwow!"

MILLIE: Cwow.

TAN: Cwow is . . .

MILLIE: Cwow!

STEVE: It's . . .

TAN: A Vietnamese word!

DOUG: What's "cwow"?

TAN: It's a lock! You hold a lock!

STEVE: Ooh, I'm perfect! I'm perfect! I'm a translator!!

The students' unabandoned playfulness with sound and language stunned me. Tan's fluent Vietnamese inspired Jon and Millie to try out their Spanish (a proficiency I had not known they possessed). Jon subsequently proclaimed his future occupation as a translator. They showed no embarrassment, no reticence to attempt a language they had not yet mastered. They simply played and let me play with them. Steve did not know another language, but he did not let that stop him. He invented his own. He was richly rewarded, inadvertently becoming a "translator" himself, stoking his enthusiasm for language and connecting with Tan—a student with whom he almost never interacted.

This language play would be almost impossible in a more traditional classroom setting where the teacher commands attention and designates speaking assignments. Here, the freedom to talk without restraint opened previously closed doors of discovery.

It turned out Steve had actually "spoken" Vietnamese a couple of times. Tan translated, and Steve continued to play with sounds and invent words. I asked Tan if she would write down the Vietnamese translation of her poem. Unfortunately, all good blabs must pass. As Millie began to share a tall tale she had written, the bell rang, and Millie was assured she would begin the next blab.

Conversation, I am now aware, involves so much more than the sterile exchange of information that predominates some sections of our classroom days. It involves a certain intimate connection among its participants: flashes of empathic recognition, exchanges of commiseration, stories that gallop off down a number of uncharted and surprising streets, laughter, argument, and passion. Conversation makes us tangible and approachable to one another. It is often the activity that transforms us from a number of random parts into a unit that moves in powerful synchrony. Conversation instructs. Conversation leads to invention. Conversation builds community.

In the days that followed our first blab sessions, I noticed changes taking place. Tan shared more portfolio artifacts about Vietnam with me, including some Vietnamese money, a Vietnamese poem, and a cover from a Vietnamese children's book. After writing a translation of her own poem, she copied it, giving one copy to me and keeping the other for herself. She searched through the class library and was thrilled to find, for the first time, a book of Vietnamese folktales.

Tan shared her life with others, too, and they accepted parts of it as their own. Suddenly, Jon's portfolio contained a Vietnamese book cover. His classmate, Shana, showed me a note written in Vietnamese that Tan had given her. Trading portfolio artifacts quickly became a hot business, indicating the conscientious formation of a shared and eclectic cultural identity.

Portfolio conversations revealed many shared interests among students. Classmates who had never associated with one another began working together, combining their knowledge and enthusiasm. Jon and a classmate, discovering their mutual admiration of sharks, raced to the library to begin a collaborative project.

Around the classroom students started experimenting with their portfolios in ways I had never anticipated. Millie and a friend discovered connections between their home lives and combined their two portfolios into one, thus clarifying those connections. No longer did portfolios simply illustrate who kids were as individuals, they also demonstrated who they were as a community.

As my final year of research begins, I see the potential of blabbing to inform how and what we teach. Consider the rich variety of topics that one conversation brought forth: Vietnam, war, foreign languages, sports, art, families, foods. All were generated and sustained by intense student interest, and they may be the first step in creating a truly child-centered classroom where students use their own lives to become co-teachers, helping to devise curricula according to their own interests and needs, and assuming the roles of experts. We teachers, in turn, may become co-learners, altering our practices as we discover what is really important to our students.

When I return to my own classroom, we will all converse and share of ourselves from the first day on, for I know that we all like to *blab it*. And we, most assuredly, are all *Go Yows*.

"O Come, All Ye Faithful"

Betty Sprague

There were no tryouts for the Templeton Elementary School faculty orchestra. Just show up for the three rehearsals and the Christmas performance. As first-grade teacher Mary Alice explained, "I think these kids are just so excited to see us there with real instruments, playing for them, that it doesn't matter how good you are."

It was my first year as a teacher, and I was grateful and enthusiastic about being in Templeton, despite the town's reputation.

It was trying at times to witness the poverty of the town. You could see it in the vehicles people drove, cars in disturbing shades of green and gold with duct tape holding on fenders, and even more disturbing people sitting in them. People whose ages you couldn't figure out. The poverty would show itself in conversations with parents as a casual reference to their apartment building portrayed a neighborhood of drug dealers. One home I passed every morning had the same load of wash hanging out on the line for two months. The teenage son had spray painted the family's name in four-foot-tall letters on the side of the home.

Templeton . . . where a guidance counselor had considered starting a support group for children who had seen people die tragic deaths.

The dark side of the town was always there, yet it was possible to detach from it—a feat made easier by the many children who were well supported and loved and a pleasure to work with. I was enjoying my first year in Templeton and had responded with excitement at hearing of this faculty orchestra.

We were pretty good: four flutes, two clarinets, a visiting oboe from another district, a violin, a trumpet, and a guitar. We all pulled together to back up the music teacher's husband on electronic keyboard. During the Sunday afternoon dress rehearsal, we had blended well with the ever-smiling, very focused, grade school choir.

The music teacher placed us in two rows. All flutes, clarinets, and oboes were in the front row. I was in the second row with my violin.

Trisha, a fifth-grade teacher and the varsity basketball coach, was placed beside me. The guitarist was on the other side of her. Trisha played trumpet. Trumpets aren't usually beside violins in an orchestra, but there we all were.

On the evening of the Christmas performance, the orchestra was warming up as the audience filtered in. Warming up really consisted of sorting pages of music, waving to other teachers in the audience, and gossiping.

To keep the audience warmed up and entertained in the minutes before the performance, the music teacher led them in a nonreligious, separation of church and state, holiday sing-along. She was backed up by her very supportive husband on electronic keyboard.

As the community audience was finishing "Rudolph the Red-Nosed Reindeer," the music teacher and the principal were backstage assisting with last-minute wardrobe repairs and backdrop maintenance. It seemed as though there would be a lull in the sing-along while waiting for the music teacher to come back to the microphone.

This would have been unfortunate. It was so festive to hear the parents and relatives singing. I didn't want a lull.

Trisha, the trumpet-playing basketball coach, and I looked at each other. She didn't want the lull either. What could we sing? How could we sing it without the music teacher to direct her husband and the audience.

"I like 'O Come, All Ye Faithful,'" I tossed to Trisha.

"I love that one. It's my favorite." Trisha lit up.

I was glad to hear that.

We called to the music teacher's husband, "How about 'O Come, All Ye Faithful?'"

He knew this was not a separation of church and state holiday tune. He played it.

In this town where 400 people had come to watch the Christmas play, the carol began.

The audience sang. They knew the words.

They had come this night to experience this season by watching their kids perform. They had come faithful to their children. Joyful and triumphant at celebrating their children and the season.

"Sing choirs of angels, sing in exultation."

There was a man in the front row dressed in black denim and a dark shirt. He sat with his arms and legs crossed, stiff and tired. He sang. He sang from the shoulders up.

This town of few privileges sang. They became the carol, the parents, grandparents, children, and neighbors. And for a few minutes on that December night, the town that people avoided was the choir of angels, and I knew their worth.

9

So, What Are These Portfolios For?

Pat McLure

"*When people read* other people's portfolios, it makes them interesting." Tom is answering my question about why he thinks we have been working on portfolios this year. He's right. The people in our second-grade class *are* interesting and we have learned a lot about each other by sharing portfolios. We learned about Jim's taking fencing lessons, and Cathy's studying ancient Egyptians with her uncle. We learned about Beth's cats and dogs, Susan's bird, Jenny's rabbits, Robert's lizards and about the many other pets that we owned. As we all took turns to share parts of our portfolios, we learned more and more about the individuals in our class.

When we began last fall, I was thinking about the portfolios that Jane Hansen had described from her research project in Manchester, New Hampshire. While portfolios can be used for many different purposes, Jane talked about some that attempted to answer the question, "Who am I?" (Hansen, 1993) The students and I decided to include anything that we considered important. The portfolios in our classroom include reflections on books, trips, members of families, activities, drawings, pets, stories that we have written, possessions, and even an imaginary friend. I suppose you might call them autobiographical. They are not the type of portfolios that are used primarily for self-assessment of academic work; however, there are some reflections about reading and writing and math. These portfolios are quite open-ended. Since this is our first year using portfolios, the students and I have been making discoveries about the possibilities for portfolios as we write reflections and share with each other.

Thinking about what we are learning and how we are learning has often been a part of the discussions in my classroom. Our regular schedule includes time for a writing workshop in which the students write about topics of their own choice. We have conferences and group-sharing times to discuss our writing. A reading workshop follows our writing time and, here again, the students make their own choices. We have conferences and discussion groups to share what we are reading, and self-assessments are often part of these discussions. "Where did you get the idea to write about that topic?" "What is your favorite picture and why is it your favorite?" "What do you plan to add to your story?" "Why did you decide to work on this story for publishing?" "Why did you choose that book to read?" "What do you plan to work on next in your reading?" "Would you recommend that book to other readers?" These questions come up all the time during conferences, sharing sessions, and in written-dialogue journals.

I introduce self-evaluation early each fall when I interview the students about their work in school. The students and I share these interviews with parents during the fall conferences. Later in the year the students write reflections about their work in school, and these reflections are included in the progress reports along with my narrative reports. When we began to work with portfolios, I wasn't sure whether we would try to incorporate some of the school-related evaluations in the portfolios. As a matter of fact, in the fall I offered to make copies of interviews for anyone who wanted to include them in their portfolios, but only one student took me up on the offer. For our class, the portfolios became a vehicle for students' sharing more of themselves than just what they do at school.

The writing my students have done for their portfolios are reflections. They have thought about the things they have done and about the people and the animals that they have known. They have written about the things they think are important in their lives. In some cases they put in a few artifacts, but the majority of entries in the portfolios are written reflections. It is common for second graders to use illustrations with their writing, and these written reflections are no exception.

I'm sure that I must have used the word "important" when I was first talking about portfolios, since many of their reflections began, "This is important to me because . . ." Cathy wrote a page about her friends for her portfolio: "This is important to me because I have known them for a very long time." Jim wrote about a book for his portfolio: "The *Scary Book* is important to me because it was my reading book and because I like being scared." "Important to me . . ." seemed to be a comfortable convention to use when they were starting to write reflections, and some of the students continue to use the phrase "important to me" in their reflections. Others may not use the phrase any more, but the idea has remained. They write about things that they value in their lives and they share these written reflections with their classmates.

Sharing Portfolios Contributes to Classroom Community

Sharing portfolios has provided the students with a very personal introduction into the classroom community. Students sign up to share their portfolios with the whole class, or they take part in small-group sharing sessions, and they are always sharing their portfolios informally with the people who sit nearby. Some have brought in photographs, some have asked for copies of book covers, but most people have drawn their own pictures to illustrate their reflections. These students view the reflections as important pieces of writing. I'm not sure why this became the established form for portfolios in our class. When I first shared the beginnings of my portfolio, I had written a few short reflections, but I had pages of artifacts without written reflections. At a later date, one of the students told me that he noticed I hadn't done as much writing in my portfolio as he had in his. These students seem to consider their written reflections as the critical element in their portfolios. I believe that the more these reflections were shared, the more they reinforced the value of the writing.

When they share portfolios, the students choose which reflections they will share. They read what they have written and show us the pictures. We listen and think about what we learn about each person. Following each turn, the reader asks for comments and questions from the audience. This request provides an opening for discussions and for learning even more about each other through these discussions. We often notice the common ground of shared interest and experiences.

As I listen to the portfolio-sharing sessions and read through the portfolios, it is obvious that pets play an important role in the lives of these children. Practically everyone who has a pet has a page or more about the pets in their portfolios. Jenny noticed that this was happening in November. Jim had shared a reflection about when his cat had died and another reflection about how he had received his turtle. When he asked for comments and questions, Jenny asked, "Do you think a lot of people are writing about animals in this classroom?" Jim answered, "yes," and then several people commented on "pet pages" that they had written for their portfolios.

The pages about their pets seem to be important because these children care about their pets and also because this common topic is shared by so many within the classroom community. Tom wrote a reflection about his cat, "Sara is my cat. She is special to me. She always sleeps with me and if you pet her she will purr." Ellie also wrote about her cat, explaining, "I'm going to tell about Rosa cause she sleeps on my bed and she makes me feel safe." Robert wrote about his lizards and told how several of them had died, "The first one died by starvation. The other one died by a horsefly because it got stuck in his throat. The third one died by my cat." Tina wrote about her rabbit's dying, then later she wrote about her new puppy. "If he wants to go out he goes by the door and goes around in circles." When she read this to the class, it prompted several stories about how other animals signal that they want to go out. Sally told us, "When my dog wants to go out, she goes to my mom's room and she turns around in circles." Then Susan commented, "When my dog wants to go outside, he just stares at the door and he whines." Every time someone shares a reflection about a pet it seems to generate conversations.

During one small group session, Beth decided to read just the reflections about her cats and her dogs. She started with her page about Alexandra, and she read, "I used to have a cat named Alexandra and she was a tiger cat and one night in winter or spring Alexandra got hit by a car. We had to bury her and we buried her in the back yard. Ever since, I've cried when I remember Alexandra because I miss her so much." Then she read reflections about the three cats she has now and another reflection about her two dogs: "My Dogs—I have two dogs. Their names are Moosy and Buffy and Buffy is twelve and Moosy is eleven. Buffy is brown and Moosy is black and white. It is hard for them to get up and down the stairs. When my dogs die, my mother wants to get a golden retriever. I would like one, too." On a second page about her dogs, she had written, "They are important to me because I've known them since I was born and they are my pets and they should be important to me."

When Beth finished reading her pages about her pets, she asked for comments and questions from our group. Here's a short excerpt from the discussion:

JENNY: What is your favorite part of your portfolio?

BETH: The one about Alex.

MIKE: I used to have a golden retriever.

PAT: Why do you think so many people write about their pets in their portfolios?

BETH: Well, I think about them as part of my family.

JENNY: My dog Rocky. . . . His eyes are like, 'Oh, please!' (She imitates the facial expression). Sometimes his eyes are like how Henry Huggins' dog Ribsy is. He's like, 'Can I have a doggy biscuit?' (Again she imitates a begging expression). Yesterday I gave my dog a bath, and he has these red spots from the fleas biting him and him biting himself . . . like on his waist he has these big red spots.

BETH: My dog, Buffy, has this big bump on his neck.

JENNY: What's it from?

BETH: I don't know.

JENNY: I think it would be from a tick or something.

BETH: You know what? How it's even hard for my dogs to walk. I feel so sorry for Moosy. She had to grow up without her father. You know why? He got shot by some cops. They thought he had rabies.

JENNY: None of my animals have never got put to sleep. Have any of your animals got put to sleep?

BETH: Yes. I had a rabbit, and she got loose, and she had a broken back, and we had to bring her to the vet.

JENNY: I think it's sad when you have to put an animal to sleep.

This conversation about the pets is not unusual in this class. The children all have questions to ask and stories to tell. With Jenny's story about her dog, she and Beth move away from the questions and comments directly related to Beth's pages in her portfolio and into a conversation about their pets. They pick up on each other's comments. They share the common topic of pets. They know what it is like to care for a pet, and they know what it is like to lose a pet. Through conversations like this one, the students learn about each other. Their discussions contribute to the community within the classroom. (Newkirk, 1989; Newkirk with McLure, 1992)

Books and Reading Are Important

Pets are not the only common topic in the portfolios. There are many reflections about favorite books. During the fall, as we were considering the possible types of entries for these portfolios, I asked students to include at least one page that would show something about their reading or their experience with books. My request prompted their initial entries about books; however, they now have so many pages I believe that books must play an important role in the lives of several students—a role that goes beyond a teacher's request. Their written reflections show the different types of connections they have made through books.

Books can provide a connection between home and school. While most of the students have written about books they have read in school, some have written about books they have read at home. Robert started writing about some of his reading at school, but then he wrote about his "number one best book"—one that he had at home. He wrote, "My number one best book is *Kermit's Mixed-Up Message*. The book goes like this: Scooter was on the phone. Kermit says something but Scooter doesn't know what he said so he goes through lots of lots of trouble." The portfolios offer many opportunities to bring students' home life into school.

In some cases, books provide a connection with another person. Jerry wrote about *Runaway Ralph* (1970), but he began by telling us how he got started with the series, "My dad bought me *The Mouse and The Motorcycle*. I finished that and got *Runaway Ralph*." For Beth, one of her books reminds her of a special friend. She titled her page "The Pet Show," but she wrote about her friend, "This girl named Tenay. She was my friend in Kindergarten. I invited her to my birthday party, and she gave it to me, and she moved away that year, and the book reminds me of her."

Other students have written about learning to read and what they have learned from reading. Laura wrote about *Moses, the Kitten* (1974) by James Herriot, "I like Moses because it was a cute kitty. I like books because you get to know words. I get to know lots of words from books." Dana's reflection included some evaluation of the reading material when he wrote, "I like *Frog and Toad are Friends* because there are some hard chapters in that and some easy chapters." Brad's portfolio includes a reflection on the *Boxcar* series. He wrote, "In the Boxcar Children series there are about thirty-five books. The Boxcar Children are important to me because it gives me ideas for my own stories and it is a neat series, too. In each book, the author picked a neat thing or adventure and a mystery, too. I like the Boxcar Children because it gives you clues so you can solve the mystery or just read the book." Later Brad was thinking about his portfolio, and he commented, "I think my portfolio tells people that I really like books because I wrote two pages about books and one was about a whole series."

Then there are connections with the characters in the books. Some students are able to think about their own lives as they think about the characters in books. Jenny has written reflections about ten different books. On one page she wrote, "I like the book *Isabel* because it is a good book and she is not afraid of anything. I like her." On another page she wrote, "I like *Five Funny Frights* because at the end of the story it is funny. That's why it is called five funny frights. My favorite story is 'Bloody Fingers'. . . . There are two boys and one girl. She is the bravest." I asked Jenny about why she liked these characters and she answered, "Well, I like 'em because I'm brave, 'cause my brother goes like, 'Will you sleep with me?' I say, 'Eugene, just go back to sleep.'" Jenny was able to see something of herself in these brave female characters. They have different reasons for including the books in their portfolios. Whether they identify with the characters or treasure the memory of the friend who gave them the book, books are valued by many of these students.

Reflections About Writing Can Lead to More Writing

Several students have included reflections about their writing in their portfolios. Some people put in general statements about why they like writing. Others put in stories they have written and then write reflections about why they like that particular story or what they like about the process of writing that story. Beth wrote about her story called "Strawberry and the Weasel." "This book is important to me because it is a very interesting book and I like the way that Strawberry [a duck] talks back to the weasel when she meets him and when he tries to eat her." Nathan wrote, "I like writing because you can make up your own story. I also like making my own pictures. I like doing my books with a friend because I like being with my friends a lot. My favorite book that I wrote was called, 'Dana and Nathan's Food Guessing Book'. I like writing because if nobody wrote, no one would be able to read."

I was expecting to see the reflections about writing. These students work on their writing every day, and they enjoy sharing their stories. I had encouraged some of these reflections by commenting on some of the first ones I had noticed in portfolios. What I hadn't expected to see were the reflections in the portfolios leading to story ideas for writing. David thinks that the purpose of portfolios is for writing short pieces, "like if you want to write about family you don't have to write a whole book on family, you can just write one page, and if you want to write about pets you don't have to write a whole book, you can just write one page." That's the way it started for most of the people in the class, but it hasn't stayed that way for everyone.

Jenny wrote a reflection about her rabbits. Then she wrote about her dogs and her cats. She wrote about her fish. She wrote reflections about every pet she had ever had. She had many pages in her portfolio before she started writing a book about all of these pets. Her portfolio still includes the reflections, but her writing folder now contains "All the Pets I Have Had" with a chapter for each pet.

Jerry worked on a page of drawings for his portfolio, and then he wrote, "These pictures are important because I like drawing because it's fun and when I do very good drawings I keep them around for a while." He explained that he had learned to do some drawings from a book called *Draw 50 Animals*. Later he told me that he had started to write his own "how to" book about drawing.

Bill wrote a page called "What Me and My Sister Do At Home." He wrote, "My sister bugs me so I throw her out of my room, and when I am playing Nintendo she bugs me, so I keep her in her room. She keeps yelling at me so I tell my mom on her, and my mom keeps her in the living room with my mom and my mom calls her a princess but I call her a devil." When Bill shared this page with the class, he received many comments from the group. Everyone with a younger sibling knew just what he was describing. Later he decided to write "Part Two," then "Part Three," and so on. He just finished "Part Five" and announced that he is going to staple these pages together and make a book.

Hannah had recently been on a trip to Australia. She commented, "Well, what happened with me was, I was thinking about putting a piece about Australia in my portfolio and I thought I would like to publish one so I thought I could do a book." Just considering a page in her portfolio started her writing a book. In some ways the portfolios have become topic lists for our writing workshop.

So, What Are These Portfolios For?

Why are we spending our time on them? What is their purpose? I asked the students about this, and they each had an answer. Some people used them for personal reflection. Beth expressed it like this: "When you're writing about you in your portfolio you can learn about you and people can learn about you." Jason describes portfolios by saying, "They're for writing stuff that you want to do or you did that's important to you. It's like a journal. I have one at home." Tom had a similar idea when he explained, "Well, it's almost like a diary because you write things that really happen and what you did." As they think about the things they value, they learn about themselves.

Other students saw the portfolios as serving a purpose by helping us remember things. Sally explains, "Well, I think you could write things in your portfolio and if you keep it for a long time you could remember things." Cathy describes her idea of portfolios by saying, "Well, the reason why you keep a portfolio—there's a lot of memories that you might want to remember because they're special memories and if you forget you could look them up in your portfolio." For many students, they see the portfolios as places to store away their thoughts about the things they value.

Some students saw the sharing of their portfolios as a way to trigger ideas for other people. Jim thought that "when somebody else reads my portfolio they might remember their cat or their pet turtle." That seems to have happened for some of the people in our class. Hannah had a similar idea when she wrote the introduction to her portfolio: "If you read about my family trips and my pets you might remember some trips you went on and you might remember some pets you once had."

I noticed that some ideas for pages in the portfolios did travel from person to person around the class. Robert and Jerry were probably the first to include pages about drawing. On one day in November, Jerry explained, "Robert's writing that he learned to do that [drawing Sonic] and I'm writing that he taught me how to do it." Once these pages were shared, we started to see other pages about drawing in other portfolios. David wrote, "Drawing is my favorite thing to do. I could draw all day. I don't only like to draw, but I'm becoming very very good at making pictures. Drawing is really important to me." He later explained, "Sometimes I just whip up something and it surprises me. I was shocked at how good I made this Sonic." Not only is drawing important, but drawing Sonic (a cartoon character) seems to be valued by the people in this class. The knowledge of how to draw Sonic has been passed from one person to another, and this little character has shown up in several portfolios.

Most students described their portfolios as a means of sharing themselves with other people. Laura said, "I think they're good 'cause you can write about yourself and share it to other people and they can learn about you." The sharing is a primary function of the portfolios. I have noticed that many students have been writing directly to their audience in their reflections. Cindy wrote, "I like reading a lot. I hope you like reading, too." Laura writes about her mother as if her mother were speaking to the class. She begins. "Hi. My name is Molly. I have brown hair and blue eyes. I broke my foot falling off a roof in the winter. I will tell you how it happened." Nathan was thinking about sharing when he wrote about Israel. His reflection includes, "My father was born there. He has an Israeli accent, like his r's sound like grzlgrzlgrzl. I put it in my portfolio because I love to tell about it."

Dana said that we have portfolios "so we can learn about more people." We have learned a great deal about the people in our class. Through their reflections, these second graders have told about their families and their pets, about their talents and their plans. We're still exploring the possibilities. I have suggested some topics for reflections in the portfolios this year, but I have left most of the choices up to the individuals. They have used this tool to explore what they value and to show themselves to the other members of the classroom community. The same students who have spent large segments of their writing workshops trying to write fiction stories about Power Rangers or Jurassic Park have written reflections for their portfolios about their grandparents and their favorite books. We even learned about an imaginary friend. Tom wrote, "I have an imaginary friend. It is a fox. It is my favorite animal, too. He won't hurt you so don't be scared." I knew that Tom was interested in foxes, but he shared a unique aspect of this interest through this reflection in his portfolio. Sharing the portfolios has helped us to appreciate the many different individuals in our class. Sharing the portfolios has also helped us to see that we share some ideas and interest. We have heard special stories from individuals. I'm not sure that we would have heard these same stories without portfolios.

Brad summed up this thoughts about portfolios when he explained, "Well i think we have portfolios because it kind of shows people what you like and what's important to you. It's like a way to tell people what's important to you—to show you."

References

Ames, Lee J. 1974. *Draw 50 Animals.* New York: Doubleday.

Barkan, Joanne. 1987. *Kermit's Mixed-up Message.* New York: Scholastic.

Cleary, Beverly. 1965. *The Mouse and the Motorcycle.* New York: Dell.

Cleary, Beverly. 1970. *Runaway Ralph.* New York: Dell.

Cole, Joanna, and Stephanie Calmenson, comps. 1991. *The Scary Book.* New York: Doubleday Book and Music Club.

Hansen, Jane. 1993. Presentation to the Summer Institute on Reading, Writing, and Learning, University of New Hampshire, Durham, July.

Herriot, James. 1974. *Moses, the Kitten.* New York: Scholastic.

Keats, Ezra J. 1972. *Pet Show!* New York: Macmillan Child Group.

Lobel, Arnold. 1970. *Frog and Toad Are Friends.* New York: Scholastic.

Nash, Ogden. 1963. *The Adventures of Isabel.* New York: The Trumpet Club.

Newkirk, Thomas. 1989. *More Than Stories.* Portsmouth, NH: Heinemann.

Newkirk, Thomas, with Patricia McLure. 1992. *Listening In: Children Talk About Books (and Other Things).* Portsmouth, NH: Heinemann.

Stamper, Judith Bauer. 1993. *Five Funny Frights.* New York: Scholastic.

Warner, Gertrude Chandler. *The Boxcar Children* series. New York: Scholastic.

Not in Our Town (in praise of Billings, Montana)

Susan Fleisher

Swastikas
nailed to
synagogue doors.
Bottles, bricks
shatter windows
where menorahs burn.
Outrage grows—
we all ask,
can this be
our town?
Dare not deny—
violence kills.

Let us
act quickly.
Bring lights
by the thousands,
our candles of hope.
All windows
cannot be broken.

Together—
hate cannot
live here.

10

Perceptions of Portfolios: What Parents and Fifth Graders Think

Margaret M. Voss

Setting the Stage for Portfolios

I wanted my fifth graders to create portfolios for several reasons. First, I knew portfolios were valuable, because they are concrete collections of work. They show students what they have accomplished—in contrast to grades or scores or teachers' comments that merely describe student performance. Another reason for developing portfolios, in fact the most important one to me, was to help students evaluate themselves—to reflect on their own work and growth and to set goals. I also believed that sharing portfolios would help us build classroom community. Finally, I hoped the portfolios would become a good bridge between home and school—a place where students could demonstrate and explain to their parents what they'd learned. Could portfolios bring parents a little more into the classroom community?

Inspired by the work of the Manchester (New Hampshire) Portfolio Project (Hansen, 1991, 1994), I first invited the children to make and share a collection of things that would show them "as people"; we would call these collections "personal portfolios." Later, we would add a section (our "academic portfolios") that would be portraits of ourselves as readers, writers, students—but first, we'd use portfolios in a broader way to get to know each other.

On the first day, I introduced myself by sharing my "personal port-folio" with the children. I reflected aloud on my selections, which ranged from family photos to items from my collection of Christmas ornaments and from my first published article to my favorite adult and children's books. As I showed items to the children, I emphasized that this was a representative collection and that making a portfolio required some tough choices. I hoped this would introduce students to the notion that to make a portfolio you must collect, select, and reflect (Paulson, Paulson, and Meyer, 1991; Adams and Drobnak, 1994). Later we would project by doing some goal setting.

Beginning the next day, children brought personal portfolios to share. Children gathered in a circle to hear about their classmates' hobbies, interests, and accomplishments. Over the next several days as children shared one by one, we learned so much about each other. We found out about Manuel's ability to repair bikes, Lauren's trip to Wales, and Betsy's love of reading. We touched David's special identification brace-let, given to him by his grandmother before she died, and we admired pictures of Brian's clubhouse. The children loved it, and they quickly became a community. They got ideas for their own personal portfolios by seeing the variety in others' collections, including the range of con-tainers: bags, backpacks, shoe boxes, and my favorites—a wooden box Seth had made at camp and Courtney's preschool bookbag with her portrait on it!

Preparing and Sharing Academic Portfolios

Later in first term, we created academic portfolios to add to our collec-tions of personal artifacts. These academic portfolios were portraits of the children as students, and they were intended to be part of the larger portfolio that also included the "personal portfolio." I told children they should select what was to be included, but that the academic portfolio must include some writing and reading.

We talked about ways to further define the academic portfolios—they could showcase best work, favorite work, progress, or simply variety. I wanted students to choose, because I saw this as a way for them to think critically about themselves and their work, to self-evaluate, and to express what was important to them. Therefore, these portfolios were not to be used for assessment, except self-assessment. They were strictly a vehicle for students to show themselves as students.

Some children decided to put in only their favorite pieces of work, others put in their best, but many chose pieces to represent the variety of things they accomplished in school, including some that were not their best. One student included an evaluation by classmates of a presentation that did not go well. Though it was highly creative, it went on too long, and she learned "to not go on and on and get silly." Some of the items students chose for the academic sections of the portfolio were finished pieces of writing (sometimes with drafts included), copies of book covers or story excerpts to represent favorite books, lists and graphs of books read, summaries of science articles, samples of math papers, spelling and math tests, original hobby dictionaries, social studies brochures and projects, notes from scientific observations, and entries from reading logs.

As students made their selections for their portfolios, they listed them, along with their reasons for selecting each item. I also asked students to fill out a "process paper," an information sheet about their favorite piece of writing, so that they would reflect on their writing process. In it, they analyzed their best piece of writing, noting its strengths, the origin of the idea, their process ("how the writing went"), and what they'd learned about writing. On another page, the children commented on what they'd learned about reading and writing this term, and they set goals for the term ahead.

Students shared the portfolios with another student and with me. Then, in November, we were ready to share them with parents for the first time. As recommended by Mark Milliken (1992), they made appointments with their parents to share the entire portfolio (both personal and academic sections). Families had to plan ahead and set a specific time to sit down and share for about twenty minutes. In a letter, I explained this to parents and asked them to write positive comments to their children or suggestions to me. (I realized later I should have been even clearer that I would especially like them to write to their children, and I will be more specific next year.) Figure 10–1 is a sample letter to parents.

Families appeared to take the portfolio appointments very seriously. Students had been encouraged to take charge of the conference, presenting first a cover letter about their choices, then sharing items and explaining them one by one. Joseph's parents commented:

Initial Letter to Parents

November

Dear Parents,

This week instead of writing a letter to you, children have portfolios to share. They are to:

1. **Make an appointment** to sit down with you at a specified time to show you the portfolio (15-20 minutes).

Date _____ Time _____

2. Tell you about each item in the academic section (red folder) and in the whole portfolio. This includes why the student chose each item. Students have also included information about some of the things they have learned and goals for next term in Language Arts.

Will you please:

1. **Respond positively** to the things your child shows you and ask questions which demonstrate your interest.

2. Write a few comments to let your child and me know how you liked this process (but especially to respond to your child).

Then **return** the portfolio to school. We will be adding to these all year.

Thank you. Enjoy your portfolio conference!

Sincerely,

Dr. M. M. Voss

There is space for parent comments on the back of this page.

Figure 10–1. *Sample letter to parents.*

We both enjoyed Joseph's appointment. He wore a red paisley tie and a blue striped shirt. He followed the outline verbatim. We liked his "Stitches Stink" story too but sure didn't like the incident (very scary). We endorse his goals. He is happy and he is learning.

Some parents wrote to me, saying what the portfolios meant to them. I was pleased that most responded to children's goals and thought processes as well as the actual schoolwork. Many indicated that they and the children had spoken quite seriously about specific kinds of progress and new goals. Eddie's mother wrote:

I really enjoyed our conference. The portfolio gave me an idea as to what Eddie thought was important to him this first term.

I've seen real progress. We are very pleased with his reading. He used to be discouraged at his reading pace but I think he's gained a lot of confidence. His writing has also improved since the start of the year and we discussed working on that more in the coming term. All in all, it's been a good start. We look forward to updated portfolios and upcoming conferences. Eddie seemed to enjoy it also.

I noticed that many parents mentioned the personal items as well as the academic work. Brendan's parents said, "It was fun to review with him some moments which are very special to us. We are pleased to know that they are also important to Brendan." Courtney's mother wrote about her child's effort, interests, and goals:

I think that Courtney's portfolio was quite interesting. She included a lot of work which represented (to me) an excellent effort! Courtney works very hard when she comes home and is very conscientious about completing her work. Her interests are varied (and surprising!) and she definitely has her preferences in order. I'm also impressed with her goals. She always wants to exceed her past performances. I think that her portfolio is a good representation of her as a person and is pretty impressive!

Quite a number of parents did write letters to their children. As in the notes to me, such letters were upbeat, with the main theme being praise and encouragement for the children. Aliza's portfolio had included an entry from her reading log in which she had figured out the symbolism of the dark thing in *A Wrinkle in Time.* Her Dad wrote to her:

Dear Aliza,

I very much enjoyed hearing about your goals for reading and writing. I know your writing will catch up to your reading and verbal abilities if you work at it.

The discussion we had about *A Wrinkle in Time* was very interesting. Perhaps I will read it after I finish the book I'm reading now. Your observation that love overcomes the Dark thing seemed very perceptive.

I also enjoyed the show of your personal mementos. The sight of you in the pushed back headband reminded me of your kindergarten days. It seems like only yesterday. Keep up the good work.

Sincerely,

Dad

Letters like that made me feel that portfolio sharing could indeed invite parents to connect more with their children's lives in the classroom. One parent questioned the purpose of portfolios and was unsure what to do, but all other responses were positive.

More Sharing with Parents

Later in the year, we revisited the portfolios, adding and deleting items, making new lists of the contents (along with reasons for their selection), writing reflections, and setting goals for the future. Small groups of students shared with me, and they also shared with at least one other student before sharing with their parents a second time, midway in Term Three.

Because not all families had responded in writing the first time, I decided to try something different in the spring. Instead of asking parents to write a letter, this time I included a brief questionnaire with my explanatory letter (see Figure 10–2). Students were asked to interview their parents. Some did, while other parents simply filled out the questionnaire in writing. Again, responses were positive. The only criticism that came up a few times was that some students' portfolios had not changed much.

Second Portfolio Letter/Questionnaire to Parents

March

Dear Parents,

Your child has prepared a portfolio which gives a portrait of him or her as a person and as a student. It does not show all that your child has accomplished or all that s/he has learned. It is a *selection* of items which are important to your child. He or she can explain to you why each item was chosen. I have asked children to create portfolios for several reasons.

- to have representative collections of the *actual work* they have done --- work which can then be shown and explained to others

- to give the children the opportunity *to evaluate themselves* and their work.

- to help children **set goals** for the things they want to learn next. Learners are more interested and motivated when they can identify the things they want or need to know and can then work toward those goals.

- to *learn about each other*. As one of the children said, "I don't always know my friends really well. Sharing our portfolios gives me a chance to know them more deeply."

Please *sit down side-by-side* with your child for fifteen or twenty minutes so he or she can show you his/her portfolio. This is a time for the child to be center-stage and for you to *listen and support* what your child has to say. *Comment positively* on your child's efforts and *ask questions* which show your interest. Your child will be asking you to respond to the questions below. Either you or the child may record the answers. I hope you will **enjoy sharing** your child's accomplishments and reflections.

****

Date and time of appointment for child to share portfolio: _____

_____

People present: _____

1. What did you find most interesting about the contents of this portfolio?

2. What did you find most interesting about sharing the portfolio?

3. What suggestions do you have for me for next time?

4. What other questions or comments do you have?

Figure 10–2. *Second Portfolio letter.*

Again and again, parents said they liked the portfolio process for their children and for themselves. About the content, Kate's parents said, "Kate really thought about her selections. She did not choose only her best work." About sharing, they wrote: "We enjoyed hearing Kate's perspective and insight pertaining to each selection." Emily wrote notes of her mom's and dad's reactions. They like "seeing what you're doing in school and reading the writing." She quoted one of her parents: "I like the writing the most because there is more personality in it than a test or something." Then, without quotation marks, she indicated their advice: Write a piece about swim team and start now.

I did not find the questionnaire responses, in general, to be as rich as the letters some parents had written to their children earlier in the year. In the future, I will continue to suggest that parents write letters to their children. As an option for someone who might not feel comfortable writing a letter, I'll allow children to take notes or make an audiotape of their parents' reactions. Someone might have a different native language, for example, and be uncertain about writing in English.

I wanted to know what parents and children thought about portfolios. In May, children in one of my two classes completed questionnaires (see Figure 10–3) giving their opinions of portfolios, while the other class held a discussion, which I taped. I sent home a one-page questionnaire to parents (see Figure 10–4), which was returned by about three-fourths of the forty-four families.

Student and parent comments about portfolios were overwhelmingly positive, yet parents and children alike made some good suggestions for improving them. There were also some differences in the ways parents and students valued the portfolios.

Parents' Perceptions of Portfolios

Parents' responses were of two main types. First, they were impressed with their children: their choices, their poise, and especially the children's thoughtfulness. They liked seeing their actual work, but the presentation and explanation of the work in the parent-child conference seemed even more important to them. Second, parents made suggestions for improving the content and sharing of portfolios.

Questionnaire for Students

1. What do you think about the non-school part of your portfolio?

    a. Do you like it?

    b. Should we share it more often?

    c. Should there be assigned times to add to them and to share them?

    d. Comments

2. What is the best thing about doing portfolios?

3. What are the advantages/disadvantages of sharing portfolios with your parents?

4. What advice do you have for me when I use portfolios next year?

Figure 10–3. *Questionnaire for students.*

Parents' Appreciation of the Children

Parents did like seeing the children's actual work. One typical response was: "I feel I have a better knowledge of what my child has accomplished throughout her school year." Parents also said they had a better understanding of their children's thoughts, as well as their strengths, weaknesses, or school progress. Jeff's mother said, "I enjoy sitting down and having a special time where Jeffrey can show me work he is proud of and go over topics that have special meaning to him. It helps me to understand his thoughts."

Parents seemed to understand the importance of the child's self-reflection. One mother cited her child's "ability to monitor his work,"

Questionnaire for Parents

****

Questionnaire about Portfolios

Name _____ child's name _____ Date _____

1. What have you liked or found helpful about the portfolios and the sharing of portfolios with your child?

2. What have you disliked or found difficult about the portfolios and the sharing of them?

3. What (if anything) did you learn from your child's portfolio?

4. Please comment on the non-school section of the portfolio (as distinct from the red folder of schoolwork), which your child may have shared. In what ways, if any, did you find this collection of non-school items useful or positive?

5. What advice do you have for me as I use portfolios in my class next year?

Figure 10–4. *Questionnaire for parents.*

while another wrote that "the subtlety of [my daughter's] observations about books and especially the characters was a pleasant revelation to us." One mother learned how her daughter gets ideas for her writing, and she also said, "I was amazed at the responsibility Sarah took for her writing and the responsibility and organization the process encouraged."

While they valued their children's thinking and responsibility, parents also said they were pleased to see their children's pride in their work, or their enthusiasm or self-confidence. Melissa's mom wrote: "I liked the opportunity it gave my child to express pride in her work." Another said that his "pride in his work has increased and he 'glows' when he has a chance to share with his family."

This valuing of the children's feelings struck me. I had expected the portfolios to give parents closer views of their youngsters as students, but I was surprised and pleased that they so appreciated the importance of their children's emotional reactions to their school performance as demonstrated in portfolios. I doubt that test scores evoke quite such enthusiasm and pride in most children. How wonderful that parents appreciated their children's love of learning at least as much as they appreciated particular skills!

Many parents enjoyed sharing the nonschool section of the portfolio and appreciated it. "It was fun to see how Brendan saw himself. How he displayed his interests." Here is another parent's response:

> This was good for her to see her interests valued by the school community for things other than academics. She's a real physically active artistic person and her intellectual school life didn't recognize it before.

Several parents were surprised at items their children had chosen and found that interesting. Said one: "It showed items that were meaningful to him that I may have taken for granted." Another wrote:

> I really got better insight as to what was important to [her] and what gave her a sense of identity. There were not [necessarily] things that I would have thought were memorable. It taught me not to slough things off as much as I do.

Some commented that the personal portfolios (as distinct from the academic portfolios) had been a good way for the children to get to know each other, as we had also discovered in class.

A number of parents commented that they liked setting aside time to go over the portfolios together with their children. Not only are parents' lives full of activity, but their children's are often overly scheduled, too. The portfolio conference gave families a time to focus on the child and to hear what he thought about schoolwork (and about nonacademics, too) in the "personal portfolio." Like reading together at bedtime, a parent-child portfolio conference became "quality time" in which to give personal attention to a child.

Improving Portfolios: More Often, More Organized

I asked parents to give me advice for next year. Most urged me to continue ("wonderful structure that encourages responsibility, ownership, and organization!"). Several suggested that I explain portfolios to parents sooner in the year, and that I organize them more clearly. ("Identify why *you* think it is a good tool to use.") Two specifically wanted portfolios to represent the progression of work throughout the year, so that they show the child's growth.

Most parents didn't indicate anything they disliked about portfolios. Of all the parents, two or three said they learned little, either because the child had not been deeply invested in the process or because they were already familiar with the things included. A couple said portfolios were difficult for their children. They were not specific about the nature of the difficulty for these particular children, but knowing the children, I think parents meant they had trouble choosing items and later articulating their reasons and processes. Still, even these parent urged me to continue portfolios.

Several asked that portfolios be shared more often, on a regular basis. Hansen (1994), too, has reported the importance of sharing. One parent explained why:

> Definitely continue to use them and encourage the children to share them more often. Often during our busy schedules we don't really sit down and *listen* to them. You can gain so much insight into their thought process and develop an understanding on what goes on in their active minds and how creative they can be. It's also important for them to have a chance to be heard.

A couple of parents wished the requirements for portfolios were more clearly focused. One wrote, "I haven't understood the criteria for choosing the pieces which were included in the portfolio—i.e., my favorite, my first one, best, etc." As the teacher, I had made a conscious decision to leave most of the selection criteria to the children, but I realized I needed to explain that better to parents early in the year. Linda Rief

(1990) speaks of external criteria (requirements set by the teacher) and internal criteria (set by the students). I learned that I must make my external criteria clearer. In the future, I intend to ask students to use the portfolios to show a range of genre and to include items from different points in the year that show growth or risk taking. I still want students to select and explain portfolio items, but I need to help parents understand that my main purpose is, in fact, student self-evaluation.

Students' Perceptions

Like parents, most students liked portfolios. They were, however, less likely than parents to comment on the ways portfolios helped them to think about their work and learning processes. They saw portfolios less as a chance to know themselves and more as a way for others, including their classmates, to "know more about" each other. They were able to identify advantages and disadvantages of sharing with parents. Like parents, students made some good suggestions for improving portfolios, but their comments revolved around classroom management issues. Like parents, they had some questions about the purpose of portfolios, too.

Sharing

Sharing was important to students, especially with classmates. Many children identified this as the best part of the portfolio (although a couple disliked sharing). A majority would like to share more often, especially the nonacademic part of the portfolio. This problem will be solved with more regular sharing and with the merger of academic and personal portfolio sections into one portfolio, as I had originally intended.

Students thought sharing with their parents was a good way for parents to see what they do in school. On the other hand, some thought sharing portfolios with parents was repetitive, because they already talk to their parents about school each day. While some students liked sharing nonschool items of personal interest, they generally did not see this as very valuable for their parents, because it was usually about things parents already knew.

Here are some sample comments about sharing with parents:

Advantages

- "You get to share a part of your life that they might know or not know."
- "They give you good comments and ways to improve them."
- "If you don't share it, they won't know what you're doing in school."
- "They know more about you."
- "Finding time to talk about it."
- "They like to see my goals."
- "You get their advice on what you should add or take out."
- "I like stopping and talking about school and how I'm doing in school. I mean we do talk but it seems it's always on the go—to soccer, piano classes, Girl Scouts. Also I have to do homework."

Disadvantages

- Parents "can't compare us with the other students to see how we are doing compared to them."
- "They already know about your life."
- "I don't like it when . . . she says things like, 'that's spelled wrong.'"
- "It was hard to explain some of the things."

Interestingly, I heard very few complaints from children that parents had criticized their work (as in the comment about spelling above). Like their parents, students generally liked the time to share. They gave me some good advice for improvements, too.

Classroom Management Issues: Time, Access, and Frequency

Students frequently spoke of the need for more time: time to sort things for portfolios, time to add things, time to think about them. I realized I need to set aside regular time, more than once a term. Next year I may incorporate portfolio sharing into our daily sharing of writing and books, or I may make it a Friday event. Somehow, I'll use Lauren's suggestion: "We should have sharing partners and trade once a month."

Most students preferred the nonschool section of the portfolio to the academic section. They liked having a place for their nonacademic selves in school because it helped others to get to know them. Because of storage difficulties, the personal portfolios were stored high on a shelf and were not easily accessible. The students wanted more access to them, so they could add things and share them informally more often.

Purpose

I thought I had clearly defined the portfolio as a vehicle for showing who the student was as a person and, more specifically, as a learner. But students had some confusion. I'd intended the portfolio of academic work to be part of the personal portfolios, but students saw them as two different portfolios. I believe this was partly because they were stored separately and partly because we sometimes shared only one part of the portfolio. All of us referred to them separately as "personal portfolio" and "academic portfolio." Next year, I will find a way to keep everything together. I am considering having large portfolios in which to collect stuff, with a smaller folder for papers inside it. Another possibility is to use loose-leaf binders as portfolios and to include only small artifacts or pictures of artifacts, along with papers.

I think I need to be clearer about my purpose for portfolios: that they are not merely portraits of the children as students, but collections that show them as learners and thinkers who can evaluate and reflect on their work and set their own goals. The students' responses showed, just as their portfolio selections did, that they can be thoughtful and reflective. I need to make clearer that I value children's ownership of their portfolios because I value their choices and want to see them truly invested in their learning.

The Value of Portfolios

Parents' comments showed that portfolios can, indeed, invite them to a closer awareness of their children's work and also of their children's reactions to that work and reflections on their learning experiences. Portfolios can bring parents and children together to share feelings not only about schoolwork but about other issues of importance. Students especially loved being center stage with parents' undivided attention and appreciation. Parent responses to their children in portfolio conferences give the children reassurance and positive feedback, so that the communication flows not only from child to parent but also from parent to child. Further refinements in my portfolio process will make that goal of communication with parents even more effective in both directions.

References

Adams, D., and M. Drobnak. 1994. "Portfolio Assessment: Collecting, Selecting, Reflecting, and Connecting." *Writing Teacher* 7 (5): 10–14.

Hansen, J. Winter 1992. "Evaluation: My Portfolio Shows Who I Am." *The Quarterly of the National Writing Project and the Center for the Study of Writing and Literacy* 14 (1): 5–6, 9.

———. 1994. "Using Portfolios." Interview with Marna Bunce-Crim. *Writing Teacher* 7 (5), 4–9.

L'Engle, Madeleine. 1962. *A Wrinkle in Time.* NY: Farrar, Straus, Giroux.

Milliken, M. 1992. "A fifth-grade class uses portfolios." In *Portfolio Portraits,* ed. D. Graves and B. Sunstein. Portsmouth, NH: Heinemann.

Paulson, F. L., P. R. Paulson, and C. A. Meyer. 1991. "What Makes a Portfolio a Portfolio?" *Educational Leadership.* 47 (6): 60–63.

Rief, L. 1990. "Finding the Value in Evaluation: Self-Assessment in a Middle School Classroom." *Educational Leadership* (March): 22–29.

11

Process-Folios in the General Music Classroom

Rosalie O'Donnell

As a general music teacher, I have been searching for ways to help students become more literate in their listening skills. Most students come to us with very few musical experiences other than listening to the radio or watching MTV. Almost none have a vocabulary that enables them to talk about the music they are familiar with, let alone the musical styles they have never heard until being thrust into a music classroom.

In 1992–1993, I was teaching general music at an elementary school in Kalispell, Montana. I had a very creative, energetic, and lively group of sixth graders. I wanted them to accept responsibility for their work as musicians. I knew that my old techniques of directing and choosing a musical play would not hold water with this class. I was searching for a way to give the students more ownership in the process of putting on our annual spring musical.

In the winter of 1993, I learned about PROPEL, an acronym for a Harvard University project having to do with assessment in the arts. I felt that this process-folio might offer a way for the students to take charge. The students enthusiastically accepted this challenge. As a result, I became a believer. The process-folio idea fit well into my belief that the process of learning music is as important as the final product or performance. Rather than a collection of the students' best work, a process-folio would reflect the work in progress. It would be a reflection of students' progress and growth as musicians.

In the PROPEL project, researchers concluded that the most valuable learning in music occurs when students generate music (performing, composing), listen to music (their own or someone else's), and think critically about what they are producing or hearing (Winner, 1991).

These three aspects of learning in the arts are a capsule of my overall philosophy of arts education. I became excited about the possibilities the portfolio process might provide in my classroom. I could see that this was the way I had been heading, and now I knew it could work.

In a performance-oriented subject, the process of assessment has always been difficult. Music teachers spend hours discussing how to assess a performance when music is so personal and subjective. I was excited to read about the PROPEL approach to assessment that maintains that assessment is ongoing and that students can be actively involved in the assessment process.

After I stumbled through using portfolios for about one year, I decided that I wanted to state what my goals should be. I also wanted to be able to explain to parents and students what we were doing and why. These goals have influenced my own goals:

1. Students will think critically about their own performances as well as those of others.
2. Students will accept responsibility for their work as musicians.
3. Students will have a chronological record of their growth for self-assessment.
4. Parents will see the process of musical growth of their children.

As with any educational tool, portfolios are meant to enhance what goes on in the classroom and to enrich the curriculum that exists. Process-folios are not meant to replace playing instruments or giving performances. I have found that the process-folios I use are still undergoing changes. The two uses I have found most valuable have been in performance and listening.

I use process-folios for setting goals and evaluating during the quarter. At the beginning of the school year, I ask students to provide a pocket folio and twenty sheets of lined paper. The first day of music class, I read a letter to the students about my personal life and what I hope to accomplish in music during the year. Students then write me a letter about themselves (see Figure 11–1).

I hand out a checklist of assignments for the quarter to keep in their notebooks (see Figure 11–2).

The classes listen to a variety of music during the quarter. Selections have included everyone from Beethoven to Eric Clapton. Ethnic selections offer the best opportunities for group discussion. African drumming music is a favorite. Gilbert and Sullivan's "Modern Major General" is also a favorite. Students describe it as "jerky," "like he was in a big hurry." I ask a variety of questions depending on the piece. Questions include, "What instruments do you hear? What is the mood? Why was this piece considered classical, or romantic, or contemporary? What do you like about the piece?" I encourage students to work together and have a directed discussion before writing answers down (see Figure 11–3).

At the close of each quarter, students choose which written assignment is their best and explain why. They also tell about any of their performances in class and how they felt they did (see Figure 11–4).

Written process-folios are kept by 150 students. Each class comes to music twice a week for forty minutes. The fifth and sixth grades are twenty-eight to thirty students strong. The folios give me a chance to learn more about the personal lives of my students and what they feel is important to them. Writing responses takes a great deal of time, but I feel that it is worth it for the special connection it gives me to those students I never seem to have enough time for.

I use the process-folios when working on a musical program. The performance aspect still loosely follows what I did with that first group of sixth graders. Students watch the videotape of the previous year's musical program. They write comments about the play in their notebooks. I ask questions such as, "What was the best part of the program?" or "What needed work or improvement?" (see Figure 11–5).

We then listen to the music and read the script for the program we are working on. The plays are chosen by me from prepared musicals available through many musical supply companies. I choose programs that can be easily integrated into classroom studies. One play, *Gonna Have an Earth Day,* deals with environmental awareness. We also did a Shakespearian play, *A Midsummer Night's Dream,* and added medieval music when a class was studying medieval history.

Dear, Mrs. O'Donnell

    It's not very fun at my house becuase I don't have any pets. I only have my bat, and my fish. I can't have any dogs or cats becaase my mom and, my sister are alergice to them. Anyway when I got out of school, My dad came and got me and we were going camping, but it started to rain and so my dad took me home. During the middle of the summer we went to ecoe lake a few times. My sister and I wanted to go to califonia but we did not have enufe money.

                    Sinsirly,
                      Jennifer

Figure 11–1. *Letter to Mrs. O'Donnell.*

Grade 5–6 Voice Unit
Assignment Sheet

Goals

1. To learn more about your own voice.
2. To develop a better singing voice.
3. To be able to perform for others.
4. To know more about choral music, terms and history.

Assignments   Points

1. Daily journal...5/day
2. Self-evaluation...20
3. Voice Worksheet...20
4. Class performace..40
   (sing one song from folder alone or in groups of no more than 3 in front
   of class or teacher.)
5. Quiz..20

   Total possible...180

Extra Credit

1. Return parent letter signed...5
2. As arranged with teacher....................................up to 20

Grade		Point Range
+	=	162–180
S+	=	144–161
S	=	126–143
S-	=	108–125
	=	0–107

Figure 11–2. *Assignment sheet.*

The class spends about six weeks rehearsing the music and learning the parts for the play. Students try out for parts or sign up as stage crew helpers and dancers if required. All students are accommodated. During this time I tape-record both singers and actors. The students analyze their own performances and evaluate the progress they are making.

While we rehearse, students design a stage backdrop and make lists of props and costume ideas. When I first attempted this, I had the incredible luck to have a mom who designed sets for a local theater company.

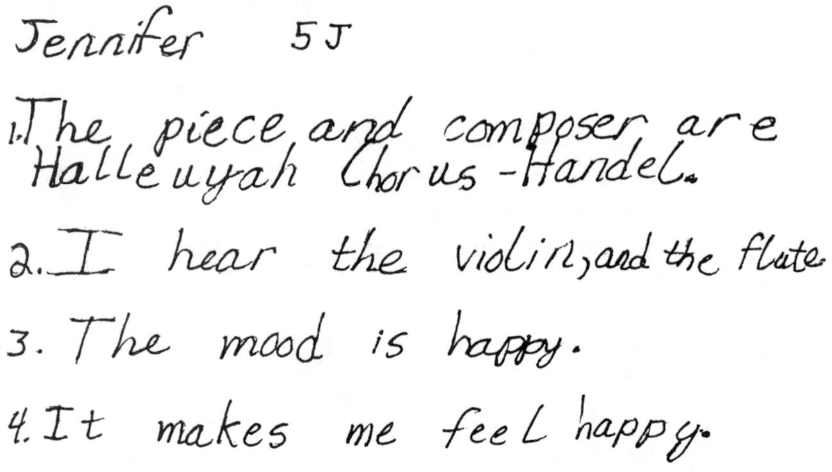

Jennifer   5J

1. The piece and composer are Halleuyah Chorus -Handel.

2. I hear the violin, and the flute

3. The mood is happy.

4. It makes me feel happy.

Figure 11–3. *Jennifer's answer sheet.*

She came into the class and explained to the students how to use a grid and what kinds of things to include on a stage backdrop. I make two four-by-eight-foot muslin panels the students use for the best design. I choose the best design; then volunteers come in after school to do the painting. This is the students' favorite part of the play; maybe I help because I buy a pop for every painter! (see Figures 11–6 and 11–7).

During the dress rehearsal, students take turns observing the choir and actors and offer suggestions afterward. Students are much more demanding critics than I. This also gives them a chance to see the things that I can't watch when I am playing the piano or directing—like the occasional student who is poking his or her neighbor! The performance is always packed with many proud parents and family members. It is an exciting and fun finale to our weeks of work.

Afterward, each class views a videotape of the performance, and then they write their impressions in their folios. Students can bring me blank videotapes to record the program for their own portfolios.

Done this way, the programs are truly the students' own creations. The children participate in every aspect of the production and feel proud of their accomplishments. Their folios reflect the work they did to create a fine product.

Nov. 10, 1993

Final Evaluation

Jennifer   5-J

1. How do you feel your performance in front of the class/teacher went? why? I think I got a B+ Becduse I was singing high so people could hear me.

2. In what way did you improve your singing this quarter? I sang higher.

3. What would you have liked to spend more time on? singing in front of the class.

4. Whitch vocal exercise worked best for you? when we had to sing ma me moo.

5. Witch song we sang in class was your favorite? A whole new world.

Figure 11-4. *Jennifer's final evaluation.*

The things that I liked were the following; some of the lines and 1 song. The song was When The Saints Go Marching In.
The things that I didn't like about the program was the dances, all the dances, and the set.
How I would fix the promblems [crossed out] is put more time into the sets. [crossed out]
Also more time on the dances then theyed be much better.

/Adriane

I liked Jess/Jessica. Her lines are good and not to long. I like the script the way it is. No; changes are neccesseary.

Figure 11–5. *Adriane's writing.*

I would like every parent to see their child's music folio during the year, so I've tried several approaches. I have sent home portfolios at the semester with a separate questionnaire for students to complete and parents to sign. This can be returned signed by parents for extra credit. I also open the music room for open houses and have the folders available to parents to view. If a teacher has a portfolio night, I make sure that the music portfolios are in the classroom with questionnaires for parents

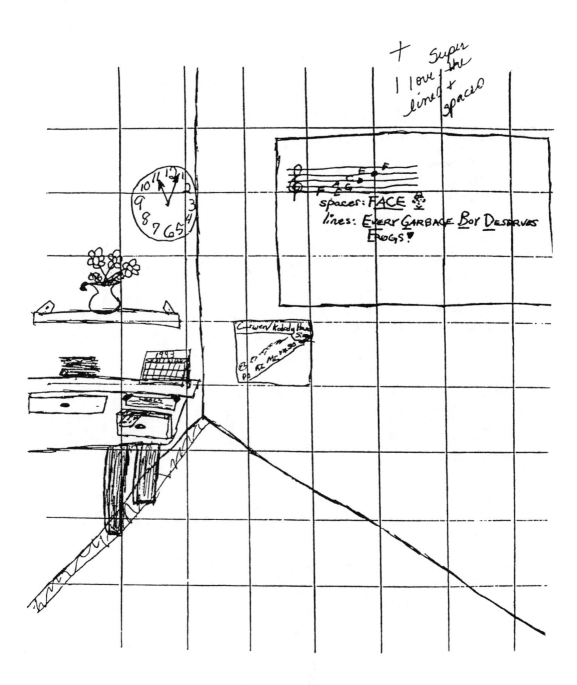

Figure 11–6. *Lines and spaces.*

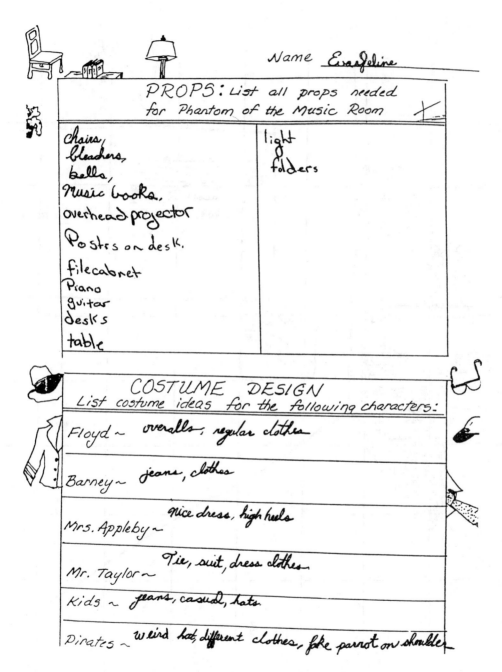

Name Evangeline

PROPS: List all props needed
for Phantom of the Music Room

Chairs,
bleachers,
bells,
Music books,
overhead projector
Posters on desk.
filecabinet
Piano
guitar
desks
table

light
folders

COSTUME DESIGN
List costume ideas for the following characters:

Floyd ~ overalls, regular clothes

Barney ~ jeans, clothes

Mrs. Appleby ~ nice dress, high heels

Mr. Taylor ~ Tie, suit, dress clothes

Kids ~ jeans, casual, hats.

Pirates ~ weird hat, different clothes, fake parrot on shoulder

Figure 11–7. *Props.*

and students to complete. Students take the folders home at the end of the school year and start a new folio the next year.

Grading is the most difficult aspect of the portfolio process. At first I tried to grade each assignment as we did it. I now have a point system. Points are given for each listening activity, evaluation, and classroom performance. Each item on the checklist is given point values at the beginning of each quarter. I have to admit that I spend hours at the end of each quarter reading and grading the portfolios. I don't know how to solve this problem, yet. In spite of the problems in grading, I am very committed to the use of the portfolio in general music both because of the growth I have seen and the insights I have gained into my students as people.

If we are to help students become involved learners, then we will have to become more involved facilitators rather than judge and jury that our grading system requires us to be. We need to make portfolios work. We need the time and commitment from everyone, including administrators and students, before we can be successful in this endeavor.

Portfolios have changed my view of myself as a teacher. Music teachers are traditionally the ones standing in front of the group waving a baton. Now I have a baton for each student, although they look suspiciously like chopsticks. Every student has an opportunity to lead and to teach each other. "When students perceive the director/teacher as collaborator rather than dictator in the rehearsal, they are empowered to work together toward common goals in performance" (Winner 1991).

References

Winner, Ellen, ed. 1991. *Arts Propel: An Introductory Handbook*. Educational Testing Service and the President and Fellows of Harvard College.

12

Celebrating Possibilities: A Valuable Experiment

Maureen Barbieri

Then I go
wandering off,
following all
of my favorite
trails
to all of the places I like.

I check how
everything
is doing.

I spend the day
admiring
things.

     (Byrd Baylor, *I'm in Charge of Celebrations*)

Our whole country is obsessed with evaluation. Education is failing, we read, let's have better tests! Let's have stricter accountability! Higher standards! But as educators, we know this is not the answer. Students caught in the excitement of risk taking worry about what external grade their work will ultimately receive from people whom they believe know more than they know. Teachers, eager to support ambiguity and tentativeness in young language learners, balk at being required to capture stories of courage, imagination, and growth in a single letter or number grade. Like Byrd Baylor, we are more interested in celebrating the surprises that occur day in and day out in the lives of literate young people. Like Mary Oliver, we want always "to be willing / to be dazzled" ("The Ponds") by the discoveries our students make in their work and share in their classrooms. And like Emily Dickinson, we want always to "dwell in possibilities."

Judging students' work, when what we seek to nurture is an attitude of curiosity, joy, and passion, has never felt right to us. In addition to my fear that my "evaluation" will not help my students improve their work, at the heart of my dilemma is the possibility that it will put our relationships at risk. How will they trust me when I urge them to pursue their own wonderings as they read, write, research, talk, and listen together and individually? How will they be able to believe me when I insist that there is no one "correct" reading of a poem or a story, no one "right" way to revise a piece of writing? How can I be their mentor, coach, and more-experienced colleague one minute and their superior, critic, and judge the next? It seems such a contradiction.

But this is the world we live in. Parents, teachers, administrators, and students themselves recognize the need for criteria for good work. No matter how reassured we are to hear William Stafford's admonition to discouraged writers—"Lower your standards."—we all know that there must always be standards. As people who love words and stories and poems, of course, we want to challenge our students and ourselves to stretch, to grow, to produce work that is stunning and vital and compelling, in the eyes of the world. Letter grades, traditionalists argue, gratify students who achieve excellence and motivate those who need to work harder. Perhaps.

Peter Elbow acknowledges the problem in his book *Embracing Contraries: Explorations in Learning and Teaching* (1986). "Evaluation is a tar-baby," he says. "To kick at it is to become stuck fast" (p. 161). Teachers cannot help but be subjective in our evaluations, according to Elbow, because we have been so involved with our students' composing processes. We ponder absolute criteria for good writing and struggle at the same time to find ways to make judgmental comments truly helpful to students.

My girls at Laurel School in Shaker Heights, Ohio, expected me to take an evaluative stance toward their writing and looked for judgment in my eyes and in my body language. I, on the other hand, wanted them to tell me what they found exciting, surprising, or moving in their own work. When we read poems or stories together, or when they read their own individual novels, they were quick and astute at citing passages they felt were beautiful, often quoting these in their notebooks (Atwell, 1987). Why was it so hard for them to bring this same ear to their own work? Their knowing that their work would be externally *graded* seemed more significant to them than anything else, and this got in the way of their own honest, specific assessment.

> The best hope for teaching trustworthy self-evaluation is to give a more accurate and explicit message of evaluation than traditional grades contain. . . ." Grades can only wither away in importance when they cease to be ambiguous and magical. The present system too often allows the student to feel them as judgements based on hidden criteria, judgements which she cannot understand and has little power over. If she is rewarded she feels she did the right things, but if the reward fails she never knows which step in the rain dance she missed. (Elbow, p. 168)

We had to demystify the grading process, but I wanted the girls' help in doing it. We worked hard to establish a class list of criteria for effective writing and kept changing the list as the year went on. *Good vocabulary* was usually one of their early priorities, along with *correct spelling and punctuation,* both manifestations of inordinate concern over surface elements of writing.

Flow seemed to be a big issue too, but when we tried to determine how our favorite authors, Cynthia Rylant, Katherine Paterson, Bette Greene, and Norma Fox Mazer, created flow, we discovered inner dialogue, concrete detail, sensory images, and graceful transition paragraphs. These became part of our growing list of criteria. As the year progressed, we added focus, plausibility, use of figurative language, seductive leads, poignant endings, and more. Our standards were high for writing; we were determined to create pieces that would move readers, just the way Cynthia Rylant's work moved us. But as we talked about the literature we loved, we realized that beautiful writing is bigger than any letter grade.

Little by little, as we wrote together every day, the girls came to understand that they could indeed evaluate themselves, not in terms of an A or a B, but in more important ways. "This bit is effective because it sounds just like a mother would talk." Or, "Here I used a good metaphor, the pomegranate." Or, "I stayed to the main point and made my readers see why I believe that using animals in medical research is wrong." They began to notice it was the writing that meant something to them personally that was also the writing they were proudest of.

At end-of-the-trimester conferences, I would ask the girls to review all their writing and to identify particular strengths and specific evidence of growth, referring in each case to our class-established list of criteria (Atwell 1987). They collected samples of their best work in portfolios (Tierney et al. 1991). But the fact remained that our school policy demanded a letter grade at the end of each trimester.

Did the girl who wrote fluently and gracefully every single time she uncapped her pen deserve an automatic A? Was growth in writing worth an A or a B? If a girl had decided to work on focus as a trimester goal and had subsequently sharpened her focus in one or more of her pieces, what would that mean on her report card? And what about a student who went beyond her announced goals, surprising herself and me by trying new points of view or a new genre altogether? Shouldn't this be worth at least an A at the end of the trimester? And what if she had not worked on focus but had instead gotten so excited by a new idea in her writing that she chose to digress and explore it in depth? How did letter grades support passion, curiosity, risk taking?

What about literature? Since we did lots of free-choice reading, was stretching oneself by reading a greater variety of texts deserving of a higher grade than last trimester's? And how about class participation? Rachel never turned in written literature responses and rarely completed drafts of writing, but she was often most articulate and insightful in any poem or book discussion. How much should that count on a report card?

There was another issue. As we sat together at evaluation conferences, before telling me what grade they felt they had earned, many girls would jot down the grades they expected in their other classes, figure out what they needed in English to make either honor roll or high honor roll, and announce that this was the grade they deserved. "I think I should have a B+" might mean that a girl's other grades were sufficiently high—

probably lots of A's—to put her on the honor roll, where she needed to be in order to keep peace at home. "What I've done deserves an A" often meant that she needed this grade to receive an honors designation overall, since not all her other grades were this high and she could count on English to bring up her average. How removed from authentic learning this seemed to me!

But honor roll is a very big deal at Laurel. On the day report cards come out, there are deluges of tears in the middle school corridors. "My mother is going to kill me" is the frequent lament among seventh graders. In light of all this, I had difficulty justifying a low grade for anyone who was making even a minimal effort in my class. Would a C or a D nudge a student to do more, or would it convince her that she was not a good reader or writer and might just as well stop trying? But, on the other hand, would a high grade for low achievement send a dishonest message? I wanted to challenge my students to push themselves toward greater engagement with literature and to discover new insight into themselves and the world as they wrote. I was absolutely confounded by the system of letter grading.

In recognition of the girls' need for some concrete and regular feedback, I graded their reading responses each week. We established tough, specific criteria for response, and grades reflected each reader's willingness to reflect on her reading in a variety of ways. Students in seventh grade often have trouble being organized, and it was the girls who neglected to turn in their notebooks whose grades suffered, not the ones who shared their thinking. I did not grade individual pieces of writing, but continued instead to confer with students about their goals as writers and their progress in meeting them, all within the context of regular dialogue about specific criteria.

We determined a writing grade which counted for half the English grade each trimester, with the other half derived from the weekly literature responses. In spite of the girls' participation in the evaluation, I knew the system was less than adequate, since it still leaned on my own external measurement of their literature responses and still had as its end product a single letter grade. Instead of building greater self-knowledge and the self-confidence so vital to girls, this approach fostered continued dependence on authority, and this haunted me.

In *Womens' Ways of Knowing* (1986), Belenky, Clinchy, Goldberger, and Tarule cite examples of educational systems that thwart girls' learning.

Incessant academic pressure may, they say, stunt rather than nourish intellectual development. "It is not evaluation per se that subverts the aims of instruction but evaluation in the separate (impersonal, objective) mode. Evaluation in the connected mode requires that the standards of evaluation be constructed in collaboration with the students" (Belenky et al. p. 207).

Our approach seemed to fit this recommendation; we collaborated on setting criteria, and we were, in some sense, connected. My goal, of course, was to help the girls need my opinion less as they internalized high standards and high expectations for themselves. And I still worried about the integrity of my relationship with them. When forced to evaluate students, Nel Noddings says, a teacher "suddenly, grindingly must wrench herself from the relationship and make her student the object of scrutiny" (1984, p. 195). This is how I felt—wrenched! Noddings understands my essential fear. "The point is that the caring teacher does not shrink from evaluating her student's work along all the dimensions proper to the field she is teaching; but she feels no need, and no right, to sum it up with a report to the world. At this point the relationship crumbles; it is altered. In many cases, it is utterly destroyed."

I dreamed of a day when I wouldn't have to reduce all that we did as readers and writers to a summary letter grade in our "report to the world," but such a time seemed far off, probably not to occur within my tenure. And then, during my fourth year at Laurel, Andrea Archer took over as director of our middle school. Coming to us from Crossroads, a progressive K-12 college preparatory independent school in Los Angeles, she was concerned from the beginning about the stress level she sensed at Laurel. After about one month, she asked the faculty to think of ways we might alleviate the situation a bit. At a seventh-grade team meeting, she wondered aloud what our school might be like if we were freed from the constraint of trimester grades. "I've always wanted to try that," I blurted. "I'd like to do narratives the way they do in primary. It would be a way to convey much more information about each kid."

At Andrea's previous school this had been the norm. Middle school teachers did not give letter or number grades, and students moved on to the rigorous upper school where grades were given. The transition from narrative reporting to letter grades, according to Andrea, was not a problem at Crossroads. She asked us if we would like to try such an experiment at Laurel, and, of course, I eagerly agreed. Gene Rosaschi, the social studies teacher, concerned about the tension the girls were experiencing, was willing to put off grading for one trimester to see if things changed. Since he was known as a traditionalist, a stickler for good grades, we were all surprised and delighted at his offer to experiment.

He and I agreed to write specific comments about each girl's strengths and growth and to make it clear to students and parents exactly how she could do better in each of our classes. I was ecstatic.

At a meeting of seventh graders' parents, Andrea announced our plan. She assured them that we would seek their reactions at every turn. The parents, equally concerned about high anxiety among their daughters, were willing to give our new idea a try. Several weeks later I asked the girls to write about the experiment in their notebooks. How did this feel to them? Should it continue? Should it be expanded to other subjects? As usual, many were ambivalent.

Marlana shares her qualms about the whole idea and uses her writing to ponder her teachers' motivation for the whole experiment, echoing Noddings' belief that it is the student-teacher relationship that really matters most of all:

> I'm not really sure how I feel about having no grades. I'm not upset. I'm not happy. . . . I do think that this makes life easier for people who try really hard and only get B's and C's. I am very curious of why Mr. R. volunteered for this. Maybe he likes us and has a heart too, but he doesn't know how to show it.

Jen M. also thinks about her teachers' behavior:

> Teachers tell students not to worry about the grades just your learning. But then they tell our parents, "Well, she got a "C" in this, etc." They never really get to the point on why he/she is getting these grades.
>
> Plus if teachers just write comments, it won't really hurt the student. If they see their grade is a D or F or something else below their standards that makes them feel bad.
>
> If we do have no grades, I feel there should be no high honors, honors, etc. That makes a student feel bad if she didn't get that award. Actually I feel there shouldn't be any of those types of awards anyway. It hurts some students to know that one person is smarter than he/she is.

Jennifer exhibits a clear desire not to be compared to anyone else as a learner. A strong student herself, in anyone's eyes, she shows empathy for others, knowing how "it hurts" to think someone else is smarter than you are. To her, a grade is often no more than a punishing "label," and she seems happy to be moving away from such a system.

Sara was thrilled:

This year my attitude on learning has changed—I LOVE IT—I like waking up in the morning and knowing I have school. I don't complain anymore.

Bernice was one of the most vehement in her objections to the whole idea, showing logical reasoning and a strong work ethic:

Grades. I don't think everybody understands them. Sure, I'm pretty certain people work for the grade—extra hard! So, it pays off. To do your utmost best on an assignment is great! I'd think that would be what every teacher would want. You're reducing stress. Too much though.

Grades show my parents and myself how I'm doing, what I have to improve, how I can help my study habits. Yes, at times it's the grade that counts, but it's paying off because I'm trying a lot harder! I don't see how working harder and more efficiently is bad, even if it is for the grade. Without grades if everyone tried just as hard in schoolwork, the stress level would be the same!! Our school is known for its academic achievement. I can go to a public school where there isn't this much stress. But we all will get used to the stress; for example my brother was really stressed out before in middle and high school. But after a while he got used to it and with grades he knew exactly what he had to improve. . . . I hope, I truly hope, that grades will always remain. . . . So PLEASE everyone, try to get grades back.

But in English, Bernice was not to get her way. Our classroom life flourished, in spite of her fears, as we continued the experiment. Freedom from letter grades challenged all of us to be even more specific in our responses to pieces of writing, and the girls became interested in making it more real, more personal. My comments or questions now seemed less like veiled instruction for revision than honest interest in hearing more. "Whose story is this?" I might ask, inviting reconsideration of point of view or focus. "Who will the reader care about most?" "Why does the character avoid talking to her mother?" "Where were the girls when this all took place?" These and similar questions attempt to clarify content. Or, to a girl who feels her piece is not grabbing a reader,

I might ask, "Have you tried writing five or six different leads?" Or, "Let's look at some of the strongest scenes in your other pieces or in stories you've read recently," to a girl working on livelier dialogue.

Because I was no longer the ultimate "judge" of good writing, the girls listened to one another more as they shared emerging drafts. They did continue to socialize a good deal, but they seemed honestly determined to help each other. I began to hear comments like, "I didn't understand why." and "I'm not sure, but you might try having more dialogue." and "I keep thinking about what the father really wanted her to do after the accident." Instead of worrying about hurting someone's feelings, they got excited about the writing of the class community, as I had hoped they would, and pulled together to improve overall effectiveness.

They also trusted their own intuition about what was working well in their pieces. "I see what you mean, but I like the title I have." Or, "The father isn't really as important to the story as the boyfriend. I want to keep the focus on him." Or, "You're right, I probably do need to add more specifics there..." Eliminating grades removed any perceived competition and lessened the girls' natural inhibitions about assessing one another's drafts honestly.

Evaluation was ongoing and rigorous, as our class list of criteria grew. Eventually, "The writing should mean something to the writer" became our number one priority. Their memoirs, their women's suffrage reports, their fiction, their letters, and much of their poetry became writing that mattered. We began to collect authors' comments about writing and hang them on the wall. Since so many of the girls were skaters, we liked Ralph Waldo Emerson: "Good writing is a kind of skating which carries off the performer where he would not go" (quoted in Smith 1989, p. 132). We were also intrigued by Maxine Hong Kingston: "Writing orders thought. It gives meaning to life. And I create beauty and help change the atmosphere of the world" (quoted in Smith, 1989, p. 103). This is what we were shooting for in Room 311. William Stafford was another favorite: "I'm not alone when I'm writing—the language itself, like a kind of trampoline, is there helping me" (quoted in Murray 1990, p. 162).

I asked the girls to select their most effective work along with anything else that demonstrated growth in literacy and to save it all in portfolios. As in other classrooms around the country, sharing portfolios helped us know each other better and brought us closer together as a community (Graves and Sunstein 1992). Our experiment was clearly strengthening relationships among us. In the absence of letter grades, true evaluation flourished.

At the end of the trimester, the girls wrote letters to their parents explaining what they had accomplished and what they valued in their own learning. Each letter reflects the idiosyncracies of its writer and reveals her individual obsessions. Christine, a shy, serious, conscientious student, had fallen in love with poetry:

Dear Mom and Dad,

Reading and writing are very important to me and are the basis of my life presently and will be in my future. Without literacy we would have limited communication with the world around us. That's why I have included magazine covers and newspaper sections in my portfolio.

I prefer poetry over stories because I feel they are more enjoyable to write. You can express your feelings and thoughts in a secretive way. Their meaning can be revealed with just a word or a winding pattern of words that fit together like a puzzle, to support one or a series of thoughts and feelings.

I've learned over the years that in order to write a poem that you and others enjoy, it doesn't have to rhyme. This type of poem inhibits you when you try to write because you can't say what you want if you're merely searching for words that rhyme.

Walt Whitman, whom I recently discovered in a class assignment, is now one of my favorite poets. I haven't read many of his poems, but the ones I have are outstanding. "There Was a Child Went Forth" and "A Noiseless, Patient Spider" are fine examples of his work. Both are very well written and thought through. They relate life with nature. He expresses two thoughts at once.

Linda Pastan has somewhat a similar writing style as Walt Whitman's, as you will notice in her poems, "Egg" and "A New Poet." Two subjects are discussed at once. This is called metaphor. I find her poems interesting, though some of them are difficult to read.

"Dog's Death," which was written by John Updike, is included in my portfolio because it conveys feeling. It is the first poem I have read that upset me, and for that reason, I did not like it initially.

"Mirage" is the first piece of poetry I wrote this year that I felt satisfied with. It flowed easily from start to finish with little effort.

Sometimes my more spontaneous creations are better than those I dwell over.

A poem by Mary Bolt, my second grade teacher is an important part of my portfolio because I feel she was my first inspiration to get involved in writing poems and the extensive reading of books. One page in my portfolio lists some of the books I've read and enjoyed over a period of time.

Writing my memoir, "Autumn Reminiscence," allowed me to reflect and record a special moment in my life.

My Williamsburg Journal displays a writing effort in diary form. Journal writing is something that I have done over the years in various classes. It's always rewarding to look back at my impressions of experiences.

English this trimester has made me a better listener and I can now read material with greater comprehension. I'm pleased and more confident with my efforts. My personal goal is to become more verbal in this class and to express my ideas and feelings.

Please read my portfolio and respond in writing. I would like to hear your thoughts and impressions about my entries.

Love,
Christine

Christine's parents were quick to comply with her request:

Dear Christine,

We were delighted to have the opportunity to read the many entries in your portfolio. Through your letter and well written pieces, we can see that you have most definitely grown as a literate person.

What pleases us most is that you have found enjoyment and satisfaction in expressing your thoughts on paper. We see great sensitivity, imagination, and style in both your poetry and story writing.

We share your pride in these writing efforts and hope that you continue to enjoy and pursue writing in the years to come. You possess a very special talent.

Love,
Mom and Dad

Often we avoid making big changes in school policy because we are afraid our students' parents will resist them. One argument against alternative assessment, "Parents need to receive frequent letter grades," may be, in some cases, a paper tiger. During our year without English grades, my girls' parents were most supportive and grateful. Surely, the portfolio and her reflections on it made Christine's strengths as a reader and writer clear. It also put her reading and writing into a personal context that was vital to her and to her parents. Other girls' letters from parents continued to encourage us with the ungraded portfolio approach. (One dad wrote to Andrea Archer in protest, however. "You are grading gym and not English," he lamented. "What do you think you are, Ohio State? He was, fortunately, in the minority.)

While most of the parental responses to eliminating grades in English were positive, opinions on continuing the policy in history were mixed. Many students and parents felt that, since the course was so content laden, and since frequent tests were very much a part of the routine, grades seemed logical and relevant. True to her commitment to listen to the girls and their parents, Andrea approved of the history teacher's decision to return to regular letter grades for the second and third trimesters. My students and I were grateful for her permission—encouragement—to continue evaluating work in English without grades.

The portfolios were ongoing. New material was added, and at the end of the second trimester, they wrote again to their parents. Wallis's letter demonstrates her growing ability to set her own goals and make plans for her writing:

Dear Mom and Dad,

I'm writing to tell you about my portfolio this trimester. I'm keeping my pictures from last trimester because good memories deserve recognition for more than three months. My two new characters this trimester are Mimi and Dad. Next trimester I'll put a picture of Poppi in.

My two pieces are a poem, "Recital," and a story, "Nightvision." "Recital" is a piece about how you can't dwell on the worst, and that you must move on in life. Sometimes one has to think, "I did my best, now I just have to go for it."

"Nightvision" got its name because the mother and daughter realize how much they need to work on their relationship. They see the reality in the dark of the night after the streetlight went off for a moment. This seems important to me.

I have my list of questions for the short stories we've read and the responses to show my beginning question and how I created a response from them. I was in a reading group with Priya and Rachel. It was hard in the reading group because if we disagreed, people would scramble to say what they thought. Then there was the problem of people complaining to me about the other group member. Over all it was nice to discuss our opinions in a small group and we all learned to deal with each other more patiently and nicely.

I think poetry is a way to express feelings and thoughts however you want. When writing poetry you're in control, whether it's writing a thought or simply choosing your own style of grammar. Poetry is untouched by everyone except you.

I think I did a better job finding things to write this trimester, instead of waiting for an idea to find me, but I would like to be able to develop a story from scratch. I think I might write a piece of fiction this trimester to practice being inside a character's mind and acting accordingly in my own story.

I'd like to try and make more time for reading. I'm presently reading a collection of fiction stories by Cynthia Rylant, and I'll be starting *Tancy*, a fiction piece about a freed slave. *Tancy* is a post Civil War book I'm reading for English and history. It's by Belinda Hurmence.

I hope we have more class discussions in the new trimester because I really enjoy them and we haven't had many this trimester.

I'll be bringing home my portfolio tomorrow, and I look forward to showing it to you.

Love,
Wallis

The girls knew that I would read their letters, even though they were addressed to their parents. They wrote to me every single week in their notebooks, so when it was portfolio time, they focused on their parents. It saved them the trouble of writing a second letter to me, and they were comfortable with this arrangement. In our portfolio/evaluation conferences, they were free to add comments or to expand on the letter, and of course, I asked lots of questions about the collected work. Reading Wallis's letter is helpful to me in ways that an exam would never be. I see her initial frustration in working with a small group for literature study; I see that there was some discord I had not been aware of and that the girls solved it themselves, learning to be "patient" and "nice." I wonder if this preoccupation got in the way of real discourse, and I make a mental note to sit in on their next discussion to hear for myself how willing they are to disagree when they examine their stories. I hear Wallis's wish for more whole-class discussions, which have indeed lessened in frequency in the weeks of the small-group meetings due to our commitment to finishing final drafts by the end of the trimester. Reading her letter, and the letters from all the girls, helps me understand what they need next from me and from our classroom environment— invaluable insight for any teacher.

Linda Rief has written, "As teachers/learners we have to believe in the possibilities of our students by trusting them to show us what they know and valuing what they are able to do with that knowledge" (1992, p. 47).

What can a B or a C or even an A help anyone see about our students' possibilities? More importantly, what can a single letter grade help a student see about herself? How does it help her believe that we value what she is "able to do with that knowledge?"

So what did we conclude after our grand experiment? The girls, even Bernice, saw real value in what we accomplished. Our year without grades challenged the girls to go beyond their perceptions of anyone's expectations. They read and wrote for their own purposes, and, freed from seeing their efforts reduced to a single letter grade, they pushed themselves in new directions. They were rigorous in their self-assessment and saw more and more "possibilities" in their work. Most important, our classroom community took on a new texture, one of greater trust and apprenticeship, and my relationships with my students flourished.

Of course, there are lingering questions. Honor roll remained, and each trimester, I had to submit a list of girls whose English achievement was worthy of this distinction. This seemed to contradict everything we were doing, and, as guilty as it left me, I had to acquiesce. Some faculty and some students in other classes began to see English as less important as an academic discipline, and this bothered me a bit at first. Then I realized that English in middle school should be *more* than an academic discipline. Becoming excellent readers and writers would certainly enable the girls to learn more in all their other classes, a goal we all shared. But there is a more important issue here. Eliot Eisner writes, "The major goals of schooling are not realized by performances on tasks defined in classrooms or within schools. The important effects of schools are located in the kinds of lives that children lead outside school and the kinds of satisfactions they pursue there" (1991).

If my girls' lives are affected in real ways by their reading and writing —and I know they are—then I am willing to endure my colleagues' perplexity, dismay, or condescension. All in all, this was a noble experiment, one that changed me as a teacher and the girls as learners. I would do it again in a heartbeat.

Now, when I remember that year—all our reading, writing, talking— I appreciate the freedom we had. Like Byrd Baylor we learned how to celebrate:

> And they came—
> dancing
> in time to
> their own
> windy music.
>
> We all started counting.
> We all started looking
> for more.

References

Atwell, Nancie. 1987. *In the Middle: Writing, Reading, and Learning with Adolescents.* Portsmouth, NH: Boynton/Cook.

Baylor, Byrd. 1986. *I'm in Charge of Celebrations* New York: Scribners.

Belenky, Mary Field, Blythe McVicker Clinchy, Nancy Rule Goldberger, Jill Mattuck Tarule. 1986. *Women's Ways of Knowing: The Development of Self, Voice, and Mind.* New York: Basic Books.

Dickinson, Emily. 1961. "I Dwell in Possibility." In *Final Harvest: Emily Dickinson's Poems,* selections and introduction by Thomas H. Johnson. Boston: Little, Brown.

Eisner, Eliot. 1991. "What Really Counts in Schools." *Educational Leadership* 48 (2).

Elbow, Peter. 1986. *Embracing Contraries: Explorations in Learning and Teaching.* New York: Oxford University Press.

Graves, Donald H., and Bonnie S. Sunsten, eds. 1992. *Portfolio Portraits.* Portsmouth, NH: Heinemann.

Hurmence, Belinda. 1984. *Tancy.* New York: Clarion.

Murray, Donald M. 1990. *Shoptalk: Learning to Write with Writers.* Portsmouth, NH: Boynton/Cook.

Noddings, Nel. 1984. *Caring: A Feminine Approach to Ethics and Moral Education.* Berkeley, CA: University of California Press.

Oliver, Mary. 1991. "The Ponds." In *New and Selected Poems.* Boston: Beacon.

Pastan, Linda. 1982. "Egg." In *PM/AM: New and Selected Poems.* New York: Norton.

———. 1991. "A New Poet." In *Heroes in Disguise.* New York: Norton.

Rylant, Cynthia. 1990. *A Couple of Kooks and Other Stories About Love.* New York: Orchard Books/Watts.

Rief, Linda. 1992. "Eighth Grade: Finding the Value in Evaluation." In *Portfolio Portraits*, ed. Donald Graves and Bonnie Sunstein. Portsmouth, NH: Heinemann.

Smith, Lucinda Irwin. 1989. *Women Who Write: From the Past and the Present to the Future.* Englewood Cliffs, NJ: Julian Messner, Simon & Schuster.

Tierney, Robert et al. 1991. *Portfolio Assessment in Reading and Writing Classrooms.* Norwood, MA: Christopher Gordon.

Updike, John. 1983. "Dog's Death." In *Poetspeak, in Their Work, about Their Work*, Paul B. Janeczko. Scarsdale, NY: Bradbury.

Whitman, Walt. 1975. "There Was A Child Went Forth." In *Walt Whitman: The Complete Poems.* New York: Penguin.

———. 1975. "A Noiseless, Patient Spider." In *Walt Whitman: The Complete Poems.* New York: Penguin.

A Simple Gift

Heather Carney

Patrick has been absent from the house for some time now, and his father is growing mildly concerned. "Where's Patrick?" he asks, and I smile to myself, for his bicycle is gone too, and I know, without being told, just where he is and what he's doing. Soon he will burst through the door, and place in my hand the treasure he brings, the first blueberries of the season, protected carefully in his hand as he bicycled over the bumps and curves of the mile of road; if he has been particularly fortunate, perhaps a stream of blue will pour from the mouth of his battered black water bottle, hastily pressed into service. "They're almost ready, Mom! And the bushes are just loaded with green ones!" Patrick is a berry picker—my companion in the field. My mother would be pleased.

My mother knew every wild spot for miles around, every patch of new growth where tangles of untamed raspberry bushes grew, every wild field and ancient cemetery where blueberries clung to the low bushes. She loved to drive the back roads of northern New Hampshire, seeking recently lumbered land where raspberry bushes sprang up to cover the piles of discarded branches, and when summer came, filled with freedom and possibilities, she could always find the bright, jewel-like berries.

As a child, free at last from school, I would join her to pick the raspberries which grew near our summer camp. We sallied forth on almost a daily basis dressed in our battered blue jeans and long-sleeved shirts, despite the summer sun, to do battle with the mosquitoes and the brush piles, which, with a snap like a bear trap, could collapse and hold our legs imprisoned. The first money I earned was for the raspberries I picked, a deal my mother struck with the owner of a local bakery whom she had known for years. I earned fifty cents a quart, and he earned the right to advertise wild raspberry pies and wild raspberry turnovers.

Through the years that followed, I would go with her to explore her latest find or to visit the old faithful patch under the power line where, once, we had found the skeleton of a black bear, clumps of hair and hide still visible among the bones. Summers free from my teaching job meant the joy of joining my mother for another day of sweat and prickers, of scratched arms and scraped shins. The hot sun beat down on our heads and backs, and the shared silence as we worked was punctuated only by the repeated five-syllable whistle of a white-throated sparrow in the shelter of the nearby woods. Often our search for the red gleam of ever bigger, ever more plentiful berries took us in separate directions, and we would work apart, but always there was the awareness of the other's presence. The rest of the world and all its inhabitants were gone from our view, gone from our minds. There was only the shared task at hand, the ruby beauty of the berries, ripe and fragrant, gradually filling our containers, old lard pails tied around our waists with string or with long strips of cheesecloth. The first plunk, plunk of berries hitting the metal bottom was replaced by silence as berries fell on the cushion of those already in the bucket, and the pull of the pail on my waist grew satisfyingly heavy. I called out to my mother, "Mine's almost half-full. How are you doing?" and always she had picked more.

Now it is I who travel the back roads of southern New Hampshire, searching for the swampy areas where the prized highbush blueberries grow, and it is Patrick who joins me under the hot sun, battling mosquitoes and branches to fill our fading green berry boxes with the silvered blue of summer's richness.

During these last summers, undaunted even by his first job, picking berries on a farm, Patrick's enthusiasm continues unabated. Muscles stretch as we strain toward clusters of sapphire berries tantalizingly high overhead, or suspended just out of reach over the mucky water. Muted voices from the nearby house built just last fall drift barely noticed through our silence. The blue builds in our boxes, and as we are lured from bush to bush, we carry them with increasing care, stepping over fallen branches with concentration, nestling them protectively in the brown leaves at the base of a tree, like colorful, speckled eggs of a wild bird, before turning to pick again.

My mother always said, "Leave some for the birds," and as Patrick and I reluctantly push our way to the road and the car, the frequent flash of blue only partially hidden by the dappled, green leaves assures me that we have left the birds their share. My mother would be pleased.

13

Sharing the Best of What We Have

Martha Horn

I just returned from two weeks of work at the Teachers College Writing Institute in New York City. The children's books that I brought there to use in my work with teachers are now replaced on the shelves in my study. In the days before the workshop, people cautioned me against sharing my own books, even my colleagues in New York. "Don't bring anything you can't carry with you each day," they warned, "we've had a history of books disappearing." I brought my books anyway. I set up a library of four hundred of my favorites in the classroom where I presented and invited the teachers to borrow them. I returned home ten days later with all four hundred.

Over the past fifteen years I have been collecting children's books. I began buying them because I wanted my students to have access to wonderful literature and the library in my first-grade classroom consisted of one sorry shelf of dusty, tattered, dated textbooks—a selection devoid of love and care. Buying books out of necessity quickly became an addiction; my collection now numbers well beyond two thousand. Each time I bought new books, I covered the paperbacks with clear contact paper and placed them on the shelves for the children to use. Then I carefully tucked the beautiful new hardcover books up on a high shelf so they wouldn't get wrecked. Years later when the focus of my work shifted from classroom teacher to staff developer, I took those out-of-reach books down from the shelves and shared them with the teachers in my workshops. Certainly adults would be responsible enough to care for them.

Three years ago, at the end of a week-long in-service with teachers in Warwick, Rhode Island, I checked off the books in my crates and discovered I was missing five. I refused to believe they had been stolen, so I wrote a letter to all twenty teachers listing the titles of the missing books, my address, and asked that if anyone found them to please send them in the mail. The following Saturday morning at 9:00, my doorbell rang. I looked out and there was a familiar woman standing on my front porch with an armload of books. "I don't know if you remember me," she said, "but I was in your workshop, and when I got your letter I recognized those titles as books I had borrowed. I went home and checked all over the place. I found them on the floor next to my bed."

Whenever I share these stories I do so with awe and surprise. Yet, why should I be surprised? I had already learned, as a beginning teacher, that when we care for the materials in our classrooms and expect our students to do the same, they usually do. Why would it be different for teachers? I recall going up to the attic in my parents' house one afternoon in late August, just days before my first year of teaching, looking for "play things" to fill my empty first-grade classroom. I came down with a box of worn stuffed animals, old games with covers torn and taped, and wooden puzzles, each with a few pieces missing. I didn't think the condition of the toys mattered because with twenty-six children using them, I expected box covers to tear and puzzle pieces to disappear. They did. Why should my students have treated them carefully when it was clear that I hadn't? The message they received was that I didn't value my students enough to give them the good stuff.

It was during that first year of teaching that I visited Mary Ellen Giacobbe's first-grade classroom. Her students shared markers, pencils, and crayons that were artfully arranged in plastic caddies. They wrote stories on custom-designed white paper that didn't tear, instead of the thin newsprint I had given to my students. And they played with beautiful games with no pieces missing.

And so I began my second year of teaching with an entirely different approach. On the first day of school I placed the bright primary-colored caddies I had bought and the new boxes of school crayons on the rug.

Together we opened each box and placed all the red crayons in the red containers, the blue crayons in the blue, etc. We opened the box of unsharpened pencils and practiced using the sharpener. And when I presented packages of brand-new markers, the children and I discussed how to care for them so they wouldn't dry out and role-played how to write gently so the points wouldn't jam. At the end of that year, we had used only a small portion of the allotted crayons and pencils, and the markers were still in good condition.

My first graders (and Mary Ellen) taught me that if I want students to treat the materials in our classroom with care, I must, as well. That lesson extends far beyond first grade. In 1991, I began teaching in the Elementary Education Department at Rhode Island College. One of the requirements in my Language Arts Methods course was for students to read three to five picture books per week and keep an annotated bibliography. I thought it unreasonable to ask undergraduates who take five courses each semester and work twenty hours (or more) per week to fit in weekly visits to the children's section of their local libraries, so I brought 450 of my books from home and placed them in crates in the entry way to my office for students to borrow. Some friends who know how much I value my children's book collection told me I was crazy. "They're college students, remember. They drink beer and eat pizza and won't think twice about setting the greasy pizza box down on top of your books." After teaching there for two years (which included seven methods courses and 109 students), all of my books were returned, and I have not yet found traces of pizza or beer.

My students learn how much I value my books through the expectations I set out at the beginning of the semester. During the first class, we read the syllabus together, taking a careful look at the page explaining the children's book requirement:

ABOUT MY BOOKS

> *The critical aspect of writing is not writing, it is reading*
>
> —Avi

For the past five years I've been carrying crates and/or boxes of books to schools throughout the country, inviting teachers I work with to take them home and read them to their children, husbands, wives, friends, or just themselves. I cannot talk about writing and reading without having examples of the best writing and reading at hand.

I try to keep current in my collection of children's books. Sometimes school libraries aren't able to get books as quickly as they would like and so I bring my books in order to help teachers become familiar with the newest books being published. It helps them in making requests for their own classrooms as well as their school libraries. I've always shared my favorites and my autographed copies, and they have always been returned. I want to do the same this semester.

One of the course requirements is that you keep an annotated bibliography of children's books. Instead of asking you to go to school and/or local libraries to get books, I brought 450 of my own books to my office. Friends who know how much I value my book collection warned me about letting college students borrow them. "Remember," one friend told me, "they're in college—they party—they'll spill beer on your books in their dorm rooms." You need to know that I take great care of my book collection and I trust you will treat them kindly, too. I hope you will get to know and enjoy them. I invite you to take them home to read to your children, your spouses, your roommates, yourselves, or anyone who will listen. And I invite you to use them in your work in the public schools.

The books are in crates in the entry way outside my office and they are arranged alphabetically according to *title*. Please find a time that's convenient for you to stop by to borrow and return books—possibly right before or right after class.

This is the procedure for borrowing books:

- You may take 3–5 books with you each week.
- When you decide on the books you want, take the transparency out of the front flap of the book and put it in the hanging file folder with your name on it. The files are organized according to section.
- Read the books to your children, students, spouses, friends, yourselves . . .
- Make notes about the books— If you liked it, why? If you didn't, why not?
- Return them no later than the following week, replacing the transparency.

- PLEASE check under your bed, under the seat of your car, in your book bag, etc., to be sure you return all of them promptly.
- If something happens to a book, *please tell me.*

I look forward to hearing your reactions to the books . . . ENJOY!

I consider it important to explain my expectations to my students as I do in this letter, but I believe they really understand the care of my books as a result of what I show them. Interspersed through the course overview on the first day of each semester, I try to read at least four or five picture books aloud. Then I place a stack of books on each table, so that these prospective teachers have a chance to look closely at a few and begin to fall in love with the literature that, hopefully, will become the core of their reading programs. I want them to leave that first class with a desire to know more about children's books and to view this requirement as something enjoyable. But I have another reason for giving my students time to look through books on that first day. I want them to see how I care for the books in my personal library.

Each book is covered with a clear book jacket. I learned from my friend and colleague Mary Ellen Giacobbe that "it is worth the time and an extra twenty-five cents per book to protect them." On one of the first pages my name is stamped with a personal embosser: Library of Martha Horn, and along the binding inside the front cover of each book, I have written the name of the bookstore, the city, state, (country), month and year in which the book was purchased. I do that as a way of keeping track of all the places in the world from which my book collection has been built. I want my college students to notice these things, because I believe that if they see I take great care of my books, they will too. And they do. Only once do I recall a student coming up to me at the end of class, talking quickly as she handed me a paper bag, "I bought you a new one because when I was getting out of my car yesterday my books slipped and there was a puddle and . . ." She had bought me a new copy of *Chrysanthemum* by Kevin Henkes.

It has long been acknowledged that we teach by example, but I would argue that we haven't begun to understand the incredible power of teaching through demonstration. At the beginning of the summer, I took care of my one-year-old niece and my three-year-old nephew for eight days. Reading books was part of our daily routine, and Patrick, the three-year-old, quickly instructed me as to how books in his house were read—the reading began with the inscription inside the cover. As he opened his autographed copy of *The Mitten,* he said, "Here's another one by my friend Jan Brett" and proceeded to read her inscription, "Best Wishes to Patrick, Love, Jan Brett." There were notes from other authors and some from his parents, but my favorites were the inscriptions written by other children. His four-year-old cousin had given him a copy of *Mary Had a Little Lamb,* the version illustrated by Tomie dePaola, because it had been one of her favorites. She had dictated what she wanted to say and her words, "Dear Patrick, Do you like animals? I bet you do. Love, Katie," written in her older sister's handwriting, were artfully placed next to the illustration on the title page. Inside the cover of Jan Brett's *Goldilocks and the Three Bears* he read the message from his seven-year-old cousin (see Figure 13–1).

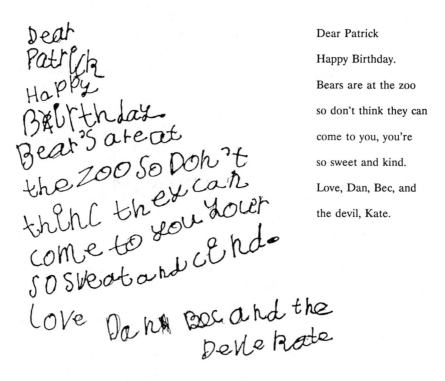

Dear Patrick

Happy Birthday.

Bears are at the zoo

so don't think they can

come to you, you're

so sweet and kind.

Love, Dan, Bec, and

the devil, Kate.

Figure 13–1. *Dear Patrick, Happy Birthday.*

And when we sat down to read *Berlioz the Bear,* Patrick recited what his eight-year-old cousin had written (see Figure 13–2).

Danny, Becky, and Kate write inscriptions like this because their own books are filled with personal messages from their parents, relatives, and friends. And Patrick demands that these messages be read because in his family read-alouds, they are read with the same reverence as the story itself.

We illustrate what we value in the way we live our lives, and certainly the same is true in the way we live our teaching. When I meet my former college students, they tell me about the newest books in their own libraries, and how many trips they've taken to the New England Mobile Book Fair (a discount book warehouse fifty minutes north of the college) since our class field trip. When students come to my office to exchange books each week, they chat about which books they read to their sisters and brothers, nieces and nephews, and which ones they loved so much that they just had to go out and buy for themselves. One day as I was working in my office, Karen arrived, her arms bracing a stack of five or six picture books. She cheerfully conversed with me as she replaced them in the crates and chose her next set.

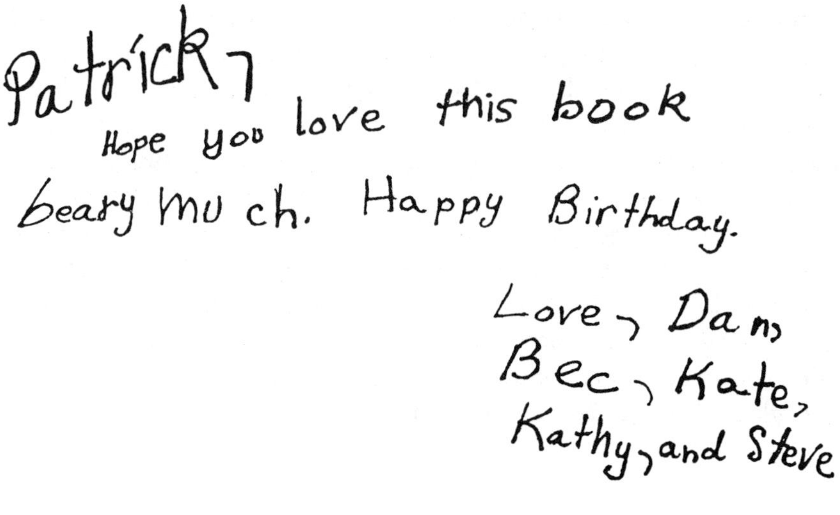

Patrick,
Hope you love this book
beary much. Happy Birthday.

Love, Dan,
Bec, Kate,
Kathy, and Steve

Figure 13–2. *Dear Patrick, hope you love this book.*

"I just loved this book," she said, holding up Audrey Woods' *Elbert's Bad Word*. "I read it to my mother when she was making dinner."

"You read it to your mother?" I asked, imagining Karen standing in her kitchen holding the book out as she knows you do when you read a picture book, her mother standing over the stove, twisting her head every now and then to take a look.

Read to my mother—you haven't heard anything!" she said. "I read to anyone who will listen. In fact, I've been reading to the guys at work. See, I work in the stock room at Apex, and lots of the time I have nothing to do so I do my homework. Last week I was sitting there reading *Wilfred Gordon MacDonald Partridge* and one of the stock boys came by and started giving me a hard time. 'You go to college huh, Karen. Looks like really tough reading!' Then they all started looking at my books and goofing. So I said, 'Sit down, I'm going to read to you' and I read them *Wilfred Gordon*. So now every day when I go in they ask, 'What are you going to read to us today?' and they sit and wait for me to read." She picked up *The Very Quiet Cricket* by Eric Carle, opened it to the last page and said, "I can't wait to read them this one!

Because I read aloud to the college students on a daily basis, Karen took her reading aloud seriously. And because I presented my books as valued possessions, teachers and college students took the care of books seriously. Now I realize that my first graders would have done the same. I often imagine myself teaching in a first-grade classroom once again, my students and I sitting together on the rug exclaiming in awe and wonder as we pour over the books that will become our classroom library. Throughout September, I would carry a box of my personal children's book collection into school each day and, just as my students and I opened those new boxes of crayons, pencils, markers and filled the caddies, we would begin each day opening a box of books—touching, smelling, reading, and arranging our library together. Ten years ago, I carefully placed my children's books on a high shelf; they were too good for my students. Since then I have discovered that by putting my prized book collection in the hands of my students I am saying, "I value you enough to share the best of what I have."

References

Avi. November 1985. Speech given at The National Council Teachers of English Conference, Philadelphia, Pennsylvania.

Brett, Jan. 1987. *Goldilocks and the Three Bears.* New York: Putnam's.

———. 1989. *The Mitten.* New York: Putnam's.

———. 1991. *Berlioz the Bear.* New York: Putnam's.

Carle, Eric. 1990. *The Very Quiet Cricket.* New York: Philomel.

Fox, Mem. 1985. *Wilfred Gordon MacDonald Partridge.* New York: Kane Miller.

Hale, Sarah Josepha. 1984. *Mary Had a Little Lamb.* New York: Trumpet Book Club.

Henkes, Kevin. 1991. *Chrysanthemum.* New York: Greenwillow.

Wood, Audrey. 1988. *Elbert's Bad Word.* New York: Harcourt Brace Jovanovich.

14

Children, Literature, Passion

Karen Smith

I love to read stories. Each day I look forward to new experiences made possible by an author who has created a story world for me to enter and dwell in. I need to read. Just as I need to garden, to dig my hands into soil and draw substance from the earth, I need to read and draw substance from words. I love talking with students about the new people I meet and the passion they arouse in me when they act or speak in a certain way. This passion is contagious—it calls forth the same passion in students and gets literature doing for them what it does for me. Passion motivated Julie to enter the classroom shouting, "You guys, you aren't going to believe this person I met in my book last night. She is awesome and bright, and she stood right up to this new boy and told him to bug off!" Passion caused Larry, a thirteen-year-old, to approach me in a quiet area of the room where no one else could hear and say, "Ms. Smith, I read *Sounder* this weekend, and I cried." It is what makes students and me look forward each day to the forty-five-minute block of time in which we quietly enter a story world and ponder, challenge, and question whatever it is our particular story has to offer.

A literature program filled with passion is what I strive for. It's a program in which participants treat literature as they treat life—they take it on and make it mean. Literature provides all of us with different ways of being in the world—it invites us in to share the experience, to enter into dialogue, and to place a value on its value (Rosen 1984). This way of interacting with text is rewarding, but it is not always easy. It puts special demands on us; we are asked to experience a story from our own position in the world. This can be validating, because it says who we are, and what we think and feel matters. On the other hand, it can be just as daunting because it may arouse thoughts and feelings that challenge what we currently believe to be true and fair and just.

Conditions have to be right to make this kind of literature program work. First of all, we have to be clear about why we use literature. We have to know what we want for and from our students. And, just as important, we have to create classroom environments that will support students and make it safe for them to respond in meaningful and passionate ways. I have three basic reasons for bringing children and literature together: (1) literature entertains; it is a marvelous way to put in time; (2) literature explores the human conditions and helps us understand who we are and why we exist; and (3) literature helps us recognize that there are many worldviews and that no single one constitutes the standard against which others' can or should be judged. This third reason is especially important—the more we explore multiple worldviews and other people's ways of knowing, the better prepared we are to live in and contribute to our multicultural and pluralistic society.

These reasons for using literature define what I value and, subsequently, what I want for and from my students. I have lots of wants. I want stories to do for my students what they do for me. I want students to meet new people and journey alongside them with questions and curiosity about who they are and what they do and say. I want them to learn to ask, "How come?" "How come M.C. and his father don't value Sarah's Mountain in the same way?" "How come Gilly is so mean to the people who care for her?" "How come Mr. Arable wants to kill Wilbur?" "How come Jonas chose to leave his 'perfect world'?"

At the same time, I want students to ask questions; I want them to be patient and to ponder and play with possible answers to those questions. What I *don't* want is for them to be too quick to judge the new people they meet and the new situations they encounter. I expect them to return to and examine carefully those events that seem unclear, that create tension, that knock against what they know to be true. I expect them to ask others about their thoughts and feelings and to use this information to inform and enrich their own understandings.

Ultimately, I want students to understand that literature has the potential to help them transcend their present situation and to move beyond what they know, believe, and imagine themselves to be. I remember clearly the day Raul, a twelve-year-old student, finished reading *Shadow of a Bull* (1964), the story of a young man who stands up for himself under difficult circumstances. Raul sat and stared at the last page of the book for a long time before he closed it and laid it on his desk. Slowly, he looked up at me and said, "I have to tell my dad that I don't want to play Little League this year." I knew the difficult circumstance Raul had found himself in during a month of playing a game he really hated. He had felt he needed to play; he needed to please his dad. I also knew what had happened between Raul and the story. The power of story had spoken.

Students need support when they are asked to give this kind of attention to story. I begin with *place*. Where we read is important. When I think of reading books that have stories tucked between their covers, I think of the special reading places in my life. In my childhood, I read good books in a tent made of blankets thrown over the clothesline and pegged to the ground with wooden pins. I also read books under the big oak tree in our family's front yard and under the thick covers on my big double bed. In college, I found a niche at the library, where the sun beamed through a window in the late afternoon and created a golden glow that gave my reading place a special warmth. In my new home, I sit on my sun porch with my book and cup of tea. It seems fitting; it feels good.

And so, I bring this need for a special place to school. I help students find places that are warm, comfortable, and fitting. I have spent countless hours and dollars making and buying pillows for students who like to lie down on a comfortable rug to read. I encourage students to find classroom "tents" (e.g. under tables, behind dividers, in walk-in closets) or other special places they can go to lose themselves in a story world.

Creating the right *mood* is equally important. Before students go to their reading place, I ask them to prepare for quiet time. I don't want them getting up and moving around. That means that if they are almost finished with a book, they should also take a new book. Or, if they have started a book but are not sure if they like it, they should take some others to look through and choose from.

Students need a large selection of books from which they can choose, especially with books written for young adolescents. Nancie Atwell's, *In the Middle* (1987), speaks to the importance of this type of book.

> The last twenty years have witnessed an explosion in the number of novels and short stories written expressly for young adults, adolescent literature of such breadth and depth that no teacher need ever apologize for building a curriculum around kids' responses to their own books. . . . As we adult readers can turn to fiction for particulars of the universalities of our conditions, our students can find their perspectives reflected and explored in a body of fiction of their own, books that can help them grow up, books that can help them love books. (p. 161)

The body of fiction I offer to students includes books that fit comfortably with their current needs and interests as well as books they can grow into. Students should be able to read the *Babysitters Club* or *Goosebump* series since they serve a purpose: they entertain, create bonds among classmates, and often support and encourage reluctant readers. They make reading easy because they are safe and predictable; the good are rewarded, and the bad are punished. But these books aren't enough. Children deserve books that provide more, books such as *Lyddie* (1991), *The Giver* (1993), and *Dragon's Gate* (1993). These books entertain, but they also broaden our awareness of unpredictable human experiences, as well as offer us experiences from other cultures and other perspectives.

It's imperative to have books that provide a multicultural perspective and, fortunately, more and more books are being written for young adolescents by people from diverse cultures. Authors such as Walter Dean Myers, Virginia Hamilton, Yoshiko Uchida, Gary Soto, and Shonto Begay write wonderful stories that accurately and authentically represent their cultures' dreams, hopes, and perspectives. Our responsibility is to give students the opportunity and time to explore and participate in these story worlds and give them what Auden calls passionate attention. Banks and Banks (1989) caution us against the dangers of not offering students opportunities to enter into these multicultural experiences, of limiting them to only an Anglocentric education.

This type of education has negative effects for mainstream students because it reinforces their false sense of superiority, gives them a misleading conception of their relationship with other racial and ethnic groups, and denies them the opportunity to benefit from the knowledge, perspective, and frames of references that can be gained from studying and experiencing other cultures and groups. When people view their culture from the perspective of another group, they are able to understand their own culture more fully, and to see how it is unique and distinct from others as well as how it interrelates to and interacts with other cultures. (pp. 189–90)

The right place accompanied by the right mood and plenty of good books is a good place to start, but students also need *support* as meaning makers. Many of us struggle with this kind of support; it's a new idea. For years we viewed students as receivers of meaning. They were expected to read and recall; the only thing that really mattered was how closely their retelling matched the meaning in the text. But now we know that a reader's life experiences are as significant to meaning construction as the text (Rosenblatt, 1976). This means I have to create a context where students can share thoughts, feelings, and sometimes rudimentary understandings without danger of being laughed at or ridiculed. Students must feel free to question others' interpretations. And as the person who is responsible for a particular group of children, I must always be wide-awake to what students' behaviors and responses tell me, so that my beliefs and values don't rule them but serve to inform my interactions with them. This kind of attentiveness is hard. Sometimes students' responses puzzle or surprise me—their interpretation of a character or situation seems light years away from my own. When this happens, I visualize myself physically moving behind the student and asking, "How did he or she come to this understanding?" For example, when six of my fifth- and sixth-grade students spent two days talking about the pole in the book *M.C. Higgins, the Great* (1974) (an object I thought unworthy of thought, much less time), I figuratively stood behind them and captured, from the eyes of an eleven-year-old child, the excitement of M.C. riding a forty-foot pole. I suddenly understood. When the same group empathized with M.C., a young man about their age, instead of his father, who unsuccessfully tries to get M.C. to understand the importance of survival and tradition (values I hold dear), I again had to "get behind" the students and say, "How did they come to their understanding? Why don't they see it the way I do?"

Students need time to read books and talk to others about what they have read. I find it helpful to provide time to share after silent reading. During this ten minutes, students pick a partner and share what they have read. I encourage them to change partners every few days, so they can hear about numerous books and get ideas about books they may want to read. Every year a network of book connections gets created. I hear kids saying, "Promise me you'll give it to me when you finish." And I find lists of book titles, with students' names listed under them, pinned to the bulletin board. These lists assure a student that he or she will be next in line to read a particular book. I stay out of these decisions and exchanges, but I always enjoy watching them unfold. They seem to give special importance to reading and add an important dimension to our community of readers.

As the year moves along, I also encourage students to form literature groups in which five or six students read the same book and talk about it. The human condition is full of complex and uncertain propositions and when students talk to other students, it usually helps them to better understand why people do what they do or feel as they feel. It took time for me to learn to value talk; it often appeared pointless and rambling. However, once I took time to closely scrutinize some transcripts of my students' talk, I found out that the seemingly pointless, rambling talk, more often than not, resulted in complex understandings.

There are always a few students who have trouble moving into the world of story and getting anchored. Sometimes this happens with less experienced readers, but it also happens with proficient readers who try out more challenging books and/or new genres. (This seems especially true with stories written by authors such as Virginia Hamilton, Susan Cooper, and Madeleine L'Engle.) To lure students in, I use a method I call *gaining momentum*. I read aloud the first chapter or two while students follow along. This seems to get the author's voice in their ear. It also gives them a chance to sort out some of the ambiguities they are facing. Students seem to naturally know when they have momentum. When they know, they slowly slip away and continue on their own.

James Britton (1978) once said that students need to learn to read more books with satisfaction and read books with more satisfaction. I agree. I want my students to be more than plot readers. It's important to me that they understand that story moves at different levels. It excites me when I hear kids discussing characters' values and beliefs or grappling with metaphors. I remember twelve-year-old Martha talking with her four classmates and me about *Shadow of a Bull.* She listened intently as Ricardo explained his anger at the men in the story who "were using Manola to satisfy their own selfish needs," and then she said, "Yeah, it was lousy of them to do that, but he [Manola] let them do it; he could have told them he didn't want to." After several minutes of trying to figure out the relationship between the "town men" and Manola, Francisco, another student, noted that the title of the story seemed to symbolize the heavy burden Manola carried as he tried to decide whether to please the men or to go with his own convictions. Martha, surprised by this notion, said that she had been thinking that the shadow was death but would now have to reconsider because, in the light of the discussion they were having, Francisco's interpretation made more sense to her (Smith 1993). I don't remember what conclusion this group of students came to that day. I'm not sure they came to any, but I do know they were reading the book at many levels.

The best way I found of helping students to recognize those levels is to *provide demonstrations* during read-aloud time. Instead of asking questions after I read, I first ask the kids what they made of what they heard. When appropriate, I share my feelings and offer some thoughts that move the story beyond plot. For example, I might talk about the title of a book and what it means to me. I like to think aloud with the students about how and when characters change. If objects in stories have meaning (for me) beyond their physical value, I talk about that. What about the ferris wheel in *Tuck Everlasting* (1975), the pole in *M.C. Higgins,* the bridge in *Bridge to Terabithia* (1977)? At first, students listen without much interaction, but usually by November I can expect a response something like the following: "You know, I've been thinking about the title *Pinballs* (1977). It's like a description of Carlie's life; they go up, they go down, just like in a pinball machine."

When children learn to explore the multiple layers of meaning, they think more deeply and feel more passionately. Each student will learn to do this at his or her own pace, of course. We can't force it and we can't require it, but we can be ready for it. We have to be wide-awake, looking with both our heads and our hearts. Sometimes we hear it when they are talking with their classmates. Or, we find it written in literature logs. But often it reveals itself in subtle ways—tears trickling down cheeks, smiles or frowns spreading across faces, and laughter spilling from hearts.

When these things happen, I note and celebrate them. They let me know the beliefs and values I hold about children, literature, and passion are guiding our classroom lives.

References

Armstrong, W. 1970. *Sounder.* Harper & Row.

Atwell, N. 1987. *In the Middle: Writing, Reading, and Learning with Adolescents.* Portsmouth, NH: Boynton/Cook.

Babbitt, N. 1975. *Tuck Everlasting.* Farrar, Strauss, & Giroux.

Banks, J., and C. Banks. 1989. *Multicultural Education: Issues and Perspectives.* Boston: Allyn & Bacon.

Byers, B. 1977. *The Pinballs.* New York: Scholastic Inc.

Britton, J. 1978. *The Nature of the Reader's Satisfaction.* In M. Meek, A. Warlow, and G. Barton, eds., *The Cool Web: The Patter of Children's Reading.* New York: Atheneum.

Hamilton, V. 1974. *M.C. Higgins, the Great.* New York: Macmillan.

Lowry, L. 1993. *The Giver.* Boston: Houghton Mifflin.

Paterson, K. 1977. *Bridge to Terabithia.* Crowell Junior Books.

———. 1991. *Lyddie.* New York: Dutton Child Books.

Rosen, H. 1984. From personal notes taken at a lecture at Georgetown University, Washington, DC.

Rosenblatt, L. 1976. *Literature as Exploration,* 3rd ed. New York: Noble & Noble.

Smith, K. 1993. A descriptive analysis of the response of six students and their teacher in literature study group. (Doctoral dissertation, Arizona State University.)

Wojciechowska, M. 1964. *Shadow of a Bull.* New York: Atheneum.

Yep, L. 1993. *Dragon's Gate.* HarperCollins.

15

Paired Learning: Toward a Culture of Collaboration

Pat McDonald-O'Brien
with Mark Klein

"*It's a ritual,* Pat, just a ritual" was the way my principal explained his model of staff supervision and evaluation. I was confused by the word *ritual,* which connoted to me visions of presents on birthdays or gobblers on Thanksgiving. The ritual Mark Klein referred to is a model of staff supervision that included a preconference, classroom observation, and post conference. My observation ritual included informing my students, "Mr. Klein is coming to watch me, not you" and a strong solicitation for cooperation. "While Mr. Klein is here I don't want to see . . ." Some of us even kept a particular lesson on file for observation day. It motivated me to straighten bookshelves, accompanied by a "company's coming" wipe of the desk and a "please close that closet door."

The anointed day arrived and Mr. Klein, legal tablet in hand and wearing a polite but serious smile, scripted and summarized my lesson. He needed to see direct instruction, on-task children, and, of course, closure, the piece I always forgot. After forty-five minutes, he waved the yellow tablet at me in false salute as he quietly backed out the door like a teenager at midnight.

When he left, the kids and I heaved a collective sigh and returned to normal classroom activity and the accompanying noise level. His observation was followed by a postobservation conference where he ladled on praise and suggested areas to improve. With the forms signed and completed, we returned to being two educators free to question our methods and strategies. It was this exchange of ideas that Mark valued.

After four years of this supervision model, Mark felt an urgency to promote professional growth, for himself and his staff. He viewed his supervision methods as a stimulus for retreating to the comfortable, the tried and true. Mark Klein was not a person who sat in the same chair long. At recess, he chased a soccer ball. That same afternoon he read van Allsburg to the fifth graders, and he was often running a little late for yet another meeting. This supervision ritual was a pebble in his loafers as he scuffled down tile floors.

Meanwhile, back in the classrooms, cooperative learning groups and reader/writer workshops were welcoming student success. Classroom libraries gobbled space like zucchini in an August garden. Special education students read their poetry at fourth-grade Author's Breakfasts. Across grade level and across curriculum, projects and literature shares were becoming weekly routines. Student mentors guided newcomers to our school. Teacher mentors lent an ear, not only to their students, but to any who needed extra nurturing. Second graders volunteered as "aides" in the art room, and my "remedial" students read to the kindergarten. The traditional evaluation model reminded us of the basics of instruction, but did not capture the craft of education. Nor did it show much of the efforts of the teachers. Much of what our staff valued was not included.

Mark began by developing a portfolio. He wrote a daily journal. He talked with other principals and read *Principle Centered Leadership* (1991) by Stephen Covey and *The Quality School* (1992) by William Glasser. While he was driving his Subaru, he listened to tapes of *Educational Leadership* and set some goals. He wanted to construct a model to scaffold the changes and innovations that were occurring in the classrooms. He wanted a climate of professional support. He believed his role should evolve from distant expert to familiar facilitator. He called his program *Paired Learning* and quipped, "If nothing else, it's a catchy title." He began to work with teachers rather than on teachers.

The Paired Learning model mirrored reading/writing workshops. With overheads and cartoons, Mark presented the groundwork to a seasoned, somewhat skeptical audience of September-busy teachers. Glances of, "Now what's he up to?" were exchanged around the faculty room. Teachers asked, "Are you saying you won't be making formal observations?"

"I am offering this as an option or perhaps, an addition to, traditional observation, not to accountability." Mark continued that we were to find colleagues with whom we shared an educational interest. With the trepidation reserved for prom dates, we meekly approached each other, "Do you have a partner for this thing Mark wants us to try? I'll do anything to avoid being observed, even if it is more work."

I found two learning partners, Nancy Dougherty and Alexsandra (Sandy) Wrigley. Nancy and Sandy are primary special education teachers and I am a reading specialist. We chose to work together because we liked each other and shared a love for children, humor, and language. Choosing to work together rather than being assigned was a vital step in this evaluation program. It enhanced trust and commitment to our goal.

Our paired learning goal was to investigate, consider and reflect upon our ideas concerning primary reading. We submitted this goal to Mark in writing, accompanied by our plan to meet it. We were brave.

We plan to meet our shared goal by

1. collecting literature and resources that promote
   - children as readers
   - emerging literacy
   - motivation and reading
   - literature based reading instruction
2. writing lessons integrating the above topics into daily reading classes
3. outlining the framework of the primary reading program

We were crazy to believe we could accomplish all of that, but Mark approved our goals.

Another group investigated portfolios by building their own collections. They attended a workshop conducted by Donald Graves and returned to school, boxes and binders at the ready. Anne Marie Pearlberg, a fifth-grade teacher, said of portfolios, "You can't expect kids to do something you aren't willing to do yourself." She had clearly heard Graves's message. Two fourth-grade teachers planned to incorporate science, social studies, and math information through reading and writing.

From a staff of forty-five professional employees, sixteen stalwart teach-ers agreed to try the program. Mark termed this a good start.

He requested that partners meet biweekly, but we simply found that hard to remember. "Is this the week we meet or did we meet last week?" So we met every Tuesday from 11:30–12:00. We began as teachers and friends, aware of our goal, but not shouldering it like a yoke. We shared information (and editorial comment) from district committee meetings. Sandy told of the trials and joys of day care and Nancy kept us aware of how the political becomes personal. I told stories of my husband's career change from the business world to elementary education. We ate lunch and without comment split any chocolate dessert three ways.

What did all this personal conversation have to do with primary read-ing? Everything. We were members, in fact leaders, of the learning com-munity we call classroom. I no longer left my life in the parking lot. I knew background knowledge directly affected student learning. Why would I pretend it did not affect mine? I believed learning and living were intertwined processes like inhaling and exhaling; why would I cut myself off from the oxygen? I asked students to collaborate and to dis-cover what mattered to them, and now I asked myself and my learning partners to till that same soil. That tilling uncovered our focus: our mutual passion for teaching reading.

Throughout the year we collected a three-ring portfolio filled with articles on primary reading. We found *Primary Voices, Educational Lead-ership,* and *Reading Teacher* to be especially pertinent. Carol Avery's *. . . And With a Light Touch* (1993), Regie Routman's *Invitations* (1991), Georgia Heard's *For the Good of the Earth and the Sun* (1989), and *With Promise* (1991) by Susan Stires were and are texts we revisited often. We chatted about authors Tomie De Paolo, Mem Fox, and Eric Carle like neighbors over a July fence. Books were exchanged in stacks to supplant each other's libraries, to extend an author study or theme, or simply because we loved them. Around mid-December, I realized I was no longer working alone.

As our evaluation process grew more personal and more relevant, we visited each other's classrooms. We began to study our students, our strategies, and our learning. It was time to implement some new thoughts, revamp, and renew. In Nancy's third-grade special education class (learning support class), we admired Judy's response log and her diligence at keeping it current. We wondered how to invite deeper thinking without thwarting budding readers. We also questioned self-selected reading for students who required learning support. Can they choose a text to challenge themselves? In an attempt to look at those issues, Nancy paired her students with Sandy's younger students for buddy reading. Children clustered on the floor, under tables, in the coat area, and a few even sat on chairs. Picture books, poetry books, fiction and nonfiction works rested on chalk ledges and tables. Quickly, the room filled with the voices of children sharing story, "Pickle things you never see, like pickles on the Christmas tree . . ." from *Pickle Things* (1980) by Marc Brown. I heard the voices of negotiation. "You read a page, and I'll read a page" or "It's your turn, I just read that page." It was hard for us to stay out of their way—so accustomed to being boss! The students read to one another, and sometimes a child found a quiet corner alone. Soon third graders were bringing books along to read to their younger peers. Buddy reading was part of the week, and a new block of literate, independent reading time resulted.

In our Tuesday meeting, we discussed books the children really loved that week. We checked with each other for affirmation, "Did you notice Jenny and Maria wouldn't let Donald join their group? What do you make of that? Is that new or have they been feuding for a while? How can we get our hands on some more funny books? What do you think about R. L. Stine? Our kids are buying *Goosebumps* to show off in the hallway."

Nancy and Sandy's students (and their teachers) borrowed books from my classroom collection. Often when I returned from a meeting, I found the children's thank-you notes, front and center on my desk so as not to be overshadowed by the coffee mug, unfinished reports, memos, plan book, and student journals. Business-sized envelopes with my name laboriously scribed by oversized pencils were sprinkled with drawings of aliens and robots. My favorite invented spelling read, "To Ms. O'Brain." Some days I found poems on my desk, a spectacular gift. These notes became artifacts to consider, to wonder about, and to value.

I began to see the advantages of "cooperative professional development." I had a new opportunity to ask the hard questions. What was my intention here? Was there another way to approach this? How did you see this? I tried to build upon what worked to entice new learning, to breathe new life into problem solving. Nancy and Sandy saw what I could not. I was working with two other teachers who were not supervising me, judging me, or completing forms for the state of Pennsylvania. Nancy, Sandy, and I worked together to find meaningful literacy education and to support one another.

"What if you read *Mr. Mumble?* That has a strong character. . . ."

"But you tried that with fifth graders, I don't know if my little ones . . ."

"How about our friend Mem, she always has something . . ."

"Yes! Mem! She'll help us! What's the one with Butch Aggie and snic, snac?"

"*Night Noises,* do you have a copy? Who else might have a copy?"

We trusted that if we delighted in the characters in *Night Noises* (1989) by Mem Fox, that the children might also see themselves in Mem's pages. So it went, week by week, some weeks more productive than others. But if we missed a meeting, it echoed through the week. I felt as though I had forgotten something, or left my glasses at home. Not that I couldn't survive, but that something important was missing.

Every week that I worked with my partners, the walls between our classrooms lowered and our community expanded. In a large school it is difficult to share even coffee with a colleague. Prior to this experience it would not be unusual for several days to pass without seeing either of these teachers. This evaluation process brought us together to shake out fresh choices. Without meaningful dialogue with interested peers, how was I to gain diverse perspectives? Isolation did not foster my teaching, nor nurture my professional and personal growth. A once-a-year, staged visit from my principal didn't either.

I set lofty goals for myself every September, and like New Year's resolutions they were soon forgotten or dressed in excuses. Now when I launched a new concept, I tried it out for a few days, and we reviewed it the following Tuesday. We made adjustments. The process of researching, brainstorming, reflecting, collecting, peer coaching, and self-evaluating was alive and changing. At the middle and end of the year, Mark required feedback on our goals. I was surprised at how much we had accomplished for our first attempt at a new program. We now have text sets for Marc Brown, Tomie De Paola, Mem Fox, and James Marshall. We did not purchase new materials to do this, we pooled our resources and discovered these treasures already in our classrooms. Reading/writing folders were revised, and I suspect they will be revised again. We collected a portfolio of current research articles. We implemented a shared reading program for across grade level, primary reading instruction, which we prefer to call "buddy reading." We talked a lot about self-selected reading for children with reading problems.

Additionally, Mark invited a paragraph or two on the strengths of this program and requested revisions and suggestions. We reported that the major strength of this process was the direct impact it had on our teaching. Feedback arrived weekly, not yearly. Sandy wrote, "Whatever question, whatever problem would instantly cause our group to form a huddle and develop a plan." She continued, "The most valuable aspect of this process is that it continually required us to question and evaluate our daily work in the classroom." We also suggested that we meet more frequently with our principal to, again, gain perspective. Additionally, I would now add personal portfolio to our evaluation. This past year we dipped our toes in the portfolio pool. We had goals and plans. We collected articles and artifacts. We wrote journals. But I believe portfolio could be our wellspring. It could help us reveal our plans as they unfold, collapse, and change. I don't know of another tool that could better reflect our work, our thinking, and guide our efforts.

I ask my students to collaborate, discuss, gather information, and break new ground. I ask them to note occasions of wonder and to dare to be curious. It strikes me that I have asked them to go first. Now it is our turn to reflect and inquire, to dare to be curious.

References

Avery, Carol. 1993. *. . . And With a Light Touch*. Portsmouth, NH: Heinemann.

Brown, Marc. 1980. *Pickle Things*. New York: Putnam & Grosset.

Catalanotto, Peter. 1990. *Mr. Mumble*. New York: Orchard Books..

Covey, Stephen. 1991. *Principle-Centered Leadership*. New York: Fireside.

Association for Supervision and Curriculum Development. *Educational Leadership*. Richmond, VA: Association for Supervision and Curriculum Development.

Fox, Mem. 1989. *Night Noises*. New York: Harcourt Brace Jovanovich.

Glasser, William. 1992. *The Quality School.* New York: HarperCollins.

Heard, Georgia. 1989. *For the Good of the Earth and the Sun.* Portsmouth, NH: Heinemann.

National Council of Teachers of English. *Primary Voices.* Urbana, IL: National Council of Teachers of English.

International Reading Association. *The Reading Teacher.* Newark, DE: International Reading Association.

Routman, Regie. 1991. *Invitations.* Portsmouth, NH: Heinemann.

Stine, R. L. 1992. *Goosebumps* Series. New York: Scholastic.

Stires, Susan. 1991. *With Promise.* Portsmouth, NH: Heinemann.

16

Teacher Portfolios: Improving the Teaching Climate

Jane Kearns

"*Escaped! That's what* I did, I escaped from that art class," I told the students, "and I'll never go back."

I was sharing my portfolio with a high school freshmen class; they knew that one of my goals was to learn something new, like watercolors. "I loved mixing the paints and sitting at the easel, but I'm just not an artist, and I'm sad about that." Then I held up my practice pages, and within seconds, the freshmen were telling me about all the good they saw in my watercolor pages.

"Oh, that's nice right there."

"I'd hang that up in my room."

"I think you did a good job, especially since this was your first art lesson."

"Look right there, see how you blended the colors into different shades. I really like that."

Dave, who is an artist, said, "You should try things like watercolors that are harder for you, to challenge yourself, and you did. I think that's great. You should continue with art."

This wasn't the response I expected; I was the teacher after all, I was trying to encourage them through portfolios, but they understood how important it is to be encouraged. I came away from that class feeling better about myself, those students, and our portfolios.

Their teacher, Linda White, said they were responding to me, as I did to them and their portfolios. This is one outcome of teacher portfolios that we love but had not anticipated.

In *Seeking Diversity* (1991), Linda Rief wrote that teachers need to keep their own file folders. Now some teachers in Manchester, New Hampshire, keep portfolios, along with their students, to model and learn, to challenge themselves, and to grow as teachers.

We ask ourselves the same questions we ask our students: What represents who you are as a reader? a writer? a learner? a whole person? In fact, teacher portfolios were considered just models for the student portfolios. But our teacher portfolios have become so much more.

Early items were personal: family histories, childhood memories, travel and hobbies, photos of friends and family. Don Graves, in talking to us, explained that portfolio keepers need to establish support structures of the past before leaping into today and the future. We looked back at what we had done and who we were, so we could move forward. "We have to have a history," Graves said, "before we can have a present and a future."

While we compile these portfolios, we also share with colleagues, interested teachers keeping their own portfolios who are willing listeners. As we share our portfolio items, we learn what interests people, we learn what others consider literacy, we learn what other portfolio keepers understand as learning.

My portfolio changed several times each year and continues to change. At first, all I did was add or subtract, very similar to beginning revisers in the writing process. Then, instead of just building onto my portfolio, for the second and third and fourth school years I started new portfolios. One reason was to always be beginning with the students, but another more important personal issue was that past portfolios initiated present and future learning actions.

Items in my portfolio over the years have included such things as:

- A list of my favorite books (updated every year and restricted to one page). (Except I have a separate page of children's books and a separate page for my mystery books and a separate page of books I am going to read).

- Letters sent (personal and professional letters; letters of praise and letters of complaint and one letter to our State Board of Education that I know will not be read) and cards, letters, postcards received.
- Articles I have had published and rejection slips from editors with no sense of style, taste, and humor!
- A poem and an essay about my mother's death (that took twenty years to write).
- Lines from favorite poems by William Butler Yeats, Gerard Manley Hopkins, James Stephens, Eamon Greenan, and Seamus Heaney; lines from favorite writers: Annie Dillard, Eudora Welty, Farley Mowat, John McPhee, and Sue Hubbell.
- Ads for writing workshops and courses I've given.
- One-pagers from our team meetings with the University of New Hampshire Literacy Portfolio Research Project with Dr. Jane Hansen.
- A monthly calendar, crowded with notations for workshops, school visits and meetings, activities with family and friends.

For each item we place in our portfolios we write reflections: How does this represent us as readers, writers, learners, whole persons? These reflections began as simple explanations, but they gradually took on more of a life; they were stories and discoveries. At first the reflections were short, one Post-it note, then two, and then reflections became whole pages, even two pages. We were experiencing what Donald Murray has talked about—that writing begets writing.

Now I think the reflections are more important than the items. The items are just concrete representations, but in each reflection we dig deeper, exploring and discovering. The writing of reflections takes us to surprising avenues of thought.

For instance, the three photos in my portfolio represent my attempt to be a student of light and texture and shade—but when I started writing a reflection, the words and thoughts poured out:

Right now I'm working on capturing the perfect wave, not as a surfer, but as a photographer. There is mystery in each wave and the perfect one eludes me but here is always tomorrow's sunrise.

My photos record who I am. They silhouette my life, what I think, where I am, how I am. They are my portraits [photographers are notoriously camera shy].

I started taking family shots, then sports and travels; now I photograph for myself—what can I see? What new vision or angles of vision can I see in the familiar near my house or on my beach. I fiddle with colors, lights, shades.

And the challenge:

In one split second to trigger the shutter and catch a bit of life. In a wink, photos become. Decisions come fast—out of a roll of thirty six, I find one or two that I like. These pictures have to speak like a clean poem, opening hues of meaning and memory.

I've studied great photographers. I walked with Jacob Ris through the New York City slums, anguished at the Lewis Hine's mills, warmed to W. Eugene Smith's midwife and angered over the stupidity of Minamata, ached at the cruel life of Dorothea Lange's migrants, admired Edward Weston's figures, the natural colors of Eliot Porter, the kind love in Brian Lanker's women and the strength and independence of William Albert Allard's vanishing cowboys, the joy of Freeman Paterson's outdoors.

Photography for me is not art but more than a hobby—soothing.

As we maintained portfolios over the years, we started to review and reconsider the items, looking for patterns and connections. Karen Harris, a resource room teacher, shared the goals her students set for their portfolios. Goals became extensions of seeing patterns, and in my case, holes in my portfolio. In analyzing my items, I noticed that I

- Tend to write pieces that I find easy to write, light expository articles.
- Read a lot of children's books, but almost no reading of books for students in grades 7–12.
- Read professional writing/reading books but no books that look at broader school topics, like questions asked by Sizer and Gardner and others.

And I sadly noticed that while I have been busy teaching, I haven't been busy learning. These patterns and gaps became catalysts for action, new goals for me to focus and act upon.

Now my portfolio is more the result of goals I set for myself, examples of trying to reflame the learner in me:

- Poems and drafts of poems I am working on.
- Two pieces of writing, harder more complicated pieces, seen in various stages of disrepair, design, and development.
- New things I am learning—Shoals Marine Lab marine life weekend; art classes; bird identification charts and books; sky, cloud, and weather information; HyperCard workshops; and books, tapes, and articles about what is jazz.

These items represent things I knowingly set out to try or do or learn. This is important as it gives me a path to weave in and about and they shape my tomorrows; the portfolio has become a deliberate focus of my literate life.

As teachers, we often get so wrapped up in teaching that we forget that in our classrooms we need to be the first learner. We forget that we need to evaluate ourselves as teacher and learners, readers and writers, as people with a whole life beyond the school door. Just as we model reading and writing for our students, we need to model learning. Teacher portfolios offer us this opportunity. Like being immersed in writing and reading processes, teachers who assign portfolios to their students need to be keepers of portfolios. Sixth-grade teacher Karen Boettcher explained that with portfolios, teachers "become members of the class community, rather than just an authority figure."

Teachers who keep portfolios create an environment of positive learning where everyone has a chance to grow and stretch and be somebody. We help students select items and then reflect by showing our work and our risk taking; we teach by being learners; we teach by demonstrating that we are making decisions similar to our students. We teach by being sensitive and receptive to a variety of inside and outside school learning.

Compiling, organizing, and presenting a portfolio, then reviewing the contents of my portfolio made me look harder at myself as a literate person, made me be more cognizant of my reading and writing and learning. I asked more questions of myself as a learner. The portfolio was the first thing I had encountered in a long time that made me self-evaluate.

Now I am working on new gaps in my portfolio: more thoughtful and challenging workshop presentations; investigating the why to my reading choices; the why to my love of jazz; the why I am better at viewing than doing art, and writing harder pieces (like this article on teacher portfolios). I'm trying to be at the right place at the right time with my camera, and as Byrd Baylor says, "Be looking!" And I continue to try writing poetry that doesn't sound like it came from an ad for a bar of soap.

The teacher-evaluation checklists always insult what teachers do every day; how can a summation of punctuality, compatibility, and other *-ities* define our roles? Even anecdotal evaluation centers on the past and never propels us into future actions. But with these self-directed and self-guided evaluative portfolios, we can blend the ingredients both in and outside school, both professional and personal, both serious and whimsical, that shape, define, and design the who and what we are.

I had been trapped in my past, but my portfolio has made me a traveler in the world of learning, loving the delight of after-rain when the world is clearer and brighter. I haven't signed up for another art class—yet—but I am wet brushing my way through the hands-on book *Watercolor for the Artistically Undiscovered*.

References

Graves, Donald, and Bonnie Sunstein, eds. 1992. *Portfolios Portraits*. Portsmouth, NH: Heinemann.

Hansen, Jane. "Evaluation: 'My Portfolio Shows Who I Am.'" *The Quarterly of the National Writing Project*.

———. 1992. "Literacy Portfolios Emerge." *Reading Teacher* 45 (8): 604–07.

———. 1992. "Literacy Portfolios: Helping Students Know Themselves." *Educational Leadership* 48 (2): 66–8.

Hansen, Jane, ed. 1993. *Researchers Reflect: Writings from the Manchester Portfolio Project, 1990–1992*. Durham, NH: The Writing Lab.

Rief, Linda. 1992. *"Seeking Diversity: Language Arts with Adolescents*. Portsmouth, NH: Heinemann.

Wansart, William, ed. 1991. "Teachers as Researchers: Creating Supportive Classroom Environments for Students with Learning Difficulties." Durham, NH: The Writing Lab.

Wilcox, Carol. 1993. "Portfolios: Finding a Focus." Durham, NH: The Writing Lab.

✑ In My Mother's Garden

Ellen H. Bryant

In my mother's garden grew many plants whose names I didn't know, not until later when I had become a gardener as well. To know my mother as a gardener one must examine old photographs through a strong lens. The photograph may be a snapshot taken in our backyard of my sister Deborah holding her two guinea pigs, but in the background is the knowledge I want: the blur of scarlet—is that *Lythrum*? The pink haze on bending stems—*Malva Fastigiata*? What did she grow in that garden that I can barely make out from the photographs taken with the Brownie "Starflex" in 1961?

While I lived in that New Jersey house I never appreciated her gift to us: the common assumption that all yards have places in them which are beautiful. Soon enough I realized that not all properties had flower beds on three sides, or *Cosmos* next to the swing set, or *Cleome* by the sandbox.

Every weeknight my father stepped off the commuter train from New York City, drove his car to our house, took off his New York City suit with its dusty smell of Pullman car and cigarettes, and poured himself a glass of scotch. With drink in hand he strolled through the backyard examining every new budding leaf and blossom. He stood in front of each plant ruminating over his day for several minutes before moving on in a clockwise manner around the backyard.

My mother no longer lives in that house. My father lives there still but with a new wife who is a banker, not a gardener. My mother left in a rush of bitter words and accusations; and in her haste, she took no time to gather up her childhood Christmas ornaments, her books saved from grade school, or the plants from her garden, many in the ground for the previous twenty years. She left in the dead of winter with her *Phlox* and daylillies covered with snow and her bleeding hearts frozen in the ground.

Several years passed with no one tending the garden. I wasn't a gardener then and besides, I lived in northern Arizona where the growing season was uncertain, killing frosts having been recorded every night of a year.

215

My mother's garden languished. The roses were ravaged by the previous season's Japanese beetles. Even the Shasta daisies stopped blooming. Then one year they didn't come up at all. The lawn mower leveled more of what was left, cutting struggling perennials into green stalks.

In early April several years ago, I spent a Saturday with my father and his wife. I had moved back to the East Coast, back to zone six in horticultural terms. I ventured out into what had been the garden at the end of the property. A few peony stalks poked up through the crab grass and a lone *Astilbe* sent up its feathery curled tendrils toward the sun. Could I dig these up, please, I tentatively asked, unclear to whom I should make the request, and uneasy with the feelings stirring in me.

I carefully dug up the *Astilbe* and wrapped it in newspaper. My father watched me from the sunporch window, his face inscrutable. I placed the plants in the back of my car and drove to Delaware. I wondered: should I sing lullabies to them and sprinkle them with infant formula? That evening I planted the Astilbe into my own garden next to the *Delphinium* and in front of the Russian sage. I planted the peony at the corner of the garage where other peonies would soon rise up in blossom.

That spring both plants struggled in their new locale. The peony did not bloom, and the Astilbe never changed its appearance; its infant tendrils remained curled through August. Neither plant survived the subsequent winter.

My mother has a new garden now. She lives by the sea and grows beach plums and *Hydrangea*. I like her new garden, but it is not a mystery to me. The garden that I long for is her garden of my youth, the one I have to search for in the old photographs of my sisters playing on the lawn.

A Teacher's Journey Among Voices

Mark J. Goodman

*with Carly Fink, Josh Michelson,
Jesse Mills, Naoko Oguro,
Alicia Pohan, Harumi Rhodes,
Alan Stone, Jessica Shapiro,
Adriana Suarez, Lara Weibgen,
and Morgan Young*

At the beginning of this year, I cared about details. I wanted you to know exactly how many steps I took walking from my house to the post office and the zip code of the person I was sending the letter to. But I didn't let you know the more important things, like my relationship with the mysterious addressee, or the feelings that I had in mailing the letter, or the hope I had for a response . . . the juicy stuff that creates the true essence of life. Not what I did, but why, and how, and what I felt like when I was doing it. One big diary all about life. You don't care that I ate french toast for breakfast, you care that it brought back memories of me sitting with my best friend in a french cafe, the smell of fresh french bread baking in the distance, the view of the Eiffel Tower shadowed in the fog. (Jessica, 1992)

It is late May. Hot. The air conditioner in the window buzzes above the sounds of spring-feverish seventh graders. It offers little relief. Jessica is on the floor, her writing circling her. She is engulfed in her own words. She leafs through her writer's notebook, reads a piece of writing she did in September, and reads her latest piece. She has hard decisions to make. Which pieces should she put into her final portfolio? Which pieces best represent who she is as a writer, as a learner? Which pieces best show the growth she has experienced this year? She looks frustrated at times. The first day I introduced the project she was one of the first ones who asked, "Can't we have an exam instead? Why do we have to do this project?" Today, she looks surprised as she excitedly turns to her neighbor and says, "Can you believe I wrote like this in September. I sound so young." I tell her, tell her class, to dig deep into the writing, allow themselves to be surprised, to discover things about themselves. Teach themselves who they are as writers and then teach me.

> When I first started to write about Alzheimer disease my feelings weren't expressed. I felt the piece did not go right. . . . At home I spent hours trying to figure out how to write this.
>
> So, I decided to go back to the beginning and figure out why I wanted to write this. The only problem with that was that I forgot why I was writing this piece. Then it hit me. I wanted to tell everyone in the world that I love my grandmother even though she doesn't know my name. Even though I don't go to the nursing home to see her a lot, I care about her a lot and that is what really matters.
>
> I remembered when the Challenger exploded that she moved into the nursing home. I was going to write my first line as "The Challenger exploded." Then all of a sudden I thought, "Why don't I write 'I remember the day the Challenger exploded' because Alzheimer makes you not remember things." (Carly, 1992)

∽

I find it easy to write about things that I am thinking or feeling about. But, I do not always write about my innermost feelings, but instead choose to stay on the surface of my feelings. I only touched the surface of my feelings. Skiing is a passion to me, and that doesn't come across in this piece. I briefly described the aspects of the sport that I enjoy, but I didn't express my love of bumps and speed, danger and excitement. My inner feelings about skiing never came out in this piece. It reads as if skiing is just another thing to do.

I do not see myself as a writer because in the first place I am too lazy. I think I could be a writer in my mind. I often write a piece "upstairs", but I lack the discipline of the writer to sit down and actually do it. My mind is where my deep feelings come out, but I guess I am afraid to put them on paper, for fear someone will read and think less of me for it. (Morgan Young, 1992)

I write this piece mostly out of love. For the past two Junes I have had my seventh graders do a portfolio, final project, self-evaluation, and reflection. Each time I have regretted it, at first. The last day of school comes, and I am faced with a huge pile of long projects that I have to grade. Why didn't I just give an exam; an exam would be so much easier to grade. Why do I always bury myself with such thankless work? I carry the heavy box of projects home with the feeling that the school year will never end, that I am Sisyphus, the teacher. But then I begin to read them and the regret and dread slowly seep away. What emerges are the honest voices of kids who know themselves as writers, who understand the process of writing, who amaze me with their insights into themselves and their own writing. Each year, these portfolio projects have brought me tears and laughter, have reminded me what is unique and special about each of the kids I teach.

What I have learned is that given the opportunity to tell you, kids know so much more about themselves, about reading and writing, than we credit them. I want you to hear these student voices, because I think they speak to the potential all of our students have. There is so much wisdom and so much poetry in these voices, the poetry of kids who are awakening to themselves.

In doing this project, I realized something that I did not write down, for it is not really about the course of my writing this year. It is about the process I went through while doing this project. I realized that I did not know myself as a writer, and that I always keep changing as a writer. I started this project thinking I would know the answer to any question asked about my writing. But when I started working on writing my opening statements, I realized that I would have to do some research on myself as a writer. As it turned out, I had to stop my writing and read over some of my writer's notebook entries and finalized pieces. After a week of studying myself, I had a couple of pages of notes. . . . I also found that my writing seemed to have changed as I wrote this project. It was extremely hard to organize this paper so it would have the same point of view in the beginning and the end. I tried to not change for a week so that I could be a good reporter on myself, but I couldn't stop my opinion from changing. In some parts of this paper I might have been lying . . . at least for a certain amount of time. But then, my opinion would change, and I would believe what I had just written. In other words, it was almost impossible for me to make up my mind about the opinion I had on my writing. It is impossible to locate the specific places int his paper where I never doubted myself. (Jesse, 1992)

∽

This year I was accepted into Dwight Englewood School not knowing anybody; nobody knowing me. I also began to take tennis lessons every Saturday with about 12 Japanese people. At Dwight Englewood School, I did not know what to do or what to say. By the middle of the year, everyone thought I was extremely quiet. Nobody even tried to know the real me, so I hid my "real" me deep inside which was filled with energy and pride. I wanted to be myself! I wanted to show everyone how wrong their judgement was! Yet, I knew it was my "mistake". . . . When I was in my tennis lesson, my eyes were speckled with millions of stars, my soul danced with the wind and my heart shone like the sun. I was myself! I laughed, I screamed, I sang, I danced, I was myself! I wanted to show everyone in Dwight Englewood who I was. Yet, I knew it was my mistake, I could not blame them.

From this experience this year, I have learned something extremely important, something I should never forget. I know how wonderful and beautiful it is to be myself and I learned this by making a mistake, from experience, and someday, somewhere I might repeat my mistake. Yet, I would know how to mend it.

I become a composer when I write. Sitting in front of a grand piano for hours, I think about my piece of music. At first I begin with a note. This note is the sound of my childhood. I am always drawn to this note because it is always in my mind. The time when I was a little girl, the time which I am able to compose into music simply by traveling back in time.

I play the note of my childhood, traveling back in time, searching for a memory. A memory, clear or vague. Once I tap the key, my fingers begin to dance. Then I find a note which doesn't fit into my music, so I rearrange all my notes and everything fits in like a puzzle. . . . The purpose of writing in my life right now is to make all my mind photographs come to life on paper so I can treasure and share all my unforgettable childhood memories with everyone. (Naoko, 1993)

I also write this piece for selfish reasons. Last June, I resigned from my job, and I am questioning whether I want to go back into teaching. I am a perfectionist, and teaching often feels like failure to me. My perfectionism has burnt me out, has blinded me to the joys of teaching. I need to remind myself of my successes, to hear these voices again. It is my students who may teach me patience and faith in myself, may open my eyes and ears to their gifts and my own. It is these voices that inspire me as a teacher and, I am hoping, these voices will call me back into teaching. In digging into their own voices and their own selves as writers, my students have forced me to dig into my own self as a teacher. In a way, their writer voices have become woven into my teacher voice.

Okay. I think to know me you must first get it into your head that—and this will shock you, Mr. Goodman—I'm completely, totally, entirely, no-holds-barred weird. To give you an idea, I like mushrooms. Mushrooms. Yuck. They grow on piles of dung and are fungus like athlete's foot. I eat relatives of toe fungus. Eeeew.
But I also think a person needs to be weird to be a good writer. I am a writer, hear me roar. Meow.
I write a lot in my spare time and I try to improve. And I have improved. The way I have improved the most is with detail. Detail to me is one of the most important parts of any piece of writing. Without detail, a piece of writing is just a skeleton. With detail, the writing can be a librarian, alien, actor, or punk rocker.
The key thing I have learned this year is that you've got to like writing something for it to turn out even half-way decently. Not just like the piece, but actually like producing it. . . . My advice to any writer-to-be is, "If you hate it, drop it. If you dislike it, drop it. If you're indifferent, drop it. If you like it, give it another shot. If you love it, cherish it and guard it like a jewel." Another thing I've learned is time is the enemy and it usually wins. A good writer shouldn't have time limits. After all, New York (or is it Rome) wasn't built in a day. So, here's another word to the wise: A story in time ruins nine.
The first sentence of a story has to be what I call a "vacuum sentence." It's got to suck the reader's face into the page and hold it there

until the reader's eyeballs begin to chafe and only then should it loosen so the reader can step back and say, "Wow." (Lara, 1993)

∞

I wish there were more time in the day so I would have more time to write . . . I love the feeling of writing as fast as you can because your mind just keeps throwing out wonderful images and ideas to your pen. I love the feeling when your muscles in your hand begin to ache, and your hand is so tired you know you are going to let go any minute now . . . but you keep on writing anyway and endure the pain. I love it when you finish writing and read over everything you wrote and feel like you just climbed a mountain and found your goal and that everything is going to be fine now. I love it when you lie back—your mind clear, and the paper cluttered with your handwriting, and you feel relieved. I love the feeling when you have no more ideas left in your brain, and you have this mixed feeling of exhaustion and happiness, and you fall asleep on the floor with the pen still in your hand—your fingers gripping it—and fall into a deep sleep.

For me the hardest is writing Haiku. I have a lot of problem finding the "perfect word," or just one powerful phrase that gives the reader an automatic vision. . . . Poetry is very frustrating for me because I know so well what I want to say, but instead I end up writing a two-page piece instead of a poem. (Harumi, 1992)

I learn so much from these students. Perhaps most important, they teach me about what kind of teacher I am and what kind of teacher I want to become. Teaching is such a demanding profession. Like me, most teachers burn out; most wonder whether they can open their hearts up yet again each September to another group of kids. These voices, if I listen to them carefully and lovingly, tell me that I can, tell me that I must, tell me that there is really nothing else to do. My life is so much richer because of these voices, because of the students I have met in the five years I have taught.

My perfectionism does not allow me to be present for these voices. It is time to let go and simply listen. If writing is about trusting words and going where they lead, then teaching is about trusting kids, listening to them, and going where they lead. I am beginning to feel that listening is the most important task I do each day in class. Without a listener, there can be no true emergence of voices. Ultimately I see myself as a voice-centered teacher. I want to create a place where it is safe for these voices to emerge out of the silence that the world often imposes. And I do believe that words, honest, reflective writing, are a key to unlock the silent spaces inside ourselves, inside our students. I am beginning to realize that this piece is as much about me, about the emergence of a confident teaching voice from the silence of self-doubt, as it is about the emergence of my students' voices. Honest voices are infectious; they make us all want to speak, to shout, to be heard. I want my classroom to be a community of unique voices, a place where all these beautiful, discordant, honest voices can be heard.

> My strongest educational moment came when I began to take Ritilin. This drug supplied by body with a chemical that I was missing. Prior to taking this drug I was not able to reach my full academic potential. In fact, I was having a hard time. There was a question as to whether or not I belonged at Dwight. Once I began to take the medicine, my whole life changed. I was able to behave well enough so that my teachers could appreciate my true intelligence. I myself started to recognize how much more I was able to learn once I was able to control my behavior.
>
> With Ritilin in my system, I began to take off with poetry. I became inspired and felt proud of the poems I was able to produce. My poetry anthology was a milestone. It was concrete evidence that I was in fact being productive and creative.
>
> I thought that putting a project like this [final project] together was a great idea. Rather than just handing in an assignment and having it done with, this experience has given me the opportunity to look back at how far I have come and how much further I still have to go. I wish there were more opportunities to do projects like this. I think that the reason the school does not do more of this kind of thing is because the emphasis is always on moving ahead and not looking back... (Alan, 1993)

∞

The thing I have learned while doing this project, that I did not know before, was how incredibly personal writing is. Having to critique my own work and write about the creative process involved forced me to see the connection between who I am and how I write.

Writing is a difficult task for me. I often don't like to write because I feel it is just another task for school, like homework. I feel rebellious about being told to do something. I would rather do something because I want to. The problem that I have is even if I think that I want to write I often don't out of laziness. I guess there is value in having someone force me to produce. When I look over my writing from the past school year, I can immediately recognize the pieces I was self-motivated to write as opposed to the pieces that I did because they were required. For example, in my piece "Do you Love me," I was self-motivated to write this because it was a way to express a lot of feelings I have been having in a more positive way. Rather than acting out at home, I felt some relief expressing myself on paper. An example of a piece I did only because it was required was "Fear." When re-reading this, it is obvious that I just did the bare minimum to get the assignment done. I did not feel like writing and I had no ideas that I felt personally connected to. Part of this was laziness and part of it was rebellion.

I write best when I am feeling extremely emotional. When I am angry or sad I find writing a really good way to vent my feelings. I come up with these ideas as a result of the conflicts that I experience in my personal life. One of Mr. Goodman's comments on my poetry anthology was that I am able to express my emotions well on paper. He also expressed a wish for me, that I come to see writing as a life-saver, as it has been for him. This comment has really stuck in my mind. It is not until this year that I truly saw writing as a means of expressing emotions in order to feel better. (Josh, 1993)

∽

Like me, Little Tree learns to open his eyes and mind because "granpa" allows him to wander off and watch nature without explaining to him beforehand what he will see and what he should expect. This year, I have also learned to open my eyes and mind. In English class, I have learned to experiment and take risks in writing. By allowing us to write what we please, you have done what Little Tree's granpa has done. You have let us wander through our minds not setting standards for us or foretelling what we were to find or experience before allowing us to put it into writing. I was always afraid to write what I wanted to. I was afraid of being told that it was wrong. My teachers had always told me that there was a wrong and right way to write. The style of writing had to be theirs, not mine, and for some reason the way I wrote was always considered wrong. I bet Little Tree would be afraid to wander off into the woods if he was told that he was going to meet up with a rattlesnake that would bite him and kill him. . . . I feel that is was not until I was allowed to express my thoughts, my fears, and my innermost feelings, that I was allowed to leave the shell of timidity that I was living in and feel confident enough to say, "Hey world. This is me. Respect my feelings and I will respect yours". . . . I am now open-minded and can see things through many perspectives. Before, my only point of view was that of my teachers. I can now speak my mind without fearing. It was almost like I was looking at a rainbow that consisted of only one color. Imagine all the other beautiful colors I was missing out on. . . . If you can remember a few months back when the school year began, I told you that I hated writing. Today I can only laugh at my attitude back then, for now it is indeed a pleasure for me to express myself through my writing. It is almost an escape from the problems of the real world or at least an attempt at dealing with them. . . . I feel I have grown a lot this year as a writer. I have learned to open my eyes and see what's really behind everyone's closed door, especially my own. . . . I thought I knew myself inside and out, but through my writing I discovered many things I didn't know existed before. . . . I had always thought I had millions of friends. I now know that it is merely a fantasy. I have also learned that I am not always the happy smiley faced person everyone thinks of me as. I have horrible days when I just feel like jumping off the tallest building and then having a big boulder fall on my head and rid me of all my problems. Writing is my psychiatrist. (Adriana, 1993)

Before writing this chapter, I thought about the approach I wanted to take. Should this be a piece of analysis? Should I talk about what I did to foster these voices, or should I analyze what these students in general know about writing? I wondered whether the fact that these students came mostly from middle-class and upper-middle families, that they were all students at The Dwight Englewood School, a private day school in a New York City suburb, should be featured information. I wondered whether I needed to tell you more about the kids, that Alicia was an intense student whose passion came out of that fiery intensity, that Josh was constantly blocked as a writer all year, but in the end was able to find a voice.

Yet, I decided that this was not a piece of analysis; this was a piece of art, a collage of beautiful voices. I value these voices more than anything else in my teaching. I see these voices as a stand against a world that wants to make everyone conform, to squeeze all individuality into a silent hum. In saying this I am reminded of an e e cummings quote I usually put on my classroom wall: "To be nobody-but-yourself—in a world which is doing its best night and day to make you everyone else—means to fight the hardest battle which any human being can fight; and never stop fighting."

When I read these projects in June, it is usually late at night, and I am all alone. So often I want to turn to someone, anyone, and say, "You've got to hear what this seventh-grade kid just wrote; this is incredible." Consider this my late night whisper to you, a lone voice of a teacher trying to remember and affirm what he does. I am like Jessica who began this piece, engulfed by the words and voices of my students, trying to teach myself who I am as a teacher, trying to remember what I truly value and why I need to keep teaching.

I conclude with a final student voice, a poem about the struggles of writing, of finding the truth:

my spring

If I began this piece
by saying "It was
a
      beautiful
        spring
          day,"
then it wouldn't
be the
same day.
That day, the water
    crept
        sleepily
along the asphalt.
That day, the
      sun

                                wasn't
        out, but I
        could feel its
        rays.
        That day the air gave birth
        to little voices
                        carried
                                by
                                        the wind.
        That day, freedom was
        at my side.
        That day, a quiet
                song rang in
                        my lonely ears.
        That soft day,
        the light
                        casted
                                shadows,
                giving
                all objects
        life. That
        day,
                was
                        my
                                spring.

                        (Alicia, 1993)

Teaching Time

Jack Wilde

Minds listening more to the clock's
    whisper of vacation
Than the math problem
    chalked on the board
The classroom suffused
    with unbidden winter sun
Bodies let go:
    crescent spines,
        legs lax,
            eyes awash
In dream-like supplication

My voice pushes the numbers
    through this light,
        against their softened bodies,
            and the clock's insistence

Into this word stream Josh floats a question—
Spoken as it is thought—
"How many factors
    can a number
        have?"
Rippling through the sunlit sea,
    brushing faces,
        it reddens cheeks.

His classmates straighten
    taking back their hands,
        picking up pencils
            in the golden light.

Maureen Barbieri, has taught middle school in New Hampshire, Ohio, and South Carolina and is now an instructor in the New Hampshire Writing Program. She has written articles for Language Arts and other professional journals and has contributed chapters to several Heinemann books. With Linda Rief, she is co-editor of the NCTE journal, *Voices from the Middle,* as well as Heinemann's *Workshop 6: The Teacher as Writer.* Maureen is the author of *Sounds from the Heart: Learning to Listen to Girls.*

Ellen H. Bryant, a classroom teacher of grades two and three for fourteen years, is currently a reading teacher for grades one through five at Tower Hill School, an independent school in Wilmington, Delaware. She loves to garden in her spare time. On one side of her computer is a box of 100 daffodils waiting to be planted; on the other side is a stack of fifth-grade reading journals waiting to be read.

She grew up in Princeton, New Jersey, graduated from Abbot Academy in Andover, Massachusetts, and from Pitzer College in Claremont, California. She received her M.Ed. from Boston University.

Heather Carney received her Ph.D. in reading education from Syracuse University in 1973. She has worked as an adjunct assistant professor in the Department of Education at the University of New Hampshire. She is currently an English teacher at St. Thomas Aquinas High School in Dover, NH.

Susan Fleisher has taught in a wide variety of classroom settings for eight years. She taught remedial reading and writing in high schools and colleges, science in middle and high schools, and all subjects in Adult Basic Education classes. Recently, she worked her way to the elementary level where she is a reading specialist and Reading Recovery teacher in Wayne, New Jersey.

Judith A. Fueyo, assistant professor of Language and Literacy at Pennsylvania State University, teaches graduate and undergraduate classes in language arts, writing research, emergent literacy, and teacher as researcher. Her research interests focus on ways of knowing and alternative assessment.

Mark J. Goodman taught seventh-, eighth-, and tenth-grade English for five years in New Jersey. Last year, despite the fact that he is not a coffee drinker, he moved to Seattle. He loves the spectacular camping and hiking that the Northwest offers.

Currently, he is volunteer teaching and tutoring at The Goodwill Adult Literacy Center. He loves this work and knows it will change the way he will approach classroom teaching. He spends a lot of time writing and finds the daily practice the most important action he has done for his writing in the past year. This is his first publication.

Martha Horn has been a classroom teacher, a staff developer in the Teachers College Writing Project, and a writing consultant in school districts throughout the country. Most recently she taught Reading and Language Arts Methods courses to prospective teachers at Rhode Island College. She is presently a doctoral student at Harvard University.

Douglas Kaufman is from Santa Fe, New Mexico. He most recently taught middle school writing and reading in Woodmere, New York, and is currently enrolled in the University of New Hampshire's doctoral program in Reading and Writing Instruction. He does not know in what state he will end up next.

Jane A. Kearns, the writing coordinator for the Manchester, New Hampshire, public schools, taught English for twenty years. A former instructor in the New Hampshire Writing Program, she says that reading Don Murray, meeting Tom Newkirk, and researching with Jane Hansen and Donald Graves changed her teaching life. An avid reader of mysteries, travel books, and newspapers, she dislikes cats, lima beans, baseball, dirty fingernails, and ice storms.

Mark Klein has taught elementary school in Churchville and Richboro, Pennsylvania. He is currently the principal of New Town Elementary School in Newtown, Pennsylvania.

Mary Mercer Krogness, a teacher who has always been a writer, is now a full-time writer who teaches. She is the author of *Just Teach Me, Mrs. K: Talking, Reading, and Writing with Resistant Adolescent Learners* (Heinemann, 1995). She is a language arts consultant to school districts.

Kathleen J. Mahan teaches seventh-grade reading and ninth-grade reading/writing workshop at Lenape Middle School in Doylestown,

Pennsylvania. Her article "My Class" was published in *Workshop 5: The Writing Process Revisited,* edited by Thomas Newkirk. She loves to read and write and tries each day to "hook" one more reluctant reader by helping them discover an author he or she really loves.

Patricia McClure teaches first and second grade at the Mast Way School in Lee, New Hampshire. She has been an elementary teacher for more than twenty-five years. She has also taught in the New Hampshire Writing Program at the University of New Hampshire during the past few summers. Her elementary classroom has served as a collaborative research site for many published projects with Don Graves and Jane Hansen, Ruth Hubbard, and most recently Thomas Newkirk.

Pat McDonald-O'Brien is an elementary literacy specialist at Newtown Elementary School in Newtown, Pennsylvania. She has published an article in *Workshop 6: Teacher as Writer* (Heinemann 1994).

Mark Milliken currently teaches fourth grade at Moharimet Elementary School in the Oyster River School District, Durham, New Hampshire. He is also an instructor in the New Hampshire Writing Program. His publications include articles in *Workshop 3: The Politics of Process,* edited by Nancie Atwell (Heinemann 1991), and in *Portfolio Portraits,* edited by Donald Graves and Bonnie Sunstein (Heinemann 1992).

Donald M. Murray is a writer who publishes novels, poetry, a newspaper column, and textbooks on writing and teaching writing.

He is Professor Emeritus of English at the University of New Hampshire where he inaugurated a journalism program, designed an advanced composition course, helped establish a graduate program in Composition Studies, served as director of Freshman English and as English Department chairperson. He twice won awards for his teaching and was awarded an honorary doctorate by the University of New Hampshire 1990 and Fitchburg State College in 1992.

As a journalist, Murray won a number of awards including the Pulitzer Prize for editorial writing in *The Boston Herald* in 1954. He was an editor of *Time* before freelancing as a magazine writer in New York City for seven years. He has served as writing coach for *The Boston Globe, The Providence Journal,* and other newspapers. He writes a weekly column, *Over Sixty,* for *The Boston Globe.* In 1991 *Boston* magazine selected him as best columnist in Boston.

His books on the craft of writing and teaching writing include *A Writer Teaches Writing* (Houghton Mifflin, 1968, 1985); *Learning by Teaching* (Heinemann, Boynton/Cook 1982, 1989); *Writing for Your Readers* (Globe Pequot Press, 1983, 1992); *Write to Learn* (Harcourt Brace 1984, 1987, 1990, 1993, 1995); *Read to Write* (Harcourt Brace 1985, 1990, 1993); *Expecting the Unexpected* (Boynton/Cook, 1990); *The Craft of Revision* (Harcourt Brace 1991, 1994).

Rosalie O'Donnell teaches general music and band in grades three through eight at Glacier Christian School in Columbia Falls, Montana. She has also taught private piano and guitar for thirty years. She teaches art to disabled students at the Hockaday Art Center.

JoAnne Rains went back to school after her children were "almost educated." She began teaching junior high English in 1988, "by default, because nobody else wanted the job." She loved it and has never left language arts or middle school since. In 1990 she received her M.Ed. and now teaches sixth-grade reading and English at Sanders School in South Carolina. JoAnne lives with her husband and her two Maine Coon cats, William Shakespeare (Will) and Queen Elizabeth I (Bess), in a geodesic dome in a heavily wooded area just outside the small town of Clinton, South Carolina.

Linda Rief teaches seventh- and eighth-grade Language Arts at Oyster River Middle School in Durham, New Hampshire. She is the author of *Seeking Diversity: Language Arts with Adolescents* (Heinemann 1992), articles in *Language Arts, English Journal, Educational Leadership*, and chapters in *Breaking Ground, Portfolio Portraits, Workshop 1: Writing and Literature, Workshop 2: Beyond the Basal*, and *Workshop 6: The Teacher as Writer*. She used to live in a heavily wooded area until her husband gave her a chainsaw for Mother's Day.

Karen Smith has a Ph.D. from Arizona State University. She was an elementary teacher in Michigan and Arizona before joining the staff at the National Council for Teachers of English as Associate Executive Director. Her publications include *Teachers Are Researchers: Reflection and Action* (co-edited with Leslie Patterson, Kathy Short, and Carol Santa), *Language Functions and School Success* (co-authored with Robert Shafer and Claire Staab), and chapters and articles in *Questions and Answers About Whole Language, Talking About Books, English Quarterly, The Reading Teacher, Language Arts*, and *Anthropology and English Quarterly*.

Betty Sprague teaches third grade at Moharimet Elementary School in Madbury, New Hampshire. She graduated from the University of Massachusetts. She has two daughters and now lives in Lee, New Hampshire.

Steve Tullar teaches third grade at Moharimet Elementary School in Madbury, New Hampshire. Previously he taught a four-five multiage class at Oyster River Elementary School in Durham and third grade at Stratham Memorial School, both in New Hampshire. Before his teaching career he worked in construction and as a dairy farmer. Both careers continue to influence his teaching and learning.

Margaret M. Voss teaches fifth grade in Marblehead, Massachusetts, and is a visiting associate professor at Salem State College (MA). She holds a Ph.D. in Reading and Writing Instruction from the University of New Hampshire and has published articles in *Language Arts* and *Reading/ Writing Newsletter*, as well as chapters in *Portfolio Portraits* and *Workshop 5: Writing Process Revisited*. She is currently working on a book about children's multiple literacies.

Carol Wilcox is originally from Colorado, where she spent seven years as a kindergarten through grade two teacher, and three years as a Literacy Resource Specialist. She is currently pursuing a Ph.D. in Reading and Writing Instruction at the University of New Hampshire. Her dissertation research focuses on assessment, particularly portfolios, as tools for helping children become independent, lifelong learners. Her publications include a teacher reflection chapter in *Windows to Literacy: Assessing Learners K-8*, by Lynn Rhodes and Nancy Shanklin (Heinemann, 1993); *Portfolios: Finding Our Focus*, a working paper published by the University of New Hampshire Writing Lab (UNH 1993); and a literacy vignette which appeared in the September 1993 issue of *The Reading Teacher*. When she finishes her doctorate she plans to return to teaching in an urban setting.

Jack Wilde's senior high English teacher took particular pleasure projecting his students' English themes on the classroom walls, then in Buckleyesque tones censure the attempts. Jack lived in dread of English class; the work on the wall more often than not was his. Working with writing as process and product has enabled Jack to write again and to find enjoyment in writing. In 1993 he published *A Door Opens* (Heinemann), which presents writing experiences he provides for his fifth-grade students at the Ray School in Hanover, New Hampshire. He is also an instructor in the New Hampshire Writing Program.